GA 9/12

KP 5/14

Books in the Politics Study Guides series

British Government and Politics: A Comparative Guide (2nd edition)
Duncan Watts

US Government and Politics (2nd edition)
William Storey

International Politics: An Introductory Guide
Alasdair Blair and Steven Curtis

Devolution in the United Kingdom (2nd edition)
Russell Deacon

Political Parties in Britain
Matt Cole and Helen Deighan

Democracy in Britain
Matt Cole

The Changing Constitution
Kevin Harrison and Tony Boyd

The Judiciary, Civil Liberties and Human Rights
Steven Foster

The Prime Minister and Cabinet
Stephen Buckley

Britain and the European Union
Alistair Jones

Pressure Groups
Duncan Watts

The Politics of Northern Ireland
Joanne McEvoy

The UK Parliament
Moyra Grant

The American Presidency
Duncan Watts

Electoral Systems and Voting in Britain
Chris Robinson

Political Communication
Steven Foster

www.euppublishing.com/series/posg

Political Parties in Britain

Matt Cole and Helen Deighan

EDINBURGH
University Press

Edinburgh University Press Ltd
22 George Square, Edinburgh EH8 9LF
www.euppublishing.com

Typeset in 11/13pt Monotype by
Servis Filmsetting Ltd, Stockport, Cheshire, and
printed and bound in Great Britain by
CPI Group (UK) Ltd, Croydon CR0 4YY

A CIP record for this book is available from the British Library

ISBN 978 0 7486 6870 0 (hardback)
ISBN 978 0 7486 2569 7 (paperback)
ISBN 978 0 7486 3112 4 (webready PDF)
ISBN 978 0 7486 6903 5 (epub)
ISBN 978 0 7486 6902 8 (Amazon ebook)

Contents

Boxes

Introduction: What are Parties For?

Contents

Overview

This Introduction sets out the ways in which political parties have been said to be beneficial to a democratic system, and how this might be true in Britain. It then summarises the debate between commentators as to whether parties in Britain are failing in these important functions.

Key issues to be covered in the Introduction

- What is a political party?
- What are the key functions of political parties in a democracy?
- How have British political parties fulfilled their functions?
- In what ways are British parties failing to fulfil their functions?
- What might be the causes of the 'failure' of parties?

'Parties', said the eighteenth-century Whig MP and conservative thinker Edmund Burke, 'must ever exist in a free country.'[1] Since then, of course, the nature of parties has changed dramatically, from loose groupings of politicians to organisations recruiting members of the public with a common outlook (or ideology) to discuss those ideas and campaign for the election of representatives to put their beliefs into effect. Our social, economic and constitutional circumstances have also altered since Burke's time but the idea that in modern society it is inevitable that organised groups become the vehicles for contrasting opinions remains relevant. In fact, mass education, media and democracy have not weakened the form and role of political parties in the last two hundred years but strengthened and clarified them: only eight of over eight thousand MPs elected in mainland Britain at the general elections of the last fifty years have not been from the three main parties or from the Welsh and Scottish nationalists.[2] A standard politics textbook of the 1960s referred to 'an established, interlocking relationship between people, parties, parliament and government'.[3] Today, Home Office advice to those preparing to take the UK Citizenship test still recognises the importance of parties, saying 'anyone can stand for election as an MP but they are unlikely to win an election unless they have been nominated to represent one of the major political parties' before reassuring us that 'the main political parties actively seek members among ordinary voters to join their debates, contribute to their costs, and help at elections for Parliament or for local government; they have branches in most constituencies and they hold policy-making conferences every year'.[4]

In the last generation, however, British parties have come under severe criticism. The last prime minister to leave 10 Downing Street in the twentieth century, John Major, complained early in the twenty-first that 'at the grass roots, our political parties are shrinking in membership from mass movements to the size of special interest groups'. Talking of a national detachment from, and distaste for, politics, he despaired: 'all the party machines are moribund, near-bankrupt, unrepresentative and ill-equipped to enthuse the electorate'.[5] A welter of journalistic and academic books has in recent years agreed – or even assumed – that the political parties are failing to fulfil their national functions. From the right came Keith Sutherland's *The*

Party's Over (2004); John Harris's *So Now who do we Vote for?* explored the dilemma of unrepresented left-wing voters in 2005; the titles of specific studies of each of the two main parties – like Ian Gilmour's *Whatever Happened to the Tories* (1997) and Andrew Rawnsley's *The End of the Party: the Rise and Fall of New Labour* (2010) – recognise the same decline; and the Power Inquiry Report of 2006 composited the views of a range of academics, politicians and commentators calling for the creation of 'a party system which is responsive enough to the changing values and demands of today's population to allow the necessary and organic creation of new political alliances, value systems and organisations which better represent those values and demands'.[6] A major inquiry under Sir Hayden Phillips was commissioned by the government into party funding but interparty talks on the proposals in its report broke down in 2007.[7] Over the last decade, the Electoral Commission has implemented new statutory regulations, seeking to make parties more transparent than before, but the challenges of the recession and coalition government have made it harder still to show that parties are serving the nation well.

To assess the substance of these criticisms, political scientists refer themselves to the functions traditionally ascribed to parties in a representative democracy – not the motivations of parties or their members, necessarily, but the ways in which they can help to promote democracy in the course of pursuing their own interests. These can be enumerated in several ways, and identified by technical terms explained below; but, broadly speaking, the useful functions of political parties can be recognised in three areas: policy, personnel and participation.

Policy

According to the doctrine of the mandate, British governments secure their legitimacy in pursuing particular policies by publicising their plans in a manifesto prior to an election and, more generally, in election campaigns. Any votes cast for candidates adopting a party's label can be taken, at least on key issues, to represent and indicate consent for the implementation of the programme set out in that party's manifesto. Thus, it was reasonable to assume at recent elections that votes cast for the Labour Party indicated support for

greater public investment in health and education; for certain constitutional reforms; and for a readiness to see the overall tax burden
rise. Those voting for the Conservatives expressed a willingness to
see relatively restrained public expenditure; to have cuts in direct
taxation at an earlier stage than under a Labour government; and to
resist constitutional reform and European integration. Those voting
for the Liberal Democrats were aware the MPs they might elect
would seek greater European integration, thoroughgoing constitutional reform, and taxation aimed at those on the highest incomes
and at environmental threats.

This gives elections greater meaning than a choice between independent candidates because those outside party structures find it
difficult to convey their policies on more than one key issue, and so
their ability to carry out the function of representing public policy
preferences is limited. Richard Taylor, the independent MP for
Wyre Forest (2001–10), was elected in opposition to the closure of
Kidderminster hospital's accident and emergency services but his
views on the arts, defence, crime and education – on all of which he
represents his constituents – are less well established than those of his
party opponents; Martin Bell (Tatton, 1997–2001) was elected on a
platform of opposing corruption but took part in protests against the
expansion of a local airport and voted and spoke in the Commons
on a range of other policy issues on which he had not publicised his
views.

Some independents are able to project a wider, if rather vague,
policy profile because they were previously members of a party
whose broad outlook they are assumed still to share: this is the case
with the socialist views of the late Peter Law, succeeded by Dai
Davies (Blaenau Gwent, 2005–10), Dick Taverne (Lincoln, 1973–4),
and S. O. Davies (Merthyr Tydfil, 1970–4) all of whom fell out with
the Labour Party over a single policy issue or with a procedure in
the party. The same could be said of Donald Robertson (Caithness,
1959–64) for whom the Conservatives stood aside, though he
declined to take the party whip. These MPs, however, have usually
had short careers and have relied indirectly on party labels to communicate what they stand for.

The result is that independents are able to claim mainly a generalised 'doctor's mandate' based upon trust and personality rather than

on specific policies for which they can be held accountable at the next election. Parties are the only organisations with the resources, expertise and public recognition to be able to communicate effectively a set of responses to most current issues. They are therefore vital to the maintenance of a meaningful electoral choice. Manifesto programmes are inevitably imperfect because they combine promises and appeals on a range of issues to a large number of voters – this is sometimes called **interest aggregation** – but they supply a reliable guide to the direction of popular preferences on more than one issue.

Parties also engage in **goal formulation**: that is, they develop new policies and give relative priorities to them. Parties have continuously active specialist research departments experimenting theoretically with new policy ideas, and then they have the ability to pilot them where they control local government. Much Conservative privatisation policy in the 1980s, and public–private partnership under Labour governments since 1997, were developed in this way; environmental policies, such as congestion charges, and educational reforms, such as school admissions 'lotteries', have been similarly tried out.

These claims by parties to offer choice in, and development of, policy are open to question, however. First there is the problem of the extent of choice between the policies of the main parties: in the 1980s, Richard Rose's study, *Do Parties Make a Difference?*, concluded that whatever their manifestos and speeches said, in office the main parties were remarkably similar to each other in the policies they pursued.[8] Following the emergence of 'New' Labour in the 1990s and the 'Modernisation' of the Conservatives in the last decade, even the promises of the main parties are difficult to distinguish. On privatisation, the shift from direct to indirect tax, social and environmental policies, there has been substantial convergence between the main parties; on other issues, such as crime and immigration, both parties seek to make the same noises, but find it difficult to bring about change in practice.

This has led to dissent from within the parties' own ranks, and concern and mockery from outside: in 2002, Transport and General Workers' Union leader Bill Morris said that 'the dividing line between our parties seems to be blurred if not erased altogether', and he accused Labour of acting as a 'pathfinder for future Tory policies' such as foundation hospitals and university top-up fees; by 2006, Melanie Phillips was complaining that the Cameron leadership of the Conservatives was betraying their supporters, saying 'one of Mr Blair's aims was not merely to win elections against the Conservative party but to destroy conservatism itself. That is precisely what Mr Cameron now appears to be doing. Remarkably, Britain now has *three* "not-the-Conservative" parties.'[9] At the 2005 election, the British Election Study (BES) survey found the lowest number of people who claimed to identify a difference between the parties since the survey began in 1964; and *Private Eye* welcomed the new Conservative Leader in December 2005 by comparing the difference between him and Tony Blair to a recent pioneering face transplant. After the Conservatives' failure to win an overall majority in 2010, Cameron was condemned by Christopher Booker in *The Daily Telegraph* for going 'to the point where, on most of the major issues confronting the country, his position has been virtually indistinguishable from that of the other main parties':

> The most important section of the electorate last Thursday consisted of those millions who stayed at home because they could see nothing in the three centrist parties to inspire them with the idea that there was any real alternative, offering genuine leadership.[10]

Parties suffer from a tension between values and **representation**: their desire to pursue the maximum vote has drawn them on to similar ground and left some of their traditional supporters feeling abandoned; yet, if they fail to respond to changes in opinion, they are dismissed as ideological and rigid. A survey by YouGov in 2007 found that over 70 per cent of the public thought that politicians never keep their promises and that 'if you vote a party into power, you never know quite what you're going to get'. Nearly two-thirds agreed that none of the parties represented their views and that 'I don't really know what the parties stand for'.[11]

This problem has been exacerbated by the condition of coalition government between the Conservatives and Liberal Democrats. Though presented by its leaders as a way of finding common ground on policies and values shared by more than half of the electorate, it has led to the abandonment by both parties of promises made during the election – to oppose tuition fee increases by the Liberal Democrats or to reward marriage with tax rebates by the Conservatives – on the grounds that their coalition partner would not support it. This has highlighted the difficulty of using parties to 'order' detailed policy change, as former MP Michael Meadowcroft wrote a year into the coalition:

> The whole concept of a manifesto conferring a mandate is deeply flawed. Quite apart from there being only a minority of electors who vote for any party, so that manifestos inevitably lack an arithmetical mandate, a much greater flaw is that a manifesto is obsolescent the moment it is written. Manifestos are important in making parties think and debate, but they can only be a snapshot of their policies. Far more important is the expression of the values and principles on which a party is based and which indicate how the party will approach present and future issues.[12]

The most fundamental critique of parties' policy function argues that each party programme is an all-or-nothing package of promises, not all of which are equally attractive to any voter. Thus, it is not possible to claim that, because a voter supported a party, that indicates support for any one of its policies. As public opinion and social identity have become more diverse and fluid in recent generations, parties have been increasingly displaced as representative vehicles of public opinion by pressure groups and campaigns with focused agendas, offering 'designer' rather than 'off-the-peg' representation, and sometimes raising new public concerns such as environmental threats that the parties have failed to identify. Professor Vernon Bogdanor set out the problem bleakly as Gordon Brown prepared to take over the Labour Party:

> Mass parties were the product of the collectivist age, so it is natural that the demise of collectivism should also mean the demise of the mass party. There has been a shift from what political scientists call 'position' politics, where parties disagree on fundamentals – nationalisation of basic industries, raising or lowering taxes, retaining or abandoning nuclear weapons – to 'valence' issues, where there is agreement on fundamental aims – an effective National Health Service, better schools – and disagreement is confined to the issue of which party is best placed to achieve them. The mass party, then, is dying on its feet.[13]

Personnel

Political parties fulfil functions known as **elite recruitment** and personal representation: what this means is that they supply the vast majority of candidates at all levels of election in Britain, and prepare and promote those who take up office at the highest levels, notably national government. They also give those in office a political apprenticeship and hold them accountable between elections by ensuring they fulfil manifesto commitments and duties to constituents.

Without the main parties, many elections would be uncontested, and certainly the most popular candidates would be absent. The three main parties contest every mainland seat at general elections, and the nationalists put up candidates throughout Scotland and Wales, thereby accounting for almost half of the candidates at the 2010 General Election. At local elections, about three-quarters of candidates are put up by the main parties. Most candidates for major parties have fought losing contests before entering Parliament and have undergone a lengthy selection and training process within their party which tests their organisation, communication and ability to respond to public demands. They may have records of office in local government by which the public can judge them (about one MP in three has been a councillor for their party).

If elected, party representatives are required by their organisation – in the case of the Commons, the whips – to stick to promises they have made to their electors and, apart from anything else, to turn up to Parliament. It is no coincidence that the small number of independent MPs have lower attendance records at parliamentary divisions than their colleagues in political parties. Against an average attendance of 75 per cent, Dai Davies was at 63 per cent of divisions, Richard Taylor 60 per cent, and Martin Bell failed to make as many as half. George Galloway attended fewer than one division in ten both as an independent (2003–5) and as the sole MP of the tiny Respect Party (2005–10). Perhaps understandably, having less impact and fewer clear commitments, independent MPs have less incentive to attend regularly but even those party MPs with little positive motivation are required by their whips to come and represent their constituents unless otherwise engaged.

Parties' structures also clarify and democratise the process of recruiting and scrutinising the executive. At general elections, voters choose not only policy programmes but also leadership teams, so that voting for a Conservative candidate in 2010 entailed supporting the appointment in office of David Cameron as prime minister, and the probable appointment to the cabinet of his senior colleagues; to vote Labour was to endorse the leadership of Gordon Brown, and so on. The leadership debates on television were possible precisely, and only, because there are parties with leaders who can be identified as the representatives of parties and the likely implementers of party pro-grammes. The public is able to see the alternative leadership teams at work in more junior offices or in Opposition before making a judge-ment: the management of reform of their own parties by both David Cameron and Tony Blair, for example, was an important test of lead-ership skill in public perception. If appointed, these leaders are then held accountable at regular meetings of the Parliamentary Labour Party or the 1922 Committee by the MPs who support them in office.

In a mass democracy, it is not possible for voters to test or disci-pline candidates for legislative or executive office on a regular basis. It is party mechanisms that carry out this work on a day-to-day basis, and their absence would deprive the public of important democratic controls over their representatives.

Despite all this evidence, however, the work of parties in provid-ing the personnel of the political system is open to question. Firstly, although they still provide a majority of candidates at general elec-tions, the main parties are faced with increasing competition from minor or non-party contestants: whereas there were only 2.2 candi-dates in the average seat in 1951 (and Labour and the Conservatives provided 90 per cent of them), in 2010 there were 6.4 candidates for each seat. In some areas where the main parties are weakest on the ground – such as the Conservatives in the urban north of England – they do not even contest some local elections.

Criticisms of party discipline concentrate on its excessive nature in both depth and scope. Many MPs complain of the periodic ruth-lessness of party whips and, though these must be set into context as potentially egocentric exaggeration, they are most telling when they argue that party whips are used not to enforce commitment to promises made to the public at elections but rather to give uncritical support to executive policies introduced sometimes against popular opinion or even contrary to manifesto commitments. The Power Inquiry went as far as to claim that 'the Executive in Britain is now more powerful in relation to Parliament than it has been probably since the time of Walpole . . . The whips have enforced party discipline more forcefully and fully than they did in the past.'[14] This was the defence made by those who rebelled against the Labour leadership's instructions on the invasion of Iraq in 2003, higher education top-up fees in 2004, and police detention powers in 2005.

Similarly, rebels on the Opposition benches objected to the Conservative leadership's policies on grammar schools in 2007, and new Liberal Democrat leader Nick Clegg's view on the referendum over the Lisbon Treaty in 2008. In both cases, frontbenchers resigned, saying their leadership was betraying its party's values. It is the party in office, however, that is most often criticised for disciplining its representatives undemocratically, and at least three Labour MPs have left the party in recent years complaining publicly of the power of the whips: Tess Kingham and Paul Marsden in 2001, and Clare Short in 2006.[15] New Conservative MP Sarah Wollaston wrote in the first year of the 2010 parliament that 'one MP told me that it was the most miserable experience of their life, always on the edge of a career advancement that never comes, constrained from speaking out but holding fire in the hope that one day they could have a real voice as a minister themselves'.[16]

Given all this, it is perhaps unsurprising that the 'elite' which is recruited by the parties is held in less public respect than it was in the past. Though the parties provide the leadership of the country, that leadership seems less effective in winning public approval than it was a generation or two ago. From allegations of 'sleaze' among John Major's Conservatives to accusations of deception over the weapons of mass destruction in Iraq and, most recently, controversy on both sides over MPs' expenses and party funding (such as the revelations leading to the resignation of Conservative treasurer Peter Cruddas in March 2012), events have strengthened public scepticism about the trustworthiness of the main parties' leaders. The Liberal Democrats exploited this distrust in their 2010 election campaign with a television election broadcast on the theme of 'Broken Promises' only to find themselves accused of the same offence later in the year over tuition fees.

This sort of evidence led a major Hansard Society study in 2005 to conclude that 'Parliament faces a crisis of confidence, power and respect. It is taken less seriously than before by the media and the public. The Commons is losing influence in the country. Satire and neglect threaten to substitute for urgent and informed interest.'[17] The YouGov survey of 2007 already quoted found that over half of respondents agreed that 'politicians are only in it for what they can get out of it'. Just before the 2010 election YouGov found that nearly half of respondents, and a clear majority of those who expressed an opinion, thought MPs 'unprincipled', 'dishonest' and 'incompetent', and over two-thirds thought them more interested in serving their own interests than those of the public.[18] Conservative MP Teddy Taylor illustrated this in the 1990s by saying that, whereas his father had proudly boasted to anyone who would listen when he was first elected in the 1960s, his own children refused to reveal his occupation to friends at university for fear of embarrassment. Parties provide leadership but it is not perceived in the same way as it once was.

The service of apprenticeship for office, which parties are supposed to provide, has been inhibited by the increased significance of the broadcast media in the last generation: dutiful service to the party has been replaced as a measure of leadership by telegenic campaign skills. This can be quantified by comparing the experience of party leaders over recent decades: James Callaghan had been an MP for thirty-one years, and a cabinet minister for eight, before becoming Labour leader; Margaret Thatcher had been an MP for sixteen years, and a cabinet minister for four. By contrast, Ed Miliband, David Cameron and Nick Clegg had been in Parliament only five, four and two years respectively before becoming their party's leader, and only Miliband had been in the cabinet, for less than two years. In this sense, Gordon Brown took an unusually long time to climb the 'greasy pole' of the party hierarchy, and significantly it is caution and lack of charisma which were the principal criticisms which did him so much damage. The high profile of the leadership debates in the 2010 election campaign illustrated graphically a trend which has been developing for years: the public no longer values long service to the party more than telegenic personality.

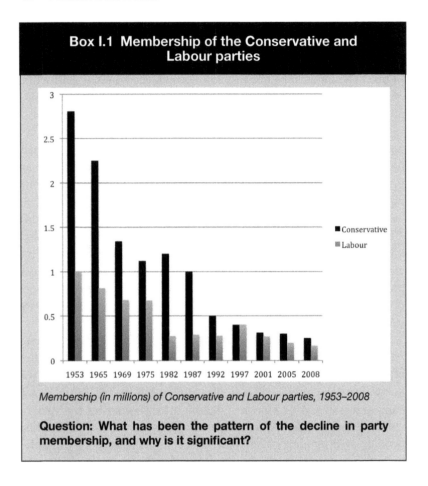

Box I.1 Membership of the Conservative and Labour parties

Membership (in millions) of Conservative and Labour parties, 1953–2008

Question: What has been the pattern of the decline in party membership, and why is it significant?

Participation

The most continuous, and therefore perhaps the most important, of parties' democratic functions are sometimes called '**mobilisation**' and '**education**'. These refer to the capacity of parties for helping the public participate in politics at elections – and beyond Parliament and between elections – and informing the public about their ideas and encouraging their discussion.

At election times, the self-serving interest of parties coincides with the operation of democracy because it is in the interest of each party to maximise its number of supporters and to persuade those supporters to vote. Parties are the only organisations capable of canvassing and motivated to do so, of mounting advertising campaigns costing tens of millions of pounds (the three main parties spent £31.1 million between them in 2010), and even of transporting voters physically to the polling station. In 1997, for example, Labour posted a video to first-time voters encouraging them to turn out; in 2001 they used text messages sent to young voters' mobiles at 11.00 p.m. the night before the election, and reminding them of the government's plans to liberalise licensing laws. It is by these campaigns that voters are not only encouraged to vote but also informed about what those in power have done and what their failings have been, and given the opportunity to question the candidates. If this process relied upon the resources of independent candidates, it would inevitably be many times more limited in scope.

Political parties are the most effective institutions through which members of the public can establish a relationship of constant access to, and influence over, decision-makers. Members of parties have rights to attend regular meetings with candidates, councillors and MPs of their party; to attend conferences, councils and policy forums where leaders can be pressurised to change or to adopt particular policies – at the annual conference in the glare of publicity; and ultimately, members can, of course, become candidates and representatives. Government policy on pensions was influenced by an embarrassing defeat at Labour's annual conference in 2000. In all three main parties, party members in the country have, in the last generation, gained the greatest or final say in who becomes the party leader, using postal ballots or electoral colleges to represent party support: over 40,000 Liberal Democrats took part in the choice of Nick Clegg as party leader in 2007; David Cameron was elected after nearly 200,000 Conservatives chose between him and David Davies in 2005; and in Labour's leadership contest of 2010, over a third of a million individual votes were cast by activists, MPs and trade unionists. Labour's membership swelled by 35,000 during the campaign, which entailed dozens of public meetings addressed by the candidates and each attended by hundreds of voters. Party members have also taken part in ballots on internal party organisation and policy, and they decide their constituency's candidate for parliament.

Parties' claims to mobilise and educate the public are less strong than they used to be, however. The membership of the three main parties, for example, has fallen by almost a factor of ten since the 1950s, leaving them with little or no organisation and activity in some parts of the country. The Conservatives had 2.8 million members in 1953 but, by 1997, the figure was 350,000; in 2007 it fell below 250,000, and the 2010 Conservative conference heard that it was as low as 177,000. Labour's individual membership total peaked in the 1950s at just over a million; in 1997 the figure was 405,000, and by 2008 it was just 166,000. Whereas fifty years ago, one voter in eleven was a member of a political party, now the proportion is one in eighty-eight. Activists, moreover, comprise only a minority fraction of membership: Seyd et al. found that 80 per cent of Conservatives, for example, took part in party activities less than once a month, and those who are active in both parties tend to have more 'purist' interpretations of party ideology, often at odds with the views of the rest of the party and the public at large.

The reasons for this are the subjects of fierce debate. Each party can identify specific episodes that explain particular phases of the decline: the enforced resignation of Margaret Thatcher as Conservative leader sapped party morale; the invasion of Iraq coincided with a sharp fall-off in Labour membership. The long-term shrinkage of parties is in part, however, a reflection of changing lifestyles and civic culture, and increasingly sophisticated policy preferences among the public. Many party members in the 1950s enjoyed the social aspects of membership as much as the political processes; in the twenty-first century these are of little significance when compared to modern leisure services and domestic facilities. As Labour candidate, adviser to two cabinet ministers and Chair of the Fabian Society, Paul Richards asked anxiously: 'How can political entities founded one hundred or more years ago possibly compete for the attention of a population which is better educated, housed, nourished and entertained than any in history? How can the local party branch meeting or fundraising Summer Ball compete with a trip to the multiplex or a couple of hours of *Tomb Raider*?'[19] Professor Robert Putnam has argued that this decline in social capital affects not only party membership but also turnout, and is reflected in a range of other collective institutions such as churches and charities or amateur musical and sports clubs.[20]

There are those who argue that the decline in party membership is more than a reflection of decline in civic culture and that, in fact, the public remains willing actively to pursue political campaigns but prefer to do so through the more flexible and dynamic process of pressure group activity.

Worse still, declining membership is part of a vicious circle in which falling individual subscriptions made parties reliant firstly upon corporate subscriptions, from trade unions in the case of the Labour Party and business for the Conservatives; then, more recently, both parties have turned to small numbers of individual wealthy benefactors, giving rise to accusations of 'cash for access' and 'cash for honours' since 1997. The controversy over this, and subsequent controls on parties' spending, have reduced their resources and activity so that the main parties spent £10 million less in 2010 than in 2005. On policy and leadership, limited membership has made parties less representative: ironically, at the very moment that extra-parliamentary parties gained control over their leaders, they were too small to use that control to convey public opinion. Hence the Conservative Party's first leadership election among party members chose Iain Duncan Smith whose public unpopularity led to his ousting by Tory MPs only two years later. Party members were also reluctant to move away from positions on Europe, tax and immigration close to their hearts but costly at the last three general elections, a syndrome identified by Pippa Norris and Joni Lovenduski as 'selective perception'.[21]

Even those who join political parties have sometimes found that the promise of influence upon their leaders has been misleading. Though key decisions are now made by postal ballot of members, these are often either limited choices or – as with Labour's vote on Clause IV of 1995, its manifesto approval of 1997 or William Hague's ballot on Conservative Party reform of 1998 – faits accomplis. In leadership contests, a wider franchise often empowers the media as much as the party membership and, in Labour's case in particular, challenge to the leadership is an unwieldy, protracted and expensive process. Beyond these rare occasions, moreover, party leaders have been streamlining decision-making processes: Labour's conference has handed this function to national policy forums and has itself become a rally at which the audience is given written cues for applause, and sometimes those who heckle ministers are bundled out by security guards. It has even proved difficult in recent years to persuade constituency Labour parties to send delegates to the conference. Within Labour, the role of the trade unions remains a controversial question, as it was only through their support that Ed Miliband won the leadership against his brother David, the preferred candidate of Labour MPs and party members.

In the Conservative Party, controversy has surrounded various attempts by David Cameron's leadership to move local activists towards the selection of more young, female and ethnic minority candidates. He has also encouraged the use of 'open' primary contests in which members of the public are invited to take part in candidate selection even if they are not party members. Under these circumstances, it is perhaps unsurprising that attempts to stem the decline in party membership have failed. As campaigner for greater democracy in the Conservative Party John Strafford argued in 2010: 'In the 45 years I have been a member of the party, I have never known it to be more centrally controlled. Members have virtually no rights, and a small group dominates. Why should anyone now want to be a member?'[22]

Box I.2 Failure of the main parties

Source A: Patrick Seyd and Paul Whiteley, 'British Party Members: An Overview', *Party Politics* **Vol. 10 (2004)**

In Britain there is clear evidence that a decline in most forms of activism has occurred . . . Whereas in 1990 almost 1 in 2 Labour members devoted none of their time to party activities, by 1999 this figure had risen to almost 2 in 3. Over a 10-year period there has been a significant growth in the proportion of members who do not work for the party in a typical month. This trend is also apparent for the Conservatives, albeit over a much shorter period of time between 1992 and 1994. We do not have trend figures for the Liberal Democrat members, but we see that 1 in 2 of them spent no time on party activities.

On the supply side, the pressures on people's time, in particular the amount of time spent at work, in domestic commitments or at leisure, make party activism less attractive. On the demand side, parties now have less need for their activists as fund-raisers and election campaigners and, as a consequence, they have reduced their incentives to become activists. For example, for Labour the activists' powers to choose party personnel, such as the party leader and parliamentary candidates, and to have an input into policy-making, have all been reduced. All three parties now elect their leaders by balloting the membership as a whole. Similarly, the selection of parliamentary candidates is by ballot of all local members rather than by local activists. These powers have been given to the members, irrespective of the time and effort that they devote to party activities, so there are now fewer rewards for becoming an activist.

Source B: Peter Hitchens, *The Mail on Sunday*, 4 October 2006

For about 25 years now, both Labour and Tory Parties have been in fatal, fast decline. Their membership has fallen, they have been unable to raise funds except by going to plutocrats. There are many reasons for this, but the main one is that the argument has shifted elsewhere. Labour and Tory no longer reflect or represent the true divisions in our society. They are elite organisations surviving by inertia. If they were commercial outfits, they would not survive at all. It is as if forgotten grocery chains, such as International Stores or Fine Fare, still dominated the retail market even though their shops were dingy, their prices high, their merchandise old-fashioned and shabby. But the rules of commerce don't apply in politics. Habit and unreasoning tribal loyalty sustain brands, which would otherwise be dead.

The Britain created by Attlee, Macmillan, Wilson, Heath and Thatcher was the result of a great national quarrel in the 1930s about class, poverty and unemployment. That argument was actually settled long ago in favour of the general idea of a welfare state that ensured nobody starved or froze, or went without necessary medical assistance. It is a reasonable idea if only it is limited to those who really need it. But the question of who needs it, and how much of it is necessary, is one of the questions that nobody dares talk about if they want a successful political career. Such questions are dangerous because they threaten the whole foundation of the political settlement in modern Britain. So, even though it would be good for the country to discuss them, they are not discussed – because it would be bad for the parties.

Source C: 'Disaffected voters turn to 'none of the above', Professor Anthony King, *The Daily Telegraph*, 5 February 2007

YouGov's latest survey for *The Daily Telegraph* suggests that the principal political divide nowadays is not between the Conservatives and Labour but between the British people and almost the whole of the country's political class. The fact that the Conservative and Labour Parties are now closer to each other ideologically than in the recent past seems not to have softened the widespread public discontent. On the contrary, the closer the main parties are to each other, the more people seem to resent the intensity – and, as they see it, the artificiality – of the ongoing party political battle.

If a majority of Britons are unhappy about politicians as a class of people, they are almost equally unhappy about the political parties. They feel unrepresented and they lack political choices with real meaning for them. The figures in the section of the chart headed 'Verdict on the party battle' speak for themselves. Nearly two-thirds of voters lament the fact that none of the parties 'accurately represents their own views' and add that in any case they 'really don't know any longer what the main parties stand for'. Almost as many believe all the parties are 'much of a muchness' and, even worse, that 'whichever party is in power, the quality of life in Britain seems to deteriorate'. Many of the disaffected are positively angry but some are just apathetic. Politics cannot anger them because they pay no attention to it.

Question: What problems of political parties are raised in these extracts, what causes are suggested, and do you think they are correct?

Lastly, the main parties have proved less and less successful at mobilising voters than in the past. Whereas between 1945 and 1970 the average turnout at general elections was 77.5 per cent, during 1974–92 it was 75.4 per cent, and in 1997 it reached a post-war low of 71.4 per cent, so that Blair's 'landslide' was actually won on half a million fewer votes than Major's narrow victory of 1992. In 2001 this trend was accelerated so that only 59.4 per cent of those entitled to vote did so, and for the first time more people – almost twice as many, in fact – failed to vote as voted for the winning party. In 2010, this figure remained stubbornly low at 65.3 per cent despite widespread use of postal voting, an eventful campaign and an extremely unpredictable result. A similar pattern of failure to mobilise has been manifested at local elections, by-elections and European elections, at all of which turnout fell by about 12 per cent after 1997. At least one parliamentary by-election campaign has enticed fewer than one-fifth of voters to the polls, and there are council wards in which turnout at local elections is below one in ten.

Even of those that vote, fewer vote for the main parties, and those that do feel less intense loyalty towards them. The share of the vote cast for the two main parties fell from 96.8 per cent in 1951 to 65.1 per cent in 2005; the number of 'very strong identifiers' – voters who tell pollsters they are very committed to their party – fell from 44 per cent of respondents in 1966 to below 10 per cent in 2005. The causes of this decline are the subject of extensive debate but, if it is one of the functions of parties to persuade us that voting in general, and voting for them in particular, are worthwhile, it cannot be disputed that they are measurably less successful than they have been in the past.

Conclusion

Analysts of the parties are divided between optimists and pessimists: some argue that parties have lost their way ideologically, lost their relevance organisationally, and cannot – however energetic their efforts – compete with modern expectations and new rivals as methods of expression of public opinion whether political, commercial or personal. Some of these critics come from the Left and call for more direct participation through campaign groups, referendums and workplace democracy; others, on the Right, regard the market as the efficient instrument for reflecting our choices in modern society, and that the whole machinery of the state and organised politics should have a much smaller say in our lives. All seem to see modern technology, the flexibility and diversity of our lifestyles, and the decline of social deference, as both causes and indicators of the obsolescence of the nineteenth-century mass party. Keith Sutherland put that case bluntly: 'the political party is an anachronism. It serves no useful purpose and we are better off without it. Furthermore, it is a danger to democracy and an affront to the constitutional dignity of our country.'[23]

There are optimists, however, who point to the fact that parties remain the major players in elections, the only continuously active and democratically structured political bodies in the United Kingdom. They question whether participation as a short-term activist in a single-issue campaign, or voting with one's resources as a consumer of goods and services, can ever be a substitute for collective decision-making and accountability in a permanent party with long-term ideological values. 'The fact remains', wrote Professor Paul Webb recently, 'that it is only the political parties that can legitimately perform the key function of aggregating demands into more or less coherent programmatic packages in democratic contexts. While this task is undoubtedly increasingly difficult, parties remain central to it.'[24]

The subsequent chapters will test these views of the role of political parties by examining each of the parties in turn, and comparing the ones with similar resources and functions – the ones of similar size – to each other. How have the parties changed in recent years? How well do they represent, organise and inspire us today? And what, if anything, could they do to achieve these goals more effectively? These issues will be the subject matter of *Political Parties in Britain*.

· ·

✔ What you should have learnt from reading this chapter

- You should be aware of the defining features of political parties, of their functions under the headings of policy, personnel and participation, and of the evidence which supports judgements about their fulfilment of those functions, including trends in party support and membership, activity, policies and leadership.

🔎 Glossary of key terms

Education Informing the public and answering its questions.
Elite recruitment Preparation and presentation of candidates and leaders.
Goal formulation Testing and prioritising of policies.
Interest aggregation Combination of different voters' ideas and preferences to produce a manifesto or programme.
Mobilisation Persuading the public to engage in political activity.
Representation The reflection of elements of public opinion by parties.

❓ Likely examination questions

What are the main features of political parties?

What are the key functions of political parties?

How do political parties in Britain contribute to democracy?

To what extent are British political parties failing?

Account for the declining reputation of British political parties.

Helpful websites

www.electoralcommission.org.uk is the website of the Electoral Commission, the body responsible for monitoring the electoral activity and funding of political parties in the United Kingdom. It gives access to research on party activity and records of donations, candidature and election results.

Suggestions for further reading

Ingle, S., *The British Party System: an Introduction* (Routledge, 2008), Introduction.

Marshall, J., 'Membership of Political Parties', House of Commons Library Standard Note SN/SG/5125 (2009, available online).

The Power Commission, *Power to the People: the report of an independent inquiry into Britain's democracy* (Joseph Rowntree Trust, 2006), especially chapter 6, 'Real Parties and True Elections'.

Webb, P., *Democracy and Political Parties* (Hansard Society, 2007).

THE MAJOR PARTIES

CHAPTER 1

The Labour Party

Contents

Overview

This chapter sets out the way in which the Labour Party was formed and developed, the different ideas and interests that co-operate and compete within it, and the reasons for its success and failure. It also tackles the question of how the Labour Party has addressed the dilemma between winning power in a capitalist society and implementing socialism in a meaningful form.

Key issues to be covered in this chapter

- How do the Labour Party's historical origins affect the party today?
- How consistent are the ideological traditions combined within Labour?
- Where does Labour's financial and electoral support come from?
- Who controls the organisation and policy of the Labour Party?
- What role does Labour now play in the national political system?

History

The foundation of the Labour Party

The foundations of the Labour Party lie in the workers' movement and intellectual socialist groups of the nineteenth century. Although the Labour Party has included more radical sections, the party has always championed parliamentary over revolutionary socialism. The Labour Party was formed in 1900 after the request was raised at the Trade Union Congress (TUC) calling for a 'distinct Labour group in Parliament'.[1] Up until this point there had been some labour representation at Parliament but the representation was not structured or co-ordinated. The most significant step towards creating a unified party was the formation of the Independent Labour Party (ILP) in 1893 led by a former miner, Keir Hardie, with the ILP gaining twenty-eight seats at the 1895 elections. It was not until the formation of the Labour Party five years later, however, that worker representation was consolidated in the long term. The party brought together trade unions, as well as socialist and co-operative groups, with the aim of raising the issues of workers at Westminster. It was decided that the organisation would agree policy and be supported financially by the union affiliation fees. Ramsay MacDonald, a prominent member of the Independent Labour Party (ILP), one of the socialist groups that set up the parliamentary party, was to be made secretary of the new group.

The Labour Party was established to represent moderate socialist opinion and avoided being too radical, dismissing calls for class war. The exact ideological position of the party was ambiguous but the party was heavily influenced by the revisionist socialism of German socialist thinker, Eduard Bernstein. The first major electoral breakthrough was in 1906, with the party winning twenty-nine seats. Most candidates were based in northern towns and were from working-class backgrounds. The party did not have a leader until 1922; until this point the most significant position within the party was the Chairman of the Parliamentary Labour Party, Keir Hardie being the first person to hold this post. In 1909 the Miners Union affiliated itself with the Labour Party allowing the party to become the uncontested voice of labour. Nevertheless, by the outbreak of World War I the party had not made the electoral impact it had hoped to achieve. Despite the Labour Party participating as a junior partner in the wartime coalition from 1915, Labour was very much the third party in the British system.

Interwar Labour politics and the first Labour government

In 1918 moves were made to consolidate the structure and the ideological direction of the party with the creation of a new party constitution. The new constitution had key democratic principles, including individual membership, and incorporated policies that would become cornerstones of the party, such as Clause IV which gave a commitment to public ownership. The clear ideological framework provided by the constitution took Labour away from the liberal influence that was present in the early years of the party's existence. After leaving the coalition government in 1918, Labour won fifty-seven seats in the general election of that same year.

By 1922 the Labour Party was the main opposition party in parliament with 142 seats, and Ramsay MacDonald was elected as the first Labour 'leader'. The acceleration of Labour's progress was considerable under MacDonald and the party was given its first, brief, time in power two years later as a minority government. Despite Labour having won sixty-seven fewer seats than the Tories, in 1924 MacDonald set up the first Labour government after the Conservatives failed to secure a mandate. Labour found itself relying on Liberal support to get bills through Parliament but did implement the beginnings of reform in housing, and made progress in foreign affairs with the Dawes plan. Nevertheless, after a couple of months, the minority government fell following the political fallout around the conduct of Attorney General Sir Patrick Hastings and Tory success at generating the 'red scare' (fear around the communist threat posed by Labour).[2] Criticisms were levelled at Labour on leaving office, particularly from the Left. Splits within the party rose to the surface and the Left accused the leadership of not being 'socialist enough' in government, an accusation which would resurface with every subsequent Labour administration. On reflection, however, the most noteworthy failure, especially in the eyes of the public, was the inability to make inroads into high unemployment levels. On Labour leaving office, there were over a million Britons out of work, much the same as under the previous administration.

Labour's problems of poor organisation and division were extensively worked on between elections. The leadership reworked Labour's programme by gaining majority decisions on policy at conference, allowing the leadership to go into the 1929 General Election with a strong hold on the party.[3] The failure of left-wingers to ignite a new period of class struggle allowed the leadership firmly to position the Labour Party on the centre ground. Conservative attempts to generate fear of radical socialism proved less successful than in 1924, resulting in Labour winning 287 seats compared with the Conservatives' 260 (despite the Conservatives winning a larger percentage of the vote – 38.1 per cent compared to Labour's 37.1). New trends made the election success even more satisfying for the party. Labour was no longer a party for the industrial north, and won seats all over the country, thus becoming a truly 'national' party for the first time. Despite winning, Labour was still a minority government which meant that getting legislation through Parliament would prove difficult. The new cabinet led by MacDonald had a number of the prime minister's key allies, but also rivals. The Labour cabinet also had a mix of experience and new blood with seven returning from the 1924 cabinet and seven new members, including the first woman cabinet member, Margaret Bondfield, as Minister for Labour. The main issue to be addressed was the economic crisis born out of the Wall Street Crash of 1929 and the mass unemployment that followed as a consequence.

Again in power, Labour failed to make a significant impact on unemployment levels and, by 1930, more than 2.5 million Britons were unemployed. In an attempt to bring about economic recovery, MacDonald introduced plans to reduce public spending and at the same time endeavoured to keep Britain on the gold standard. The policy of reducing government spending had little support in cabinet and led MacDonald to go to King George V to offer his resignation. The king, however, persuaded MacDonald to continue as prime minister at the head of a 'National Government' which would be a multiparty coalition rather than a Labour administration. This betrayal saw MacDonald thrown out of the Labour Party and forced to form the new National Labour Group with a few of his colleagues that had followed him into the National Government. With the National Government in power, the Labour Party returned to Opposition.

Opposition in the 1930s

The despondency of losing office caused the Labour Party to reform, focusing on funding levels which were much less than the revenue secured by other political parties. New funding plans led to a wave of union financial injection after it was agreed at conference to increase union affiliation fees. After failure in government, Labour looked to reinvigorate itself with a return to the 'fundamentals'. With moderates like MacDonald gone, agreement within the party would seem to be easier to achieve; actual policy initiatives were few and far between, however. Initially substance was limited but, eventually, moves to resolve this issue came with the publication of *For Socialism and Peace* which proposed a move away from MacDonaldism towards a highly planned economy and large state. At successive conferences moves were made to put meat on the bones, with the backing of policies such as nationalisation, as well as passing a resolution opposing taking office as a minority administration again. Policies generated at conference also included a socialist take on the anti-war culture of the 1930s, calling for a general strike to prevent Britain from becoming involved in further conflicts. Despite some discussion of the need for emergency powers in the form of an 'Enabling Act' in case of a national emergency, there was no evidence of a strong desire to leave behind the parliamentary socialism that formed the basis of the party.

Electorally, the 1930s was a dreadful period for the Labour Party. Its change in strategy failed to capture the mood of the country, with the party making few gains. Labour's failure to win votes was largely attributable to the fact that the leftist policies did not appeal to an electorate that, on the whole, was content with a National Government presiding over relative stability and rising living standards. The origins of eventual victory lay in the election of Clement Attlee who became leader of the Labour Party in 1935. As a politician, Attlee was in stark contrast to MacDonald; rather than oozing charisma, Atlee was seen as a quiet but sincere, proficient politician. Under Attlee the party became heavily influenced by the ideas of social liberal economist, John Maynard Keynes, with the party accepting capitalism but believing that government management of the economy should be the basis of development of a socialist society.

Wartime coalition

On the eve of war a political truce was called in the United Kingdom with the Labour Party supporting the Conservatives in their decision to go to war with Germany. During debates in the Commons, it became clear that the Labour Party was more eager than the government for a declaration of war. The majority of the parliamentary party was supportive of the leadership's calls for a declaration of war, with only twenty Labour MPs voting against. Labour eventually joined the wartime coalition when Churchill became prime minister. Churchill had taken a similar tough stance against Germany from the start and was believed by Labour to show the fighting spirit essential for a wartime leader. Labour was given considerable power in the government, despite its reasonably small representation in the Commons, with two of the five positions in the war cabinet. Being part of the war cabinet was an important step in Labour gaining power after the war. Firstly, it revived public trust in the Labour Party's ability to govern after the difficulties of 1929–31 but, secondly, gave a number of key Labour figures ministerial experience. With peace on the horizon, Britain's population was ready for a change of administration and the first Labour majority government.

Labour's first majority government and political consensus?

The Labour Party in power between 1945 and 1951 introduced the widest programme of socialist reforms in British history, with the implementation of a mixed economy, the founding of a welfare state, and a commitment to full employment, as well as prompting greater equality in society. Under Labour, much of industry, that had previously been in private hands, moved over into the state sector. This was part of a policy of creating a mixed economy with a mixture of state and private ownership. Under Labour, coal (1946), electricity (1947), railways (1947) and gas (1948) were among the major industries to be nationalised. The motivation for nationalisation was to ensure that companies were run in the interests of the people, with profits from these industries fed back into society in the form of welfare. When Labour left office, around 20 per cent of industry had been nationalised under the Attlee government.

The money generated from nationalised industry was used to fund an extensive welfare system set up under Attlee. The system included the flagship policy of the NHS (National Health Service), founded in 1948, that made healthcare free at the point of need. Existing welfare structures were also expanded, with reforms to family allowances, unemployment and sickness benefits, as well as education. The government also began to undertake a new house-building scheme that would provide homes for soldiers coming back from war and for those who had seen their houses destroyed during the conflict. The housing project also included clearing of slums, with state housing provided to remove people from living in squalor. As well as providing welfare support for those too ill to work and the unemployed, the Labour government also committed itself to achieving full employment. To a large extent, the commitment to full employment was met firstly by the creation of jobs as a result of expansion of the state sector and secondly through strict targets that meant that unemployment never rose higher than 3 per cent.

As a socialist government, the Labour administration of 1945–51 also committed itself to creating a greater level of equality within society through the use of a distributive tax system. High progressive taxes were introduced to even out inequalities, with tax contributions increasing for higher wage earners. The government also intervened in the economy to ensure that depressed areas, such as the north-east, received extra funding, and with government job-creation schemes set up to meet full employment targets. By the end of the 1940s, however, cracks in the Labour government were becoming clear. The Labour Party was burdened with an economy that had been left in an unhealthy condition by war and was struggling to meet demands for rebuilding. Post-war austerity measures were unpopular with the voters who resented the limitation of goods and the continuation of rationing. The control and the bureaucracy that remained were damaging to an Attlee government which gained a wider reputation for botched financial management.

Splits within Labour and back into Opposition

The Labour Party lost the 1951 election by a narrow margin despite securing 14 million votes (which was a larger percentage of the vote than they had managed to obtain in the previous election). Once in Opposition, existing splits came to the surface and Attlee's worsening health meant that he was unable to hold the left and the right wings of the party together. When Attlee retired later in the year, Hugh Gaitskell, from the **revisionist** wing of Labour, became leader. Throughout the 1950s Gaitskell came into increasing conflict with those on the left of the party, led by Aneurin (Nye) Bevan, who also had considerable support within the parliamentary party and among the trade unions. The conflict between 'Gaitskellites' and 'Bevanites' seriously damaged the Labour Party and limited its effectiveness in providing a first-rate Opposition to the Conservatives. The rift that caused the party so many difficulties after Attlee's resignation was never sufficiently patched up. As a result, 1951 to 1964 can be seen as a period of Conservative dominance, despite the limited abilities of Tory leaders or policy competence.

With Gaitskell as leader, Labour policy during the 1950s was heavily influenced by social democratic ideas (Box 1.1) leading to a promising election campaign in 1959. The 1959 election ended with an unanticipated loss for Labour, however, who neglected fully to exploit the failures of the Conservatives' 'stop–go' economic policy. As well as splits, explanations for the failure in 1959 centre on Labour's relationship with the unions and with radical social movements, as well as the failure of the party to reform its internal democracy. The unions had always had a strong power base within the Labour Party but during the 1950s and early 1960s there was growing anger within the unions at Labour leadership policy and pressure from the unions to alter the direction of the party in accordance with union requests.

Labour's failure to modernise

Towards the end of the 1950s, the Labour Party tried to reform but failed to gain enough support to modernise the party; to a large extent this was because of union resistance to change. In 1959 Gaitskell attempted to reform the Labour constitution and remove Clause IV, the commitment to state ownership of industry for the workers. Strong opposition from the unions and other members on the left of the party, however, meant that Labour did not seize the opportunity taken by other socialist parties in Western Europe to become a more centrist, '**catch-all**' party. Instead, this move would be undertaken in a radical way by Blair in the 1990s.

Box 1.1 Comparison between social democracy and democratic socialism

	Social democracy	Democratic socialism
Collectivism	• A mixture of collectivism and individualism. • Favours a classless society.	• Emphasises the importance of collectivism, with people working together to the benefit of all. • Class based.
The economy	• A mixed economy, embracing neo-liberal principles and reducing government intervention in the economy. • High taxation to allow for redistribution of wealth.	• **Keynesian** economic policy with considerable government intervention and nationalisation. • High taxation to allow for redistribution of wealth.
Equality	• Equality of opportunity.	• Equality of outcome.
Welfare	• Welfare with conditions – e.g. 'rights we enjoy reflect the duties we owe' (Revised Clause IV Labour Constitution).	• Extensive welfare provided at the point of need.
Key proponents	• Anthony Crosland, *The Future of Socialism* (1956). • Anthony Giddens and The Third Way. • Tony Blair and 'New Labour'.	• Attlee Government 1945–51. • Tony Benn, *Arguments for Socialism* (1980). • 'Old Labour'.

Harold Wilson and the return to power

With Gaitskell's unexpected death in 1963, Harold Wilson became leader of the Labour Party. Unlike his predecessor, he largely managed to keep internal disagreements under control but was also helped by a change in attitude within the party which had become weary of conflict and disappointed with more than a decade out of office. In 1964, Wilson secured a narrow victory with 44.1 per cent of the vote compared with the 43.4 per cent of the vote gained by the Conservatives led by Sir Alec Douglas Home. Labour's power was consolidated with another election in 1966 in which Labour won 47.9 per cent of the vote. Labour in power was not the radical force that some had predicted when the 'left winger' Harold Wilson won the leadership. Instead, policy under Wilson would show a continuity with many policies of the previous Conservative government, and pragmatism rather than a dogged attachment to socialist ideology. The reason for the move towards the centre was partly because Wilson had one eye on the re-election of Labour but also because of fiscal constraints. Britain's economy was in a poor state by the end of the 1950s with many Conservative policies being short-term fixes to huge long-term problems. Wilson was under considerable pressure from the Left to continue the socialist transformation of the state begun by Attlee but the Left was firmly informed by their leader that 'socialism costs money'.[4] Some reforms, however, did emphasise the party's commitment to nationalisation, such as renationalisation of steel. There was also a promise made by the leadership to the party faithful that further socialist reform would come after economic recovery. The British economy would continue to struggle, however, showing little sign of an upsurge.

To view the Wilson government as purely pragmatic or a continuation of Conservative ideas is unjust. Between 1964 and 1970 fundamental changes were introduced, championing equality of opportunity and empowering sections of the population previously under-represented, including women and poorer members of society. Despite economic constraints, the Wilson government introduced a range of policies which reflected the liberalised attitudes of 1960s Britain and that also met key socialist egalitarian aims. The most pioneering reforms were those that increased choice for the individual, with important changes to the laws regarding abortion and divorce. The Abortion Act, 1967 liberated women from the dangerous and shameful fate of 'backstreet' abortion; at the time of reform, around 100,000 illegal abortions were being carried out each year. The Divorce Reform Act, 1969 ended the need for guilt or fault, with a further act coming the year after that for the first time recognising that a wife's work, whether inside or outside the home, made a financial contribution and so should be considered in the settlement of property. Considerable reform also occurred within education. In 1966 the government led the drive to encourage the growth in comprehensive schools which took students regardless of academic performance. By 1970, 1,145 comprehensive schools had been introduced, with one in three students attending one.

Nevertheless, there were limits to reform, with the government allowing other types of school to continue to exist, including academically selective grammar schools. The abolition of grammar schools was a thorny issue for Labour with Wilson unmoving on the issue, stating when asked about the subject that grammar schools would be abolished 'over my dead body'. The reason why the subject was so contentious was that many of the party were mindful of the fact that they themselves had benefited immensely from a grammar school education. There were other areas that generated disagreement: for instance, the postponement of raising the school leaving age split the cabinet along class lines. Cabinet members such as George Brown, who came from a working-class background, were furious at middle-class colleagues who failed to recognise the significance of the policy that had been promised in two consecutive Labour manifestos.[5]

Shock defeat of Labour in 1970

The shock result of the 1970 General Election saw Labour lose to the Conservatives under Ted Heath. The Tories managed to secure 330 seats compared to Labour's 287, despite the fact that Labour had led in the polls throughout the whole election campaign. The Conservatives introduced a radical economic policy based on the beliefs of the modernising **New Right** faction of the Tory Party that took many of its economic principles from the classical Liberalism. In following New Right ideology Heath broke the post-war Keynesian consensus. Despite two years on a new economic path, however, in 1972 Heath performed a U-turn and dropped many of his more radical policies when the economy hit trouble and unemployment rose to the then unthinkable level of one million.

For the next two years the Conservatives followed a more moderate path but came into increasing conflict with the unions and, after failing to curb union power, Heath was forced to call an election in 1974. The Conservatives went to the polls looking to restrict the influence of unions which had threatened to dictate the direction of the government. Heath's campaign asked the electorate, 'who runs the country'; the majority of voters decided it was not him, which saw the Labour Party in power once more under a minority government led by Harold Wilson. After another election later on in the year, Labour secured an outright majority, though at just three MPs, that majority was tiny. The small majority put the leadership under considerable pressure as the left of the party aimed to make the most of the fragile position by pushing for a radical socialist programme. MPs, such as Michael Foot and Tony Benn, pressed for unilateral nuclear disarmament and an increase in state control of the economy through a new wave of nationalisation, as well as withdrawal from the European Economic Community (EEC) which Britain had joined the previous year. What made the threat worse was that the pressure to move away from the centre was not just coming from troublesome backbenchers but also from members of the cabinet. Despite Wilson's reputation for strong cabinet control, he appeased the left wingers of his party by calling for a referendum on EEC membership under his own newly negotiated terms. The leadership allowed all within the party a free vote; notable cabinet ministers including Tony Benn spoke out against EEC membership. The referendum put to the British people in 1975, however, resulted in overwhelming support for EEC membership, with the majority in the country deciding that the United Kingdom was best served inside rather than outside the EEC.

Callaghan's leadership and Labour in decline

Weary and worn out, Wilson resigned in 1976 and was succeeded by Callaghan which signalled a calculated move back to the centre for Labour. Successive by-election defeats removed Labour's majority, forcing the Labour Party to seek support elsewhere and form the 'Lib–Lab' pact. The pact with the Liberals that was in existence from 1977 to 1978 was not an official coalition but, instead, it was an agreement for Liberal support for legislation going through Parliament on a bill-by-bill basis. The most significant event of the Callaghan premiership was the need to ask the International Monetary Fund (IMF) for financial support. This humiliation of having to ask for financial support showed acceptance of the dire straits that the British economy was in as a consequence of poor economic management and industrial decline in the United Kingdom since the war. The unhappy task of asking for outside help fell to the Labour prime minister in 1976 and, consequentially, Labour policy was severely restricted by limitations placed on the government by the IMF. The most important restrictions included: a reduction in public spending; vetoing of nationalisation and part privatisation of BP; as well as imposed monetary targets with all departments having their spending capped.[6] Despite strict guidelines, the set of harsh economic measures introduced by Callaghan did not have the impact desired. Trade disputes with the unions became a serious problem for the government, with the unions continuously rejecting government pay proposals, leading to widespread strikes among the transport and public service unions. The disruption caused by strikes, along with the harsh money-saving measures enforced by the government, led the winter of 1978–9 to become known as the 'winter of discontent'. The desperate state of Britain finally led the public to lose faith with the Labour Party and consequently the party lost the general election in 1979 and would not return to power again until 1997.

Opposition and radicalisation of the 1980s

The splits within Labour between the Left and the Right that had historically divided the party came to a dramatic head in the 1980s. In 1983 Labour would suffer its worst post-war electoral defeat following a lurch to the left by the Labour leadership which took few Labour supporters with them. The rift began to bubble up following electoral defeat to Margaret Thatcher in 1979, with differing opinion within the party on how to rebuild. Differences were so great that some members would choose to leave Labour to set up a new party. The signs of another seismic split were clear after the prominent moderate, Roy Jenkins, in all but words proposed the setting up of a new centre-left party. A breakaway of Labour moderates seemed almost inevitable after Callaghan resigned and Michael Foot was appointed leader. With the election of a leader from the left of the party, the final push was given to moderate Labour MPs and, in March 1981, Jenkins, Owen, Williams and Rodgers known as the 'gang of four' launched a new party, the Social Democratic Party (SDP) whose ten MPs followed the 'gang of four' over to the new party.

Despite the departure of some moderates from the Labour Party, there was by no means complete domination of the party by the Left. In 1981, many 'left-wing' candidates failed to gain re-election to the National Executive Committee (NEC) so domination of the direction of the Labour Party could not be guaranteed. The Labour leadership was more radical than it had been for some time but its power over the party as a whole was relatively fragile, partly because of the 'bottom-up' nature of Labour but also because of the way in which Michael Foot was elected. Foot had won the leadership largely on the basis of union support but had gained less support within the Parliamentary Labour Party that was, by and large, more moderate.

Removal of the militants

The frailty of the British economy in the early 1980s had made the Conservatives seem vulnerable but, with the 'jingoism' resulting from success in the Falklands War in 1982 coupled with infighting within Labour, the Conservatives were ensured victory. Labour policy had also contributed to the party's defeat. Voters overwhelmingly rejected a radical left-wing manifesto that was dubbed 'the longest suicide note in history' with Labour gaining only 209 seats. Policies – with such ideas as the five-year economic plan having overtones of soviet economic management – failed to appeal to the public. Many policies were also out of touch: for example, the call for the United Kingdom to leave the European Economic Community (EEC) was not a prominent issue for most voters. Labour also failed to connect with a wide enough demographic and was damaged by a focus on industrial democracy and renationalisation which failed to appeal to all but a small section of the electorate. Added to issues of divisions and unpopular policy was the lack of personal appeal of the Labour leader, Michael Foot, who, when interviewed, seemed uncomfortable and amateurish compared with the Conservative leader Margaret Thatcher (who had previously been ridiculed as unconvincing). The final result, of winning only 27.6 per cent of the vote, was Labour's worst performance since 1918, with Labour even losing out in their traditional heartlands and among the section of society that the party had been founded to represent, the working classes, with a considerable percentage of that section's vote going to Thatcher. The political impact of Thatcher caused Labour to react, accepting the change in the political landscape. Defeat in 1983 shocked the Labour Party into change and, though the swing to the left was not as great as sometimes maintained, there was after 1983 a definite shift back towards the centre. That shift was marked by the election of the less radical Neil Kinnock as Labour leader, with Roy Hattersley as his deputy.

Labour move to the centre ground

The decision for the Labour Party to move back to a more moderate stance was taken after the catastrophic defeat in the 1983 election and begun under the guidance of Neil Kinnock. Kinnock reshaped the internal workings of the party, changing rules over the election of candidates and centralising power within the party. Over nine years, he was able to reduce significantly the power of the militant Left, and changed the policy direction with a move away from the traditional commitment to nationalisation, withdrawal from Europe, nuclear disarmament and protection of trade union power. The move to take the party to the centre ground, however, and the development of Labour into a modern 'catch-all' party occurred under the stewardship of John Smith and then, after Smith's untimely death, under Tony Blair. In the 1990s Labour would be rebranded as 'New Labour' and, rather than drawing on traditional socialist ideology, would take on a new stance more akin to social liberal thinking. New Labour would take the seminal work of sociologist Anthony Giddens, *The Third Way*, and use it to modernise the politics of the Left, taking on a fusion of ideas including 'stakeholder capitalism' and **communitarianism** as well as the 'duties' owed to society.

Blair's social democracy and modernisation

Tony Blair envisaged a type of 'one-nation socialism' that would benefit all, not just the rich. Blair believed that the market economy could be used to help groups that had become socially excluded.

'One-nation socialism' would also create a robust, relatively free market that could generate wealth which could be taxed and used to amend social inequalities. The state could use the revenue from tax to provide an extensive welfare system thereby removing the causes of social exclusion. Unlike previous Labour rhetoric, however, plans to tackle poverty emphasised social responsibility as well as support. Campaign slogans, such as 'tough on crime, tough on the causes of crime', that become central to the 1997 election campaign captured this 'rights with duties' ethos of New Labour.[7]

The third way in action saw fundamental changes to Labour as an organisation and in its policy direction. The biggest reform for the party was the alteration of the constitution with the removal in 1994 of Clause IV, the commitment to nationalisation, that had existed as a core principle of Labour since 1918. Gaitskell had attempted, and failed, to make this amendment thirty years earlier. The changing of the constitution under Blair firmly established that the balance of power within the Labour Party had moved from the left to the more moderate centre ground. The new Clause IV referred to rights but also to the 'duties we owe', reflecting the responsibilities of citizens as well as privileges.

New Labour and the embracement of the market

Under Blair, economic management had many similarities to policy under the previous Conservative government. Enterprise was mostly private but industry was to be scrutinised by the establishment of regulatory bodies such as the Competition Commission. The market was accepted as the best way of creating wealth so assets that had previously been in the hands of the state were transferred to the private sector, with moves such as the privatisation of air traffic control. There was also a withdrawal of the state from economic management, with the intentions of the New Labour government established from the off with the Bank of England being granted independence in 1997.

New Labour had considerable success and proved, initially, to be popular with the public. Under New Labour there was a greater role for the state in welfare provision and, to facilitate the commitment to the state provision of services, a growth in the numbers of those employed by the state. Between 1997 and 2005 41,000 more teachers, 66,000 more nurses and 14,000 more police were provided, to support Labour's continued commitment to public services. Waiting lists in hospitals, that had been such a hot topic when Labour came to power, were cut by ten months. The commitment to assisting the poorest members of society was addressed by an increase in welfare, with spending going up year on year. The foundation of schemes, such as Sure Start, aimed to level the playing field and provide a solid platform for children from a range of backgrounds thereby furthering equality of opportunity.

The decline of New Labour and Brown's leadership

Despite increased spending by the state, the Labour Party under Blair was becoming increasingly unpopular; criticism over the morally questionable war in Iraq, along with a reluctance by Blair to relinquish the reins, caused a slump in popularity as shown by opinion polls. When Blair finally did resign, and Gordon Brown took over, prospects initially looked promising, with Brown boosted by the perceived effective handling of a national crisis, the outbreak of foot-and-mouth disease. The public also seemed to like the break from the 'sound-bite' culture that characterised Labour under Blair and, for the first couple of months of Brown's premiership, Labour's standing in the polls improved. The 'Brown bounce' was relatively short lived, however, as Brown's dithering over whether to call a general election or not turned the tide against the new leader and, from that point on, the Labour Party popularity declined in the polls.

The Labour Party led by Gordon Brown into the 2010 General Election was beset by difficulties. Short of money and with the lowest memberships in years, the signs of a party coming to the end of its time in power were apparent. Heavy losses in the 2007 council elections, the London mayoral elections and in European elections coincided with significant defeats in by-elections leading up to the general election. By-election losses in Labour heartlands, such as Glasgow, as well as in Nantwich and Crewe, were unhappy omens for the failure to come. The country that the Labour Party presided over had deep-set problems; in recession after a worldwide financial slump, unemployment levels were growing and, with a lack of finance, the government had to accept the necessity of cuts. General public discontent with the political class was also at an all-time high with the expenses scandal hitting Westminster damaging all parties. Although Brown himself did not lie accused of abusing the system, some of his cabinet colleagues, such as Hazel Bleers, did as did many members of the Parliamentary Labour Party who were also found to have exploited their positions and, most damaging to Labour's electoral chances, were often unrepentant about their actions.

Brown and the 2010 General Election

Going into the 2010 election, Labour Party policy saw a leap back to traditional Labour ideals with faith placed in the merit of Keynesian solutions to economic problems. Labour chose to borrow and to cut taxes to provide incentives for the public to spend Britain out of recession.[8] The decision by Brown to bail out the banks was widely considered to be a sound one. Nevertheless, the policy left the Labour government unpopular with the public as the help to the banks was perceived as allowing bankers to 'get away with it'. Brown also opted for Keynesian solutions to regenerate industry, using state funds to stimulate the private sector with a £1 billion innovation fund that would provide private-sector funding. A popular but temporary measure was the reduction in VAT which was introduced to encourage spending and stimulate the economy. The consequence of Chancellor Alistair Darling's economic measures was moderate success in refreshing the economy, and Britain's growth was higher than that of many other European countries. Short-term successes did not mean that Labour was not criticised, however; national debt was considerable at 62.1 per cent of gross domestic product (GDP) and Labour suffered attacks from the Conservatives and from the Liberal Democrats that tainted perception of the Party's economic record and increasingly swayed public opinion towards believing that it was 'typical' Labour economic mismanagement.

Policy since 1997 had broken the association of Labour with economic crisis which had plagued the party historically but the financial crisis that started in 2008 threatened to destroy the reputation secured by more than ten years of economic growth. Despite the success of Labour's opponents in convincing the voters of Labour's frailties, in reality Britain's situation was not as bad as was feared. National debt was high but, put into context, it was not as high as that of other strong economies, such as Germany where national debt was at 64.9 per cent of GDP. This said, Britain had problems that other countries did not have to overcome; for instance, Britain's deficit remained high at 10.4 per cent of GDP.

Despite the Labour government's relatively steady management of the economy, the 2010 election saw Labour unable to get across the message of the party's firm economic management under the circumstances. In the 2010 election campaign opposing parties successfully painted Labour as having 'bankrupted the country',[9] leading to their eventual defeat at the polls. Brown then resigned as Labour leader. Even though many big hitters entered the race to become Brown's successor, the comparatively inexperienced, former energy minister Ed Miliband won a leadership run-off against his considerably more experienced brother David. Ed Miliband won the election largely on the vote from outside the Parliamentary Labour Party, causing disquiet in some ranks about his ability to command the party and fears about his being able to mount a successful opposition to Cameron's Conservatives. However, Briefly after his election, however, Ed Miliband did overtake Cameron in the opinion polls. The direction of the party under Ed Miliband is hard to gauge at present and a 'policy review' is currently being carried out. Comments made by Miliband on policy so far, however, suggest no drastic move away from policy under Brown's leadership.

Ideology

There can be no point in searching the encyclopaedias for a definitive meaning of socialism; it has none, and never could.[10]
Anthony Crosland, *The Future of Socialism*, 1956.

As established by Crosland in *The Future of Socialism*, socialism as an ideology is too disparate to pin down because of the wide range of groups that refer to themselves as socialist. Interpretations have ranged from seeing socialism as an economic model favouring state ownership to more recent interpretations that see socialism as an ideology that ensures equality by harnessing the market and distributing wealth (Box 1.3). Despite such a wide range of interpretations of the ideology, key features are common to all strands, notably the commitment to equality, a positive view of human nature and a belief in the moral obligation to ensure fundamental rights to all. The type of socialism championed by the Labour Party has varied over time. The socialist traditions associated with the Labour Party in Britain, however, have tended to be influenced by evolutionary, rather that revolutionary, socialism. This section will explore the development and key components of socialist ideology.

Box 1.2 Utopian socialism, Marxism and revisionism

Utopian socialism was based around the premise that humans were innately good, proposing it was the natural instinct of human beings to co-operate, rather than compete for scarce resources. In the early 1830s the growth of utopian socialism was headed by followers of the French philosopher Saint-Simon and the British industrialist Robert Owen who referred to their egalitarian and co-operative theories as socialism, meaning the term 'socialism' was in common use in the UK by the 1840s. Charles Fourier was one of the first thinkers to advocate living in a utopian community. Fourier based his theory on the principle that collectivist living was the natural solution to conflict caused by competition in the modern world.

Marxism, shaped by the German Karl Marx, was an alternative to utopian ideas and favoured scientific socialism which took a distinct 'scientific' approach to analysing society and the historical course of change. Marx predicted a 'proletariat' (workers') revolution once the workers developed class consciousnesses (recognition of their exploitation as workers). Marx was writing with the backdrop of the 1848 revolutions that had sprung up throughout Europe challenging the rule of absolutist monarchs. At this point in history, throughout Europe workers seemed to have little alternative to revolution as all political avenues were denied them, with control resting in the hands of traditional political elites. The right to vote was coupled with property qualifications and, though the growing industrial middle class was beginning to challenge traditional elites, Marx felt this did not go far enough; for Marx it would take revolution to overhaul the system completely. Once the workers had removed the capitalist state, there would be a temporary period of transition which Marx called the 'dictatorship of the proletariat' where previous inequalities would be broken down and industry would be temporarily placed in the hands of the state to ensure that the profit went to the workers. Eventually, once socialism was established, the state would wither away to leave a classless communist society. Although Marx has proved to be the best-known socialist philosopher, Marxism was not taken up by the UK Labour Party. The development of social-ism in the UK was forged under different conditions in which the development of capitalism accompanied cautious democratisation which in turn led to a slow improvement of working class conditions. The growth of working-class institutions, such as trade unions, and the growth of socialist political groups caused mainstream British socialism to move away from revolutionary Marxism to a more evolutionary formula.

Revisionism grew out of the work of Eduard Bernstein who revised Marxist thought. Bernstein's book, *Evolutionary Socialism*, was the first piece of revisionist literature to be released. For Bernstein the development of the democratic state left the call for revolution redundant and, using the vote, socialist political parties would come to dominate the political arena owing to the numerical superiority of the workers. This revisionist approach would become the eventual basis for mainstream political groups, including the British Labour Party, throughout Europe.

Question: To what extent is it true to argue that revisionist socialism is the only relevant strand of socialism in the United Kingdom today?

View of human nature and the importance of collectivism

Socialists have a positive view of human nature, seeing humans as essentially social creatures whose actions are shaped by the society they live in rather than being dependent on intrinsic characteristics. Therefore, socialists reject the idea that a person can be inherently 'bad'; instead they believe that 'bad' behaviour can be provoked by conditions in society. Socialists see human nature as malleable, shaped by experience, and argue that 'nurture' in the development of human character overrides the significance of nature. As social-ists prioritise the importance of social interaction, their political outlook is widely shaped by the importance placed on collectivism. Collectivism is used by socialists to rationalise the actions of people within society and to justify the power of collective organisations, and collectivism is promoted as a way of assuring fairness through the redistribution of wealth. The premise that it is a natural instinct to

act in a collective manner is used by socialists to explain the organisation of society. As human nature leads people to seek interaction, it
becomes inevitable that groups will form. Socialists argue that groupings within society become relevant political entities whether it is as
a class, a nation or an ethnic group. Socialists promote collectivism
on the basis that collective human effort is of greater practical and
moral worth than individual, self-serving goals. An example of collectivism in action is the work of trade unions. Since the nineteenth
century, unions have tried to improve the pay and conditions of
workers rather than leaving each worker to negotiate individually.
Traditionally, trade unions collectively have won considerable concessions; for instance, in 1963 under the Conservative government
of Harold Macmillan, the Contracts of Employment Act was passed,
guaranteeing basic employment rights together with wage rises.

Collectivism and the redistribution of wealth

Socialists believe that one of the fundamental benefits of collectivism
is a commitment to a shared responsibility for poverty alleviation
which encourages redistribution of wealth. As well as being a natural
preference, socialists argue that collectivism is also more desirable
because it is fairer and more beneficial than it is to encourage competition where individuals seek to meet personal goals. Welfare systems,
where everyone is expected to pay into a system through tax and
which allow access to all according to their own need, provide good
examples of collective action in practice. Essential to socialist ideas
of a collective welfare system is that contributions should be calculated according to how capable someone is of paying. Linked to this
is the premise that each individual has responsibility for the welfare
of others in society and no one should be left to go without. This has
led socialist governments to introduce collective systems, such as the
NHS created by the Attlee government in 1948.

Often collective action is interpreted as the state acting to uphold
the collective good. The ability for all to reap the benefits of the
wealth created in society is realised in collective ownership of states
assets in the form of nationalisation. The Attlee government of
1945–51 undertook the biggest nationalisation project of any British
government, with 25 per cent of industry coming under state ownership. This involved bringing natural monopolies, such as railways and

gas, public utilities, such as electricity and telecommunications, as well as heavy industry, such as iron, coal and steel, under state control. Within the Labour Party a commitment to collectivism, in the form of state ownership, was enshrined in the 1918 constitution stating, 'we aim to secure for the workers . . . the full fruits of their industry and the most equitable distribution thereof that may be possible upon the basis of the common ownership of the means of production.'[11]

Egalitarianism

Egalitarianism, the belief in the importance of promoting equal political, economic and social rights for all people, is an underlying principle of socialism. The importance of equality means that, for socialists, everyone deserves equal rights including equal chances to succeed in society. Socialists champion equality as a way of ensuring social cohesion. Socialists believe that the root of conflict within society has always been unequal distribution of resources whether this is between individuals or, on a grander scale, between countries. Therefore, socialists maintain that equality is desirable because it allows for co-operation and for genuine community. Views on equality have varied between socialists and have evolved over time within the Labour Party, with Brown being the first Labour leader to state categorically that the Labour Party no longer believed in equality of outcome, favouring, instead, equality of opportunity.

Box 1.3 Equality of opportunity and equality of outcome

Equality of outcome proposes that equal treatment must result in people ending up with the same conditions. Equality of outcome takes into account the circumstances of each individual before distribution and adjusts the amount owed appropriately.

Equality of opportunity advocates that each person should be equally positioned with respect to opportunities to complete for a good on a level playing field.

Question: To what extent is the goal of equality of outcome possible in a modern society such as that of Britain?

The Labour Party's assertion of a preference for equality of opportunity has been mirrored by most modern socialist groups. The socialist understanding of equality of opportunity differs from traditional understanding of the concept, however, which can be described as a 'simple' equality of opportunity. Rather than 'simple' equality of opportunity that provides equal legal rights (as proposed by classical liberals and conservatives), socialists favour a more 'complex' form of equality where maximum opportunity is given to everyone. A more 'complex' form of equality proposes that legally defined equality has not given equal access to opportunity and, rather than assuming differences in society come from natural abilities, proposes that social factors, such as schooling, family, access to resources and encouragement given to an individual, have a greater impact on an individual's ability to fulfil potential.[12] 'Complex' equality of opportunity can be realised through equal access to resources that have an impact on life chances. On this basis, for a person to have the best chance to succeed, it is essential that there is the opportunity of access to quality education and welfare, and for protection at work to be assured. In practice, the Labour Party has encouraged equal opportunity in education with the drive to encourage comprehensive schools, as well as in health care with the foundation of a universal NHS providing help at the point of need. It can also be seen in the attempts to improve conditions of work, including reform of employment law to ensure equal treatment, such as the national minimum wage that was introduced in 1999 to ensure just reward for work. [13]

Social Justice

Social justice is the idea that fairness should be applied to the social reality to ensure that burdens and benefits are distributed equally within society. For socialists, society at present is not equal because of underlying inequalities based on traditional social structures and historically uneven access to economic resources. Therefore, as equality has not yet been achieved, socialists maintain that the goal is to create a society based purely on merit. The social democratic branch of socialism has been influenced by the work of the social liberal, John Rawls, who advocated the need to consider common requirements for fairness as part of distributive justice. Distributive justice is proposed as the most effective 'tool' to create an equal society based on talent rather than simply to leave distribution to the market alone. With distributive justice, worth is attributed to an individual's work in society, and distribution is undertaken through a progressive tax system with higher earners paying a larger proportion of tax. Different levels of tax ensure that people contribute according to their ability to pay. Tax is then used to reduce inequalities through a welfare system that provides opportunities for the least well off.

As well as distributing resources in society, achieving social justice might also require the engineering of opportunities to overcome inequalities. Methods, such as 'positive action' which proactively intervene to aid disadvantaged groups, can be used to ensure justice. An example of a 'positive action' is the choice made by some London schools with high immigrant populations to teach lessons in the mother tongue of pupils. The aim of intervening is to overcome the immediate barrier of language, thus allowing pupils to achieve qualifications that will make them competitive in the job market. As well as positive action, positive discrimination can also be used to tackle inequality. Positive discrimination implies using specific criteria for the selection of people of different social groups as a way of addressing inequality within society. Positive discrimination was used by the Labour Party with the creation of an all-women shortlist before the 1997 election.

Class

Traditionally, class has been vital to socialists because the ideology has been dominated by concerns for the oppressed working class. Though the ideology may be interpreted in different ways, all types of socialism have a common class-based origin. The importance of class within socialism was immensely influenced by Marxist thinking. For Marx, class was the basis of inequality within society because class was economically determined and wealth was divided unfairly. Marx proposed that the proletariat (working class) was being exploited by the bourgeoisie (property owners) and, because there was such disparity in goals, that class interests were irreconcilable. Therefore, for Marx, the only solution to overturning inequalities between different classes in society was revolution. Although the revolutionary aspect of Marxism never gained prominence in Britain, the importance of class and championing of the rights of the oppressed worker did ring true. The British Labour Party was founded on class lines, and the commitment to the worker was enshrined in Clause IV of the constitution which promised to, 'secure for the workers by hand or by brain the full fruits of their labour'.

Nevertheless, with the reduction of class identity, increased social mobility and the desire for broader appeal, socialist parties, such as the Labour Party, eventually abandoned rhetoric that was based on class lines. The most important work on the subject within the **revisionist** Left in the United Kingdom was Tony Crosland's *The Future of Socialism* (1956) which maintained that, 'Marx has little or nothing to offer the contemporary socialist' and argued that Britain was a 'classless society'. Today, social democrats play down class ties, preferring to appeal to the classless centre. Evidence of this move away from class identity can be seen with the British Labour Party which removed the mention of 'the workers' in Clause IV of the constitution in favour of a commitment to 'live together, freely'.

The right to work

As the workers lay at the heart of socialist ideology, the importance of work as a means of survival, as well as an identity (as your work defined your class) became fundamentally important. Utopian socialists argued that involvement in the economy gave identity and pointed out the value gained by working because of natural human instinct to create. This creative spirit was jeopardised with the coming of the Industrial Revolution as a person's creative experience of work was destroyed and replaced by the monotony of factory work. Marx rejected utopian ideals in favour of scientific socialism but shared the concerns of early socialists about the threat to identity caused by the onset of capitalism. Marx maintained that work often created alienation in a capitalist society owing to the obligation to undertake repetitive tasks. Marx also observed, however, a development in fraternity that came about because of conditions in an industrial society that required people to work together on the factory floor rather than at home alone.

Because work had acquired an elevated status in socialist theory, socialist political parties enshrined the importance of work in their foundations. This can be seen with the British Labour Party and the defence of the 'right to work'. The concept of the right to work lost favour towards the end of the twentieth century, however, and changes in employment levels meant that some members of British society had never worked so had failed to forge this connection between their identity and employment. The option not to work was made possible largely because of the welfare system introduced under Labour in 1948. Labour created welfare on the assumption that all people would want to work but, if they were sacked, the state would offer support in the form of unemployment benefit to avoid destitution. The principles on which the welfare system was created assumed that people would want to avoid being out of work at all costs, because work was a large part of their identity, and that they would apply for unemployment benefits only in desperate circumstances. In modern society, however, this identity through work was not as strong as it once had been and, what was more worrying to many, was the attitude among some members of society who were choosing not to work. Successive governments have tried to deal with the modern problem of generations of people who had never been employed, and aimed to break the cycle of people using benefits as an alternative to paid employment. In a radical move that disappointed those on the left of the party, Labour under Blair dropped the 'right to work' in favour of the idea of 'rights and duties' which placed a heavier emphasis on obligation to make a contribution to society.

Property and attitudes towards the economy

Historically, property has been seen in a negative light by socialists on the premise that property is the root of inequality. According to Marxist theory, property was power, and the concentration of property in the hands of the bourgeoisie, and the absence of property for the proletariat, formed the basis of all ills in society. Marx maintained that a fair society could be achieved only through the abolition of private property. Though socialism in Britain has not developed along Marxist lines, the Labour Party traditionally took the view that the unfair distribution of property was detrimental to assuring equality. Consequently, successive Labour governments have proposed that a considerable amount of property, in the form of business, should be owned by the state to ensure that the power was used to guarantee the best for all in society. Nevertheless, even the most socialist of governments, such as the Attlee administration, nationalised only 25 per cent of the economy, and Labour in power has never advocated the confiscation of private property. Instead, socialists in Britain have favoured distributive methods that aim to redress the balance of property ownership across the population. British socialist governments have used the tax system to require individuals to give up some of their own money (technically their property) to the state and have redistributed property through welfare. In recent decades, social democrats, such as the New Labour government, have softened the party's approach to private property, encouraging the accumulation of wealth and the formation of a 'property-owning democracy'. Under Labour in the 1990s, privatisation of previously state-owned property took place, and ensuring fairer distribution of property was seen as a long-term project, helped by the creation of equality of opportunity, which would allow everyone to own property if they wished to do so.

The economy and property

Socialist views on the economy vary considerably and have developed over time as the rhetoric of modern socialist parties, such as Labour, has moderated and moved towards the centre ground. Initially the economy was viewed as an arena where the workers remained isolated owing to their lack of property and the means to generate wealth. Revisionists proposed, however, that managing the economy effectively could promote egalitarian values through redistribution, and the accumulation of wealth could act as an incentive to provide motivation within society. The existence of a mixed economy, which included both private and public ownership, has been the economic system favoured by the British Labour Party in power, accepting the need for private property to exist. Under Blair, this idea was developed with the removal of Clause IV from the Labour Party constitution. Capitalism became accepted by Labour as an effective way of creating wealth and welcomed as long as social justice was maintained and the poorest provided for. Blair called this 'one nation socialism'.

Recent Labour policy reflects this change in attitude; for instance, in Britain today enterprise is mostly private with large-scale industry regulated by bodies such as the Competition Commission. There has also been considerable privatisation under Labour, including the Bank of England in 1997 and air traffic control.

> ## Box 1.4 Labour economic policy since 1997
>
> - Freeing up the labour markets, e.g. EU Amsterdam Treaty 1997.
> - Low taxation to reduce boundaries to wealth creation and economic growth, e.g. VAT was cut to 15 per cent to ease the recession under Brown.
> - 2010 manifesto highlighted economic growth, not fiscal austerity, as the key to tackling Britain's £178bn deficit.
> - Increasing the Pension Credit to a minimum of £130 a week.
> - Extra cash to encourage employers to recruit people without jobs.
> - Those earning more than £150,000, pay income tax rate of 50 per cent.
>
> **Question: To what extent has the Labour Party embraced the role of market forces in control the economy?**

Support

This section explores the traditional demographic of the Labour vote and the changes to support over time, as well as exploring Labour Party support in the 2010 General Election. Historically, Labour's support has come primarily from the working class, as the section of society that the party was founded to protect, with a sizeable segment of working-class support coming from the trade unions. Labour has also always enjoyed a larger share of the ethnic minority vote owing to the perception of Labour as a more inclusive party that actively promoted ethnic minority rights. Furthermore, there is evidence to indicate that Labour rhetoric has a tendency to attract more male voters than females. Nevertheless, because of changes in society and in the political landscape, patterns of party support have also altered, challenging the traditional understanding of voting behaviour.

Traditional links between Labour and the working classes

Research into party preference traditionally emphasises the belief that, rather than being chiefly influenced by 'issues', voters are more strongly swayed by 'generalised attitudes'. In practice, this translates as the 'attitudes' the public associates with particular parties. 'Attitudes' of parties rest in the core values and characteristics that shape their identities. For Labour, this includes issues such as welfare, state intervention and high taxes but, most significantly, voters have traditionally identified Labour as the party of the working classes. Therefore, political scientists have maintained that the strongest determinant effecting how individuals vote is class. The importance of class is emphasised by Pulzer, who claimed: 'Class is the basis of British party politics; all else is embellishment and detail.'[14] With the Labour Party this argument has considerable weight because the party was founded on a class basis, promising to further the rights of the working person. Through studying voting behaviour in elections, the division of voters according to class seems to play out in practice, with around two-thirds of the working class consistently voting for Labour. This said, the working-class vote has become less of a guarantee over time, with a change in the social and economic make-up of the country, meaning identity through class is not as strong as it once was. Consequently, rather than voting for 'their own party', many working-class voters have voted Tory. Nowadays, there is a trend towards **partisan dealignment**, and traditional patterns of voting no longer apply. The biggest switch of the working-class vote away from Labour occurred under Thatcher. The Conservatives managed to secure the support of up to 36 per cent of the working-class vote. Despite the loss of some traditional supporters, significant patterns remain. Those people who live in council accommodation are more likely to vote Labour – as was the case for Brown in 2010. The numbers voting from council areas fell in the last election, however, meaning that the core vote in many areas is no longer engaging in the political process in the way it once did.[15] Despite continued support from trade union members, the numbers of voters in trade unions also declined dramatically.

Winning back the traditional Labour vote and appealing to 'Middle England'

The recognition that the working-class vote is not guaranteed Labour support is a pattern increasingly understood by political scientists, as it is by the Labour Party itself, causing a shift of party policy to assure the retention of votes. The attempts to win back the working-class vote, however, have not automatically focused on 'typical' working-class issues. Instead, the Labour Party has often changed to appeal to working-class voters seeking social advancement. The decline in class rhetoric has been a conscious move by Labour to attract working-class voters who had switched their support to the Conservatives. The move away from class-based electioneering is not just a trend under New Labour; calls for Labour to become a 'classless' party go back to Anthony Crosland during the 1950s and 1960s. The percentage of manual workers voting for Labour had already begun to decline, as observed by Crosland in the 1960s when around 62 per cent of them voted Labour.

The case for avoiding class-based electioneering has become stronger with time. The change in the type of employment within the United Kingdom, with the continuing decline in British industry, means that the numbers of people in unskilled or unionised work have fallen sharply, so the core base of support no longer exists. Steven Beackon called this shift a, 'fundamental change . . . in the relationship between the Labour Party and its traditional supporters', with the majority of manual and non-skilled workers no longer confined by union demands but concerned with a whole new set of issues and, in many cases, a desire for social progress.[16] Rationalisation of this decline in Labour's core vote reveals a link with the change in the British economy but also shows that social mobility leads to a fall in the numbers of those who identify themselves as working class. Many people, who would once have been employed in manual jobs, now work in the private sector and are home owners with one or more cars. Along with changes in lifestyle and job patterns has come an alteration in politics which, in the 1980s, led this section of the electorate to vote Conservative.

By 1997, however, these socially mobile voters with working-class roots were once again voting Labour, largely because of a deliberate move by the Labour Party to win these voters back. Blair made a conscious move to rebrand to ensure that the party would regain the supporters it had lost to the Conservatives in the 1980s. The decision by Blair to target the socially mobile electors, who had become part of 'middle Britain', was shaped by his experience in the unsuccessful 1992 Labour election campaign and by a meeting with a former Labour voter who had switched to the Tories. Blair found the man polishing his Ford Sierra in front of the house that he now owned. As he listened to the man's explanation of why he had shifted to the Tories, Blair realised the need for Labour to appeal to the social climbers who had once been the core of Labour's electorate. After reflecting on that incident, Blair said later 'people judge us on their instinct about what they believe our instincts to be'.[17] For Blair, support was not solely about the manifesto or the speeches made during the election campaign but about the 'brand': if Labour were to win support people's acceptance of the brand was vital. The success of this change in outlook was great and, with the brand 'New Labour', Blair managed to win support from all sections of society. At conference in 2005, Blair triumphantly proposed that 'twenty years ago we gifted the ground of aspiration to the Tories; today we've got it back, and we'll never yield it up to them again'.[18]

As well as appealing to voters who had left behind their working-class roots, the attempt to appeal to traditional 'Middle Britain' also won over a large percentage of more typically middle-class support. Labour Party appeal to middle-class voters is not in itself a new phenomenon. As early as the 1960s, one in six middle-class people supported the Labour Party, and the proportion grew to one in four by the 1970s. During the 1980s, the percentage of the middle-class vote declined but a similar pattern across all votes could be indentified during this period. Under New Labour, many voters switched their support to Labour largely because of the successful performance of the government's economic policy up until 2008, and because of the limit on the tax increases that would had scared away middle-class voters in the past.

The significance of gender and race on the Labour vote

Trends over time have shown that men have been more likely to vote Labour. Historically, this can be explained by the greater numbers of men in paid employment and belonging to trade unions, coupled with the fact that women tended to prefer the social conservatism offered by the Conservative Party. In 2010, however, this trend was reversed with more women than men voting for the Labour Party, and Brown received 31 per cent of votes from women compared with 28 per cent from men.[19] Probably the most significant factors in explaining the increase in the number of women voting Labour are the family-friendly legislation of Labour governments from 1997 to 2010, including increased spending on schools and hospitals, as well as the promotion of women's issues through equality legislation. In addition, some female voters may have been influenced by the attitude of the party towards women, with important strides made in increasing women's representation in Parliament, including all-women shortlists in 1997 and family-friendly parliamentary sitting times. The impact on voters' choice as a consequence of changes to women's roles at Westminster is difficult to measure, however, and the effect is almost certainly small, with reforms likely to appeal only to a specific type of female voter. Whether the increase in the female vote for Labour is a long-term trend is also yet to be established.

Existing voting patterns reveal that ethnic minorities are more likely to vote Labour than for any other party. The reasons for this concentration of votes for Labour include the disproportionate percentage of the Pakistani, Black and Bangladeshi population working in manual jobs and, consequently, disproportionally disadvantaged by poverty and social deprivation. Research also shows that ethnic minorities from Pakistani, Black and Bangladeshi backgrounds are more loyal to Labour and consistent in their support by coming out to vote. In addition, other explanations for strong support for Labour within ethnic minority communities have centred around the fact that Labour as a party has led race-relations legislation and, historically, has taken a more moderate attitude towards immigration. Despite strong support for Labour within ethnic minority communities, there is a growing disparity between the voting behaviour of Indians and other ethnic minority groups, with Indians increasingly likely to vote Conservative owing to Tory support for small and medium-sized businesses and the popularity among Indian voters of the Conservatives' traditional moral values. Although there are strong patterns of ethnic minority support for Labour over time, the 2005 election saw a dip in that support, with a notable fall in the percentages of Bangladeshis and Pakistanis voting Labour. Issues such as the war in Iraq and the War on Terror, as well as asylum legislation, can help explain the blip. During the 2005 election a large percentage of the ethnic minority vote shifted to other parties, including the Liberal Democrats and the Respect Party in London. Discontent with Labour was high enough, in 2005, to lead to the party losing the safe seat of Bethnal Green and Bow to the Respect Party; Labour retook the seat in 2010, however.[20] Despite historical patterns of strong turnout from particular ethnic minority groups, the ethnic minority vote overall was down 0.2 per cent in the 2010 election. This decline could suggest that, running up to the 2005 election, Labour's policy might not have just caused a blip in support but that, in the long term, Labour may not be engaging with ethnic minority voters in the way the party once did.

Support at the 2010 General Election

During the 2010 election, Labour lost many of the supporters it had managed to win from the Conservatives in the previous two elections, as well as losing the support of liberal middle-class voters to the Liberal Democrats. Eventual defeat for Labour was predicted but the election did not play out exactly as many had envisaged it would. Despite some ups and downs, the support for Labour in the second half of 2009 going into 2010 was increasing but the party remained behind the Conservatives in the polls. New to the election campaign in 2010 were the three television debates, with 9.4 million people tuning in to watch the first one, providing the opportunity for a charismatic and articulate party leader to boost support. It was predicted that the debates would not be Gordon Brown's forte and that the media aspect of the election would boost support for the Conservatives because of their more polished leader, David Cameron. Cameron's failure to shine in any of the three television debates, however, led to a much closer election than many had predicted.

The election on 6 May 2010 resulted a decline in support for Labour which won 29.7 per cent of the vote with a 5.1 per cent swing from Labour to the Conservatives. Labour lost eighty-seven seats to the Tories and did not gain any. What was clear from the result was that Labour had failed to retain its previous supporters, with many people who had switched to Labour under Blair returning to the Conservatives. The most noteworthy aspect was the loss of votes from the Labour Party to the Liberal Democrats who were picking up previous non-voters, the youth vote and liberal middle-class protest votes. As well as losing votes to the Lib Dems, the Labour Party also lost out to smaller parties such as the United Kingdom Independence Party (UKIP), and even lost some votes to the British National Party (BNP) though not as many as was feared during an election campaign that was dominated by immigration. The Labour Party lost a significant section of support in its heartlands in Wales, the Midlands and the north, with the percentages of the vote falling most significantly in the north-east where Labour support fell by 9.3 per cent. The only area in which Labour gained support was in Scotland with the Fife-born prime minister proving to be more palatable than his predecessor.[21]

Overall support for the Labour Party is at a low ebb after electoral defeat but the poor performance in the 2010 General Election was unsurprising, coming as it did during a recession and with Labour seeming weary, having been in office for thirteen years. The level of support for Labour under their new leader, Ed Miliband, is uncertain and, though some patterns can be drawn from the 2011 local elections, it is too early to make conclusive judgements but the initial signs were not encouraging. An unimpressive performance during the 2011 local lections saw few Labour gains and a failure to win over voters unhappy with the harsh cuts made under the coalition. What seems to have happened is rather than disgruntled voters – especially those who voted Lib Dem in 2010 – registering a protest vote with Labour, many, including traditional Labour voters, chose to stay at home.

Funding

Historically, securing funding has always proved more difficult for Labour than for the Conservatives because of the lack of big donors and because of the party's traditionally less well-off support base. Traditionally, the unions provided most of the Labour Party's funding which, alongside the party's structure, explains the strong role of the unions for most of the twentieth century. As a result of internal democratisation within the Labour Party, however, the power of the unions has declined, as has their financial contribution, comprising about 30 per cent of all Labour funds.

Most of Labour's funding, about 40 per cent, comes from its members in the form of membership fees and donations. Traditionally, members of the party have been of a similar demographic as its voters, including working-class members and a sizeable proportion from a specific type of middle-class background, namely intellectuals, civil servants and other people employed in public services. The smallest percentage of funds, 10 per cent, is raised by the Labour Party from its commercial activities. A further 20 per cent of funds comes from the '1000 club' donors, so called because they contribute £1,000 or more during a year. Under New Labour, big donors became increasingly controversial as the press highlighted links between positions gained within Parliament and large cash donations. Prominent cases included that of Lord Sainsbury, who became science minister under Labour, having previously deposited a large amount of cash into Labour Party funds. Other accusations suggested that large cash donations could influence policy when, shortly after a £1 million donation to Labour from F1 boss Bernie Ecclestone, Formula 1 motor racing was exempted from a new cigarette advertising ban.

Funding from membership
After such difficulty for the Tories in the 1990s over sleaze and bribery campaigns many were shocked at Labour's questionable judgement over funding deals that came to tarnish New Labour's whiter-than-white reputation. However, closer examination of Labour's finances reveal why Labour were prepared to risk speculation with big money donations. During recent years membership of the Party has declined rapidly and, with Labour relying on members for the largest percentage of its funding, the fall in support was catastrophic. At its peak Labour had over a million supporters but, over time, numbers have reduced sharply as the Labour Party faced the common problems of a decline in popular attachment to parties and a reluctance to associate closely with a political party. Under Blair, membership levels started to rise again, bucking the general trend, and peaked at 405,000 after Tony Blair came to power in 1997. The recovery was short-lived, however, as membership figures fell to 198,026 in 2005. In recent years, the downward trend has continued, and the deterioration of support means that the Labour Party has, in effect, lost 27,000 members a year since the beginning of the decade, causing considerable damage to funding levels.

Much has been made of the fact that the Labour Party does not have the big donors that the Tories rely on and, consequently, the dwindling membership is more disastrous for Labour than it is for the Conservatives who have similar issues of declining membership. It is true that the Conservative Party does have more money than the Labour Party but Labour has begun to emulate Tory tactics to improve finances, encouraging more large donations with the setting up of the '1000 club', and even 'Red' Ed Miliband has accepted donations from big business. The playing field during has been levelled slightly, with the Neill Report setting a limit of £15 million on party spending during an election campaign. During the 2010 election, the Labour Party spent £8,009,483, around half the amount spent by the Conservative Party.[22] Nevertheless, the finances of the Labour Party remain an issue, and the party has admitted that it was facing 'cash flow problems', with debts of £23.4 million putting its already fragile monetary resources under further pressure.[23]

Structure and organisation of the Labour Party

This section will look at the structure of the Labour Party and examine the different components of its internal organisation, including the National Executive Committee (NEC), Parliamentary Labour Party (PLP), the Constituency Labour Party, as well as assessing the role of the leader and party democracy. Labour was founded as a grassroots movement and, consequently, power was exercised from the base upwards. Over time, however, the structure and organisation of the Labour Party have become more hierarchical, transferring more power to the leader, taking away the influence of conference and the unions in an attempt to sharpen up the party machine.

The National Executive Committee (NEC)
The Labour Party is different from other mainstream British political parties in that its origins lie outside Parliament. As a result, its structure continues to reflect this extra-parliamentary foundation, being a 'bottom-up' party (in theory at least) rather than a 'top-down' party like the Conservatives. Labour was founded in 1900 with the joining together of trade union groups and socialist organisations, including the Fabian Society, the Independent Labour Party (ILP) and the Social Democratic Federation (SDF). Consequently, these separate organisations retain considerable independence when they come together during a party conference. As a 'bottom-up' party,

conference traditionally had huge significance for Labour because it was the time when all strands of the party met and when the NEC was elected. The party structure was shaped with representatives from the union and socialist organisations uniting as part of that National Executive Committee to oversee its work. The structure was formally set in the Labour constitution drawn up in 1918. The NEC was to be elected at each annual conference with seats allocated to socialist groups and to union representatives, distributed according to size; as a result, a majority went to trade unions. The creation of the party structure, along with the large union financial input, consolidated trade union dominance of the Labour Party.

Over time the Labour Party structure has developed to reflect changes in the political climate. The party's shift to the left during the 1980s led to calls for reform from those sections of the party that wanted to move Labour back to the ideological mainstream. On the back of electoral defeat in 1983, reforms altered the balance of power within Labour to create a more 'top-down' party and break from traditional grass-roots control. This more centralised structure saw power move away from extra-parliamentary elements. The NEC now has a leader and deputy; the trade unions hold 50 per cent of the votes at conference, and twelve of the thirty-two seats on the committee. The reforms aimed to reflect all aspects of the Labour movement, with separate representation for the Constituency Labour Party, the front bench, and the Parliamentary Labour Party, together with the European Parliamentary Labour Party (EPLP). There is also representation on the NEC from socialist societies, such as Young Labour, as well as five spaces reserved for women who are elected by conference, as well as the party treasurer.

The NEC also plays an important role in organising the party and has significant influence over the selection of candidates. Under Neil Kinnock, the process of making Labour more electable included the removal of the 'Militant Tendency' within the Party, and this ultimately meant intervention in candidate selection. The NEC also controls the Labour Party outside Parliament and, despite the encroaching influence of the leadership, it remains the official job of the NEC to run the party machine. Under leadership guidance, the NEC was tasked with reorganising the party machine, including reworking the Labour 'brand' to improve the presentation of the party to the electorate. The change in emphasis and the move to portray a more professional and organised party were led by Larry Whitty as general secretary and Peter Mandelson in the new role of director of campaigns and communications. Mandelson also went on to set up the Shadow Communications Agency, using public relations experts to modify Labour's image. The rebranding of the Labour Party was completed with the controversial abandonment of the historical socialist red flag as the party logo in favour of the more 'voter-friendly' red rose. There was also an attempt to portray a more businesslike image which involved meticulously planned policy launches that became part and parcel of a multimedia age. Under Mandelson the New Labour way of working was established, with glossy presentation and strict organisation. Reforms began to make Labour more electable but the change was not without critics from all areas within the party. The new, precise organisation was predictably disliked by many of those on the left of the party but it was not popular either with some of the more moderate characters, such as Mandelson's successor as director of campaigns and communications, John Underwood, who later resigned in protest over disappointment at the triumph of style over substance.

The Parliamentary Labour Party (PLP)

The Parliamentary Labour Party refers to those Labour members at Westminster who accept the Labour whip. Within the PLP smaller factions represent different elements of the party but, as a whole, the PLP has the role of putting forward Labour issues in Parliament. Originally, the PLP was largely working class and, during the first half of the twentieth century, three-quarters of Labour MPs came from manual labour occupations. Post-war, however, the nature of the PLP has changed and the majority of the PLP is now from a middle-class background. Analysis of previous occupations reveals that most, 35 per cent, were in professional jobs and only 2 per cent now came from a manual background.[24] To a considerable extent, the pattern can be seen as part of a general trend within Parliament and across society; the PLP remains much more middle class than the country as a whole, however.

Another trend that has been used to question the representativeness of the PLP is the continued pattern of the majority of it being middle aged. The average age of Labour politicians increased again in 2010 with 60 per cent now over fifty; this pattern is in contrast to the other parties where the average age of MPs is going down.[25] Women and ethnic minorities remain underrepresented in the PLP, with levels of representation slow to increase and, in some cases, declining during some parliaments. Despite the general trend of increased female membership, the number of women is disproportionate to that in the country as a whole. That said, Labour is still leading other parties in becoming more proportional, holding the record for the largest number of women in the Commons, with sixty-four 'Blair babes' elected in 1997. Worryingly, however, the number of female MPs has declined since 1997 and, of the current PLP, just 28 per cent are women. The pattern of underrepresentation can also be seen in the ethnic makeup, with Labour having only forty-six MPs from ethnic minority backgrounds but this is a number that has been steadily rising in successive parliaments.[26]

Constituency Labour Party

The Constituency Labour Parties (CLPs) have the role of gaining support for the Labour Party, supporting the local MP, generating funds for the party and electing candidates. Though election campaigns are guided by the centre of the party, the majority of the work of canvassing and promoting the Labour Party in the constituencies is done by the CLP. The CLP offices also have a vital role in supporting MPs, with a large percentage of constituency business dealt with at local offices, along with the implementation of party-wide initiatives. Everyone who wishes to be a member of the Labour Party can join centrally but becomes a permanent member of the party only if there are no objections from the local party to the prospective member becoming part of the CLP.

The CLP is organised into ward parties that elect delegates to represent the ward on the ruling body of the CLP, the General Committee. Members of the CLP's General Committee then elect an Executive Committee to deal with the running of the party. Each CLP also has an additional type of membership, just as on the national level, with affiliated societies including union braches but also other groups, such as the local branch of the Young Labour or the Co-operative Society.

Recent drives by the national party have tried to encourage more action and fundraising at CLP level because, historically, the CLPs have failed to be as active as their Conservative counterparts. At present, just over 40 per cent of Labour's funding comes from members' applications and small donations at CLP level. The membership of CLPs is disproportionately male and white; nevertheless, they have a larger ethnic mix than the other mainstream parties. The characteristics of the CLP have changed dramatically over time, largely due to the decline in working-class participation in the Labour Party at CLP level, following a wider trend of reluctance to associate closely with political parties. An interesting shift in CLP membership has been the move towards more middle-class members, characterised by Peter Jenkins as 'lumpenpolytechnics' referring to the fact that around two-thirds of the party are now 'professionals' and less than a quarter comes from manual occupations. It is the increasing number of middle-class members of the CLPs, including public-sector workers, teachers, lecturers or local government civil servants, who have become the main activists at CLP level.[27]

Since 1993 parliamentary candidates have been elected on the basis of one member one vote within the constituency. Parties are provided with party lists from which a shortlist is created. The election of a candidate must always be approved by the NEC, with the NEC reserving the right to veto any candidate – though this rarely happens in practice. The threat of NEC interference has encouraged constituencies to choose leadership-favoured candidates to avoid conflict with the NEC. Some controversy around the selection process has been raised, especially the reduction in grass-roots power, with the CLP limited by party lists and NEC checks. The primary motivator for more control from the centre, however, was the wish to drive out militant elements from the party and avoid hard-line candidates. Nevertheless, the concern that has been raised by reform is the new issue over party lists that have increased control by the centre of the direction of the Party. This said, the use of lists has not been purely a tool to promote candidates that toe the party line. The use of lists has also been important in ensuring one of the most important socialist goals of Labour, that of greater equality, with the use of all-women short lists in 1997 boosting the number of women representing Labour in Parliament.[28]

Internal party democracy

Much criticism has often been levelled at political parties for failing to have internal party democracy. Assessments of the Labour Party's internal democracy have focused on the disproportionate amount of power traditionally held by the trade unions. Criticism prompted reform of the NEC and a decline in the percentage of funding gained from union subsidies. Despite the commitment to parliamentary socialism, set out with the foundation of the Labour Party, the party has, at times, had issues with its militant wing, and it was not until reforms of the 1980s that the antidemocratic element was removed from the party once and for all. Concerns still remain about some elements of union control, most notably the role of the unions in electing the leader. A recent example of this controversy, is the election of Ed Miliband who was able to win the leadership contest on the basis of union support without much support in the PLP. Attempts to modernise internal party democracy have led to new problems, most notably, the potential dominance of the leader and the worryingly tight control of the party machine as a result of reforms to the NEC and election of candidates, so that the party centre is far stronger than it once was.

The party leader

The Labour Party leader has traditionally been weaker that the Conservative counterpart but, with the reform of the NEC, the powerbase of the leader's office, and access to the communications team, the influence of the leader has been able to grow over time, and has become ever more powerful in recent years. Historically, the Labour Party's culture has revolved around the independence of different sections of the party and around open discussion and influence over policy at conference, rather than around any emphasis on unity or loyalty to the leader. So, traditionally, the Labour leader has found it more difficult to exercise control over the party especially when compared to the internal hierarchy and resulting deference historically enjoyed by the Conservative leader. Nevertheless, Kinnock and Blair have been held up as examples of leaders who have 'taken on the party and won'. Kinnock's ability to shape the party was extensive. Over nine years, he managed to marginalise the militant Left and changed the course of policy with a move away from the traditional commitment to: nationalisation, withdrawal from Europe, nuclear disarmament, and protection of trade union power. Kinnock's reorganisation and reform transformed Labour into a modern social democratic party, and this laid the foundations for further changes under Blair with his New Labour brand.

The creation of the communications team allowed considerable leadership control over how the party and how the leader was presented to the electorate, with public perception of the leader now crucial to party success. Now, more than ever, when voters assess the parties, much of their judgement is based on how much they like the leader and whether or not that leader would make a good prime minister. In seeking office in 1997, Blair presented himself successfully to the public, creating a confidence in his ability to run the country. Not all leaders have been as successful in playing the media game, however. In the 2010 election campaign, the BES survey revealed that only 25 per cent of those asked said they would prefer Gordon Brown as prime minister, compared to 33 per cent who chose Cameron.[29]

A Labour leadership election can take place either when the existing leader stands down or when a challenge is made to the incumbent. If a leader stands down, a contest is triggered automatically, with new candidates being put up for nomination. To take part in a leadership election, potential candidates require support from 12.5 per cent of Labour MPs. A challenge to the leader may also lead to a leadership election, but a potential candidate requires 20 per cent of the vote. The change from only 5 per cent to 20 per cent was agreed upon in 1988, following Tony Benn's unpopular challenge to Neil Kinnock as leader. These regulations were brought in as a sequence of reforms aimed at reinforcing the power of the leader. The increased level of support needed to mount a challenge to the leader also helped Gordon Brown fight off a leadership challenge in 2010. The challenge from the Blairites' faction, led by Geoff Hoon and Patricia Hewitt, came to nothing because canvassing opinion among MPs revealed there was not the 20 per cent needed to trigger a contest. Further reforms to leadership elections also made the process more democratic by removing the larger weight of the trade union vote (which amounted to 40 per cent of the total vote until 1993). These reforms meant that every member of the party had an individual vote in the leadership election rather than the block votes that existed within the CLP and trade unions before 1989 and 1993 respectively.

The selection of a new Labour leader takes place at conference; if the party is in government, a leadership election will take place only if the majority of conference requests it. The voting procedure involves an electoral college, with the party divided into three blocks. The blocks include: section 1, MPs and MEPs; section 2, individual members; and section 3, Labour's affiliated organisations (most of which are trade unions). Each block is granted a third of the votes. The MPs and MEPs are granted one member, one vote (OMOV); the individual members of the party are allocated one vote each as part of a nationwide ballot, which is then registered as a combined vote; and members of affiliated organisations cast OMOV, which is then aggregated from a national total. The candidate who wins more than half of the votes overall is then declared leader. If no candidate gains half the votes on the first ballot, further ballots are held on an elimination basis, with votes redistributed according to preferences indicated on the ballot paper.[30]

Despite the reforms during the 1980s, the leadership voting system remains controversial. The extent of this controversy was revealed in the leadership election of 2010 which saw Ed Miliband becoming leader on the back of union support and ahead of his brother. Ed Miliband failed to gain the majority of votes in the parliamentary party, calling into question his right and power to lead the party at Westminster. In response to the criticism of his reliance on union support, and his resulting nickname of 'Red Ed', in December 2010 Ed Miliband announced leadership reforms. Proposed changes included reducing the weight of the trade union vote.[31] Nevertheless, other problems with the leadership voting system remain, including the fact that some votes are 'more valuable' than others because of the different sizes of the various sections of the electoral college. For instance, a PLP vote is worth 0.1 per cent of the electoral college compared to 0.0013 per cent for a CLP vote and 0.000008 per cent for each vote of members of affiliated organisations.[32] In addition to procedural failures, critics have also pointed out that the process, though more democratic than the previous system, is costly and time-consuming, diverting attention from political activity. In the summer of 2010, the preoccupation with Labour's leadership election allowed the newly elected coalition government to remain unscrutinised during its early stages.

Formulation of policy

Theoretically, formulation of policy is supposed to take place at conference but, in actuality, such a high level of grass-roots control over policy does not, and has never, truly existed. In reality, the leadership of the party has been the main driving force behind policy, with leadership power over policy formation increasing with reform. Nevertheless, despite increasing influence, the level of control over policy by the leadership within the Labour Party is not as great as that enjoyed by Conservative leaders. Within Labour, leadership control of policy is shared with the National Executive Committee, with NEC proposals, forged in its committees, forming the basis for many of the proposals to be debated during conference. Traditionally, alongside the parliamentary leadership, the NEC has also been central in drawing up the party manifesto. Nevertheless, as part of streamlining process begun in the 1980s, the policy-making role of the NEC has declined. The creation of a joint NEC–(Shadow) Cabinet Committee was designed to facilitate parliamentary steer-ing of policy, giving the front bench a constitutional role in policy creation. NEC influence over policy has also been reduced by other centres of policy, such as the National Policy Forum, created in 1990 alongside further independent policy groups that have become more prominent since the early 1990s.

Reforms under New Labour reduced party-based policy-making still further. In 1997, Blair created 'partnership in power' which was a two-year programme of policy-making. 'Partnership in power' left the formulation of policy to the leadership, and then ideas were sent to the NEC, finally being put before conference as part of the last stage of policy-making. This method allowed far more control of policy-making, and of the direction of the party, because the content of policy was decided by the leadership. Despite being criti-cised for reducing internal democracy within the Labour Party, the new method of policy-making has improved the image of the party because it has avoided the public confrontation within it that had dogged the image of the Labour in the past.

Current Labour policy

Election defeat and the appointment of a new leader in 2010 mean that the policy direction of the current Labour Party is still being forged. Ed Miliband has given early signs of general direction but, as yet, there is little detail as the party conducts a 'policy review'. On being elected leader, Ed Miliband proposed the 'need for change', seeming to distance himself from Labour under Brown, yet initial indications fail to show a real change in the party's direction.

In contrast to the coalition's wide range of cost-cutting measures, the Labour Party under Ed Miliband has opted for a continuation of the Keynesian approach used under Brown, highlighting the need to encourage economic growth, not fiscal austerity, in tackling Britain's £178 billion deficit. Under Miliband, Labour has vowed to introduce plans to create jobs, choosing to intervene in the economy to stimulate revival. Other economic policy proposals also indicate a return to traditional socialist values, such as the pledge to introduce a living wage of £7.60 an hour which is designed to protect workers' rights and give a boost to those members of society in most need.

The Labour Party has accepted the need for some reduction in public spending but favours increases in taxes, rather than cuts in welfare, to reduce the deficit. Under the new leadership, the proposal to raise income tax rates to 50 per cent for those earning more than £150,000 a year remains Party policy. Ed Miliband has made it clear, however, that this is purely an emergency measure, and maintains that this policy would end once Britain was out of economic difficulties. Analysis of economic policy suggests that Ed Miliband is not as 'red' as many supposed; he has also ruled out renationalisation and the practice of accepting donations from 'big business'. On many economic issues, Miliband seems firmly to have accepted New Labour ideas, proposing 'capitalism that works for the people',[33] which appears to be a very similar idea to Blair's vision of 'stakeholder capitalism' in which the market economy works to benefit all, not just the rich.

In some areas of policy, Miliband seems to use rhetoric more commonly associated with the Conservatives, calling for a renewed commitment to the values of family, community and decency at work – certainly he would find common ground with Cameron in this area. Such statements reveal a similar commitment to morally

Box 1.5 Two views of Labour's strategic position

Source A: Tony Blair, *A Journey* (2010)

The Labour Party won power when it was New Labour. It lost because it stopped being New Labour. This is not about Gordon Brown as an individual. It is true he is unsuited to the modern type of political scrutiny in which characters are minutely dissected. He was never comfortable as the 'normal bloke' sort of politician. He didn't need to be. He had strengths: he was regarded as hard-working, with his heart in the right place, intelligent, and definitely committed to the country. Had he pursued New Labour policy, the personal issue would have made victory tough to achieve but it wouldn't have been impossible. Departing from New Labour made it so. Just as the 2005 General Election was one the Labour Party was never going to lose, 2010 was one Labour was never going to win – once the fateful strategic decision was taken to abandon the New Labour position.

Source B: Len McCluskey, General Secretary of 'Unite' trade union, *The Guardian*, 16 January 2012

Ed Balls's sudden embrace of austerity and the public-sector pay squeeze represents a victory for discredited Blairism at the expense of the party's core supporters. It also challenges the whole course Ed Miliband has set for the party, and perhaps his leadership itself. Unions in the public sector are bound to unite to oppose the real pay cuts for public-sector workers over the next year. When we do so, it seems we will now be fighting the Labour frontbench as well as the government. The political elite that was united in promoting the City-first deregulation policies that led to the crash is now united in asserting that ordinary people must pick up the tab for it. It leaves the country with something like a 'national government' consensus where, as in 1931, the leaders of the three main parties agree on a common agenda of austerity to get capitalism – be it 'good' or 'bad' – back on its feet. This confronts those of us who have supported Ed Miliband's bold attempt to move on from Blairism with a challenge. His leadership has been undermined as he is being dragged back into the swamp of bond market orthodoxy. And this policy coup may not be the end of the matter. Having won on the measures, New Labour will likely come for the man sooner or later. And that way lies the destruction of the Labour Party.

Question: What pressures have come to bear on the policy position adopted by Ed Miliband?

conservative values that were also present in Blair's rhetoric. This suggests that Miliband's ideological source might not be the Right but the New Labour favourite Anthony Giddens's *The Third Way*, which championed communitarian ideas that emphasise support for the community and the social importance of the family unit.

On welfare policy, Labour has maintained strong support for substantial welfare provision, choosing not to propose harsh cuts to departmental budgets. Miliband's promise to make Britain 'more prosperous, more equal, more fair and just',[34] reveals an ongoing commitment to providing social justice, inferring support for the use of distributive justice, through a system of progressive tax and welfare provision. The party has also promised to 'prioritise' the NHS; the claim to be 'prioritising' the NHS, however, has been made by every mainstream political party at present, leaving the policy failing to stand out. In the Commons, Miliband has called Cameron's promise to revise the NHS reforms a 'sham'. As a party, Labour is overwhelmingly opposed to government reforms to the NHS that would see 80 per cent of the budget being placed in the hands of GPs.

It is hard to gauge in which direction Ed Miliband will take the Labour Party, not least because, having held the modest position of energy secretary in the last Labour government, there is only that, the leadership campaign, and his modest record so far to assess. Although Miliband called for 'change', in reality there is considerable continuity with the previous administration and, at the 2011 Labour Party Conference, Miliband gave interviews insisting that he was not 'left wing'. It could be that, just like many other politicians in the current political climate, Miliband is calling for 'change' as it seems to be deemed compulsory to secure election. What is clear, through the existing policy and through the actions of Ed Miliband since becoming leader of the Opposition, is that the term 'Red Ed' was an inaccurate interpretation of his outlook. With no distinctive ideological break from New Labour.

• •

 What you should have learnt from reading this chapter

- The Labour Party was founded as a loose coalition of socialist groups and organised Labour and would grow to become a successful social democratic party. Because of its roots, the Labour Party traditionally drew its support from the working classes but, over time, the party has become 'classless', winning votes from a wide demographic. After electoral obscurity in the 1980s, reform under the banner 'New Labour' led the party to a landslide victory in 1997, before losing power in 2010 as the public fell out of love with the Labour and desired change.

- Even though some sections within the Labour Party have been more radical, the party has always championed parliamentary, over revolutionary, socialism. Although the 'type' of socialism may be disputed, throughout its history, key ideas can be identified in Labour, including: a collectivist nature; a fundamental belief to ensure that equality can be achieved; and a commitment to distributive justice, accepting the role of the state in ensuring fairness.

- The balance of power within Labour has changed radically as a result of structural reforms, and Labour is no longer (nor ever truly was) a grass-roots party. The most fundamental shift in the power relationship within the party has been in changes to policy-making. Conference is certainly no longer the centre of policy decision-making, nor is the NEC; instead, reforms have given the leadership constitutional rights to drive the direction of the party. Policy direction under the current Labour Party is hard to interpret because the party is currently undertaking a policy review. So far, however, ideas show no great divergence from the policies of New Labour.

 Glossary of key terms

Catch-all party A party that seeks to draw its support from a diverse cross-section of society. For a catch-all party, the number one concern is to maximise votes rather than to stick to a distinct ideology.
Communitarianism A theory established by Etzioni which focuses on the importance of community. The idea established the rights of the individual but also emphasised the importance of duty to society.
Keynesian economics A theory propounded by John Maynard Keynes that the state should play an active role in the economy to ensure stability and continued growth.
New Right A political movement in Britain associated with Margaret Thatcher that took classical liberal ideas about economic management, limited state, and priority of individual freedom while maintaining traditional conservative moral values.

Partisan dealignment A phenomenon identified by political scientists that shows that short-term factors, rather than historical attachment to parties, are the biggest determinant of voting behaviour.

Revisionism A type of moderate socialism which came about through revision of Marxist thought. With democracy established in many states at the turn of the century, revisionists believed that Marx's call for a revolution was outdated and that socialists should use the democratic system and vote to secure their aims. Socialists who have aimed to revise the direction of socialism to meet modern circumstances are referred to as revisionists.

Third Way A political theory created by Anthony Giddens that aims to offer the best of opposing post-war political trends. The 'third way' was an substitute for the 'first way' of Keynesian economics favoured by the Labour Left and the 'second way' of the New Right taken up by Thatcher.

? Likely examination questions

'The Labour Party has moved firmly to the centre in British politics.' Discuss.

'Traditional socialist principles have seldom been apparent in Labour's policies in government.' Discuss.

'Labour's understanding of equality, market economics and social justice draws little from traditional socialism.' Discuss.

To what extent has the power balance within the Labour Party firmly moved away from the grass roots to the leadership?

'Policy-making within the Labour Party is now the sole remit of the leadership.' How far do you agree with this judgement?

To what extent do reforms in the structure of Labour mean that party can no longer be considered a grass-roots party?

To what extent have recent reforms to the structure and organisation of the Labour Party weakened internal party democracy?

Helpful websites

www.labour.org.uk/home Labour Party Home has information on Labour policy.

www.labour.org.uk/history_of_the_labour_party The Labour Party's own webpage about the history of the party discusses the development of the Labour Party up to present day.

www.parliament.uk/documents/commons/lib/research/briefings The Parliament document page has information about the internal democracy of Labour.

www.unionhistory.info.php The unions' history pages have information about the development of the workers' movement and union relationships with the major political parties.

 ## Suggestions for further reading

Useful articles
Fisher, J. and Cowley, P., 'The Labour Party (History and Future)', *Politics Review*, 10.1 (September 2000) .

Hirsch, D. and Miller, J., 'Labour's Welfare Reform' (Joseph Rowntree Foundation Publications, 2004).

'Tony Blair's "New" Labour Party in Modern Britain', *Politics Review*, 16.4 (April 2007).

Useful books
Beech, M. and Hickson, K., *Labour's Thinkers: the Intellectual Roots of Labour from Tawney to Gordon Brown* (Tauris Academic Studies, 2007).

Beech, M. and Lee, S. (eds), *Ten Years of New Labour* (Palgrave Macmillan, 2008).

Griffiths, S. and Hickson, K. (eds), *British Party Politics and Ideology after New Labour* (Palgrave Macmillan, 2010).

Pugh, M., *Speak for Britain! A New History of the Labour Party* (Vintage, 2011).

Rawnsley, A., *The End of the Party: the Rise and Fall of New Labour* (Viking, 2010).

Reeves, R., *Why Vote Labour* (Biteback, 2010).

Thorpe, A., *A History of the Labour Party*, 3rd ed. (Palgrave Macmillan, 2008).

The Conservative Party

Contents

Overview

The Conservative Party is Britain's oldest party, and the party most associated with defending the past and with representing the social elite; yet it has prospered in an age of democracy and continues to govern. This chapter examines the principles that have held true for Conservatives and the issues that have divided them. It also explains where their support has come from in a changing society, and the way the party decides how to respond to its challenges.

Key issues to be covered in this chapter

- How much has the Conservative Party changed over time?
- Which issues divide and which ideas unite Conservatives?
- Who has voted Conservative at recent elections and why?
- What have been the effects of the recent modernisation of the Conservative organisation?

History

Foundations of the conservative political movement and the Conservative Party in the nineteenth century

The modern conservative movement came about in response to the radical change threatened by the French Revolution of 1879. The revolution in France sparked off fear within Britain that the country could soon experience a similar revolution to that which had occurred across the Channel. The most prominent opponent to the revolution, who captured the concern felt by many conservatives among the British elite, was Edmund Burke, considered by many to be the founding father of modern political conservatism. In Burke's important work, *Reflections on the Revolution in France* (1790), Burke championed the social order that existed in Britain and the stability and economic prosperity it brought to the country. He argued that the protection of traditions, including social hierarchy, created strength and was what made the nation great and the envy of the rest of the world. Burke highlighted the importance of preserving the existing state of affairs, based on a sceptical view of human nature, believing that humankind did not have the power to predict what was best for the nation, so that it was wise to look to experience from the past and make decisions based on existing prejudices. Burke did not see prejudice in the same way as contemporary understandings of the term, that is, as an example of discrimination. Instead, what Burke meant was the advantage in using 'pre-judgement', that is, in using an idea that had already been thought through thereby giving merit to reasoning.

Throughout the nineteenth century the primary base of support for the Conservatives was the Protestant, land-owning classes and, consequently, for a large part of the century, the party's policy was shaped to meet the needs of this elite section in society. It would not be until there was a substantial reform in the voting franchise, and reforms under Disraeli, that the party would broaden its programme to become a 'one-nation party' (Box 2.1). Between 1828 and 1830, and again in 1834 the Tory Party divided. These splits were increasingly damaging, and it was not until reforms were undertaken by the then leader, Sir Robert Peel, that the issue was satisfactorily resolved (at least in the short term), with Peel encouraging the party to reform or cease to exist. It was Peel's *Tamworth Manifesto*, issued in 1834, that called for a change in the outlook of the party, away from being a purely backward-looking organisation.

Box 2.1 Strands of Conservatism

Paternalistic conservatism
- Emphasises the moral obligation of the ruling elite to care for the population
- Anti-revolutionary, discouraging change unless it is inevitable
- Protectionist economic policy

One-nation conservatism
- Gives prominence to mending divisions within society that can be destructive. Disraeli identified the danger that British society could becoming divided into 'two nations between whom there is no intercourse and no sympathy'. The idea of one-nation policy is to be inclusive, recognising the importance of appealing to all groups in society to avoid social revolutionary forces
- Unity throughout the nation, with emphasis on its great achievements and the importance of protecting British identity and stature on the world stage
- Pragmatic economic policy

The New Right
- Limited state with the state viewed as the 'nightwatchman', protecting individual property rights. The New Right believe that many roles traditionally taken on by the state, including encouraging economic growth and employment, should be left to the market.
- The New Right draws on classical liberal ideas about economic management and has a monetarist economic policy based around the ideas of Milton Friedman's *Free to Choose* (1979). Economic policy focuses on controlling inflation by monitoring the increase in the money supply.

Question: To what extent can Cameron be considered a one-nation conservative?

Disraeli and the birth of 'one nationism'

Benjamin Disraeli became Britain's prime minister in 1868 and would go on to be one of the most influential of conservative thinkers. Disraeli would establish a more inclusive type of conservatism, one that aimed to attract all classes within society, rather than allow Britain to divide into two nations of rich and poor. Disraeli would unite social classes under his philosophy of 'one-nation Toryism'. As well as changing the political landscape, Disraeli also fundamentally changed the organisation of the Conservative Party. After the passage of the 1867 Reform Act, it became clear to the Conservative leadership that the focus of the party was going to have to change if it wanted to attract the broadening electorate. The creation of the National Union of Conservative and Constitutional Associations in 1867 amounted to the first mass organisation of a modern political party and allowed the Conservatives to organise its supporters, as well as campaigning, and gave rise to considerable control. In the same year, Disraeli also established the Conservative Central Office which was linked to the National Union and shared the same headquarters. The creation of the Central Office allowed control from the top down and ensured that party workers in the constituencies were following the official party line. The reorganisation, helped by structural reform, reaped rapid rewards, with the Conservatives winning the 1874 election.[1]

The early twentieth century

By the twentieth century, the Conservatives had successfully made the transition from a party of the land-owning classes to a party for property-owning people in general. Supporters now included the land-owning middle class in the cities as well as aristocratic and rural landowners. It became clear to the reformers within the party that the Conservatives would have to broaden their appeal again if they were to win over the newly enfranchised working classes and hold off the threat of socialism. The need to modernise, however. was not an idea favoured by the 3rd Marquess of Salisbury who was the leader of the party at the beginning of the twentieth century. Salisbury favoured reactionary policies that glorified Victorian values and traditions, and sustained social hierarchy and distinctions between the classes.

In the face of growing support for socialism, Salisbury chose to bury his head in the sand and avoid dealing with the problem. The rise of socialism was a phenomenon that could not be ignored, however. The creation of the Labour Party in 1900 would prove to be most significant, long-term threat the Conservatives would face, as the power base of Labour was set to enlarge with each extension of the franchise. Socialism encroached on the freedom of the individual that the Conservatives were eager to preserve. It limited individual freedom because the ideology favoured a major role for the state and a reordered, government-controlled economy, and was concerned with advancing the concerns of workers rather than those of the propertied classes.

At the beginning of the twentieth century the structure of the Conservative Party still reflected the strict social hierarchy of Edwardian England. The Conservative Party leadership was controlled by social elites, the replacement of Salisbury by his nephew, Author Balfour, summing up the extent of elite dominance within the party. Under Balfour, there were moderate reforms intended to pacify calls for more wide-ranging change. Legislation, such as the 1902 Education Act, established secondary and technical schools and put education under the control of local authorities. Balfour's time in office would be cut short, however, after old wounds reopened and the party split once more over protectionism, just as it had done in the nineteenth century. Unable to unite the party, Balfour resigned as leader and was replaced by Andrew Bonar Law in 1911. Under Bonar Law, the Conservatives joined the wartime coalition led by the Liberals under Asquith and later Lloyd George.

The interwar years
The Conservatives were the dominant party of British politics between the wars, governing either as a majority government or as a leading partner in a coalition. Despite short-lived Labour minority administrations in 1924 and in 1929–31, the Conservatives were nearly always in government. Between 1918 and 1922 the Conservatives were in government as part of a coalition led by Liberal leader, David Lloyd George, before deciding by 185 votes to eighty-eight, at a meeting held at the Carlton Club, to leave the Lloyd George administration.

In the 1920s, the leadership of the Conservative Party favoured slimmed-down government, with the party keen to dismantle structures that had been put in place during wartime and to reduce taxes that were high as a result of the cost of war. The Conservatives were also pragmatic in government, however, and did not reverse the legislation introduced before the war and by the coalitions ensuring welfare provision. The negativity and reactionary policy of Salisbury were replaced by a desire to introduced moderate social reform with an acceptance that the government had some responsibility to relieve the suffering of the working population. Between 1924 and 1929, Tory governments added to the foundations of earlier social reform by introducing state benefits including a widows' pension, poor-law reform and legislation to improve conditions in the factories. The introduction of welfare legislation was justified by the Conservative leadership as being part of their paternal responsibility to care for the people but it also served to counter the growth of the Labour Party by appeasing the working classes. As well as moderate reform, Conservatives also used scare tactics – including the 'red scare' during the 1924 General Election – to warn people away from voting Labour. Other more aggressive antisocialist propaganda emphasised the international links of the socialist ideology. In Harold Begbie's 1925 work, *The Conservative Mind*, Begbie warned of the danger of socialism, describing it as a 'mushroom forced by Russian atheism on the dunghill of German economics'.[2]

The 1920s and 1930s were a difficult time in Britain, with Conservative governments having to deal with economic stagnation and decline in Britain's economic power. The Tories introduced quotas on foreign goods and provided subsidies for British companies, as well as providing aid for regions which were particularly hit by the difficult economic conditions. During this period, the Conservatives under Baldwin were either in government by themselves or a majority player in the national government. Baldwin was much more successful than previous twentieth-century leaders had been in harnessing splits over the issue of protectionism that allowed the Tories to stay in power. Coalition, which had existed in the form of the national government, was turned to again with the outbreak of war. After the appointment of Churchill as prime minister, the coalition also included the Labour Party. Under the wartime coalition, the government waged a successful war but also managed the home front effectively. The signs of an extension in welfare provision were also evident in the wartime coalition, with education reform though the Butler act of 1944 and the drawing up of plans for the welfare state in the Beveridge Report.

Post-war consensus

Election defeat for the Conservatives in 1945 was not as unexpected as is sometimes argued. Despite the popularity of Churchill's wartime leadership, polls taken during the war revealed that Labour was ahead of the Tories on issues such as housing, health care, and in promoting full employment. When defeat came for the Conservatives, the margin was large and there was a landslide giving the Labour Party an overall majority of 146 seats. Consequently, there was a need for an overhaul of structure and approach by the Tories. Towards the end of World War II, many within the Conservative Party had begun to support the ideas of liberal economist John Maynard Keynes who had criticised the boom and bust that had characterised large periods of the pre-war period. With electoral defeat, the reformist wing of the party came to prominence, and it became more widely accepted within the Conservative Party at large that the government should manage parts of the economy to ensure stability. The Conservatives' aim in the post-war climate was to realign themselves as a party that did not stand for laissez-faire economics but for a small state with both private and public industry existing side by side.

The move towards a mixed economy, with both public and private industry, was an example of the Conservative flexibility when faced with the inevitability of change. Nor was it surprising but just an example of the Peelite tradition of acceptance of change when it was unavoidable.

Policy generation was put in the hands of modernisers such as Richard Austen (Rab) Butler who had introduced the 1944 Education Act, legislation that had set the tone for change. Butler became chairman of the revived research department that functioned like a think tank to forge the new direction of policy. These changes were reluctantly accepted by Churchill after overwhelming support from the party as a whole which wholeheartedly backed the policy at conference in 1946. The 1950 election manifesto showed this shift in policy, and also contained a continuation of popular policies pursued by the Labour government, such as house-building projects. However similar the party policies were, ideas about how to implement policy remained different, with the Conservatives pledging to build houses using public, as well as private, contractors and emphasising speed rather than quality.

Modernisation of the party and return to government, 1951–64

This change of tactic meant that, by 1948, the Conservative Party had reorganised itself and was able to form a credible Opposition to the Labour government. The Conservatives grew in strength, reducing the Labour majority to five after the 1950 election, and eventually returning to office in 1951. Such a rapid turnaround was made possible because of policy reform but had been made a reality through a reorganisation of the party. During the 1945 campaign, funds had been low by pre-war standards and hardly any professional staff were employed. After the Conservatives were defeated, central office began a recruitment drive that aimed to create professional units in the constituencies, and nearly 300 people had qualified as constituency agents by 1950. There were also funding and recruitment drives giving the party around three million members by the 1950s. Many of the new members were younger than the traditional membership had been, with the growth of the Young Conservative movement. Perhaps more significant to party finance than the increase in funds that came with a growth in membership was the boost provided by big donors. The increase in funds provided money for candidates but it was also pumped into reinvigorating public relations (PR). It was the reform of policy and the reorganisation of structure and finances that eventually put the Conservatives in a position where they were ready to win a general election.

On returning to office in 1951, the Tories set out a number of reforms that drew the party towards the centre ground with a continuation of many of the changes brought in by Attlee's government. Popular with the public were the pledges to remove rationing and to increase the number of houses built. The public was eager to have its share in the new consumerism the Tories promised and people were happy to have the opportunity to buy their own homes. The

Tories also made sure that they would maintain public support by retaining the NHS reforms with only slight alterations, such as the introduction of charges for some health services. Keynesian principles dominated the economic programme with high public expenditure and intervention on interest rates. Not all industry was allowed to stay in the public sector and the government chose to privatise road transport and the steel industry. The 1950s and early 1960s were characterised by 'stop-go' economics in which periods of growth were followed by government-stimulated deflation. The inability to manage the economy successfully saw the Conservative Party defeated by Labour under their new leader, Harold Wilson, in the 1964 General Election.

The experiment with New Right economics and the U-turn under Heath

On returning to office under Ted Heath in 1970, the New Right method of economic management seemed to have triumphed with the abolition of controls that had been introduced by the Wilson government such as the National Board for Prices and Incomes (NBPI) which aimed to allow the government to set prices and, potentially, wages. Other radical moves made under Heath during his first two years in office included the removal of a fixed rate for the pound thereby allowing the market to determine value. In addition, the Conservatives passed the Industrial Relations Act, 1971 that introduced restrictions on the activity of unions, including the right to strike, giving rise to hostilities with the unions that would continue throughout the decade, leading to almighty conflict under Thatcher. The United Kingdom also entered the free-trade organisation, the European Economic Community (EEC), a personal triumph for Ted Heath who had been chief negotiator during failed attempts to join the EEC a decade earlier. Despite the vigour with which Heath approached reform from 1970 to 1972, the removal of state-imposed limits did not have the desired affect, and the abolition of the NBPI gave the green light to an increase in wages and in spending. The rises in wage and spending levels led to inflation of 9.4 per cent by 1971, causing Heath to lose his nerve and drop his New Right economic programme.

As part of this huge U-turn in policy, the government began to intervene in the economy once more. The Conservatives set up the Pay Board, that closely monitored wages, alongside the Price Commission which managed price increases. There was also government support for struggling businesses, with bail-outs for Rolls-Royce and for the Upper Clyde Shipbuilders. Heath was widely criticised for his volte-face but the problems that had led him to introduce radically different policies during the second half of his premiership were not all of his making. The difficulties that had arisen by the early 1970s were a result of decades of mismanagement by both Labour and Conservative governments and Britain's failure to keep up with foreign markets.

There was also a need to reshape the British economy in its entirety because it was no longer fit for purpose and the workforce did not have the skills needed in the modern world. Heath recognised the impact of economic decline and the need to redirect economic policy; as a result, money was pumped into retraining the workforce. This measure was expensive, however, and took place alongside other costly government policies and, eventually, spending levels reached a rate that could not be sustained. The final straw for the Tory government was the increasing number of strikes by the unions whose members were angry at legislation brought in to monitor wages. The result was widespread picketing at the coal mines and also at power stations. Railway workers followed suit, causing the conflict to come to a head. With the government's policies proving unpopular with unions and with the public at large, Heath was forced to go to the polls and lost the election.[3]

1979 Thatcherism: the Conservatives become ideological

Under Thatcher Conservative policy direction changed fundamentally. The most significant thing about Thatcher, compared to previous Conservative leaders in post-war Britain, was that she was an ideologue. During her term in office, Thatcher would apply to the market **monetarist** principles of the New Right to fix Britain's economic decline. Just like Heath, Thatcher had become absorbed by New Right theorists such as Milton Friedman and F. A. Hayek but, unlike Heath, Thatcher would keep to these principles even when the economy seemed to hit crisis point. In a famous 1980s conference speech, in response to criticism of her handling of the economy,

Thatcher triumphantly stated 'You turn if you want to. The lady's not for turning!'[4]

The economic mismanagement of the previous decades meant that there was a feeling of desperation, creating the conditions which would allow the government to take a risk by introducing a radical new economic programme. The New Right programme had a different outlook on the role of the state, relations with the unions, and attitudes to employment. Rather than taking the view that the state had a role to play in managing and intervening in the economy, Thatcher believed that acceptance of a mixed economy had been a mistake.

Once in office in 1979, Margaret Thatcher introduced the most wide-ranging reforms ever attempted by a Conservative government. In her first term in office, Thatcher had a large majority and a powerful mandate for change. The long period in office, from 1979 to 1990, enabled a huge programme of reform to be introduced without interruption. Under Thatcher, the economy was restructured with her guiding principles for reform being those set out by her monetarist heroes Friedman and Hayek. Thatcher followed the monetarist principle that controlling the money circulating in the economy was the crucial concern for economic efficiency. Although the Thatcher government failed always to meet monetarist targets, the Conservative administration stuck doggedly to the plan of limited intervention, instead placing trust in the market to fix difficulties, often with huge social consequences. Under Chancellor of the Exchequer, Geoffrey Howe (1979–83), the government did not intervene to stimulate the economy artificially by creating more jobs, despite the increasing problem of unemployment. Unemployment would continue to rise until 1985 and, at its peak, would see four million out of work. But, as a monetarist, Thatcher's main concern was not limiting unemployment; instead, the focus of her economic policy was managing the money flow.

Other New Right principles were applied to the British economy: public expenditure was reduced and interest rates were raised to fund low income-tax levels. The ideological principle behind this tax policy was a single rate for all; indirect tax which was set at the same rate for everyone created fairness within the taxation system. The desire for fairness within the tax system was a fixation for Thatcher and would eventually see her pursue her ideological principles to an extent that would prove unpopular with the voters. The attempt to introduce a flat-rate tax at a local level, the **poll tax**, was so disliked that it became pivotal in Thatcher's fall from power.

One of Thatcher's primary concerns was to limit the role of the state within the economy; this was achieved in part through **privatisation**. During Thatcher's time in office, there was huge constitutional change, with the introduction of legislation that allowed Rolls-Royce, British Airways, British Gas, British Telecom, British Leyland, Jaguar Cars, and the British National Oil Corporation to be privatised. Privatisation did reduce state expenditure but also fulfilled the ideological goals of ending monopolies and creating competition in the hope of improving profits and reducing prices. The government also sold off thousands of council houses in its effort to encourage property ownership which Thatcher believed would lead to more social responsibility and create a sense of duty to the community.

The biggest battle undertaken by Thatcher was to curb union power that had proved to be the thorn in the side of the two previous administrations. The role of the unions in the workplace was reduced, with changes aimed at shrinking union membership. In some industries, there were 'closed shops' in which all members of the workforce were required to be members of the union. New legislation meant that this could not happen unless four-fifths of the workforce agreed through secret ballot. Government reforms also made strike action more difficult to achieve, with the requirement for a secret ballot before a strike could take place, a secret ballot for the election of officials, and a secret ballot to endorse the gathering of union funds. In addition, secondary picketing, where union members would picket in support of other striking unions, was banned.

The disputes with the miners during strikes in 1984–85 were violent and, after much conflict, pits were closed and industries were sold off. The harshness of the government in dealing with the unions was seen as unjust in the eyes of many. The lack of government support to help miners find alternative employment after pits were closed or to regenerate former mining areas was, in the long term, politically unwise and it generated difficulties for future generations. Though the power of the unions needed to be reduced, the government's methods were brutal and led to huge social problems in former mining communities which the government made little effort to address.

Despite the unsympathetic nature of some Conservative policy, the Tories won a comfortable victory in the 1987 General Election, with 375 seats compared to Labour's 229. By 1987, the market had begun to recover, with regeneration in areas, such as the southeast, and the finance and banking sectors enjoying a boom with unprecedented profits. Though the market was beginning fix itself, as New Right theory predicted it would, not everyone in the United Kingdom shared in this new prosperity. Huge sections of the population, who had had to deal with the consequences of the decline in the British industrial sector and lack of employment opportunities, did not see the rewards of market recovery. Young people, ethnic minorities, as well as parts of the north, the Midlands, Scotland and Wales were hit disproportionately and remained neglected by the government. The decline in the role of the state meant that support for those who were struggling was limited; after cuts in funding for housing, transport, and social services, the authorities were less able to provide relief. Some of the measures put in place to deal with welfare issues were considered inadequate. Youth training schemes and the use of private companies to provide work for those without a job were controversial. In an attempt to encourage private investment, companies were given the right to pay lower wages in depressed areas but the policy did not have the desired effect and, instead of encouraging investment, it increased the disparities between different areas of the country.[5]

The decline in Conservative dominance under Major
Under John Major the Conservatives lost their reputation for being the party of competent government and sound economic management. The early period of Major's premiership had proved to be largely successful, with strong leadership during the first Gulf War in 1991 increasing his popularity. In 1992, when Major successfully led a very unpopular and tired Conservative Party to a surprise victory, credit was given to the prime minister because the success had been, in part, a result of his approachable and down-to-earth personality

which appealed to the public. Major's popularity would not last, however, and the huge policy failure of Black Wednesday which saw the pound falling out of the Exchange Rate Mechanism on 16 September 1992, was a pivotal moment in the break in trust between the public and the Conservative government.

By 1992 cracks had started to appear and signs of division became clearer. On leaving office, Thatcher commented that she expected to continue as a 'back-seat driver' but, much to her disappointment, Major's pragmatic approach was in stark contrast to her own. Major's consensual style of leadership had been a direct response to Thatcher's authoritarian approach. Major allowed debate within the party, choosing to be a 'first among equals' in the cabinet. The choice of **cabinet government** in an attempt to foster agreement, however, allowed splits, between what Thatcher referred to as the 'wets' on the left of the party and the more radical 'dries' of the right wing, to become more apparent. Divisions within the party were played out very publically for all to see in Parliament and in the media. During Major's time in office, the number of rebellions increased and many Tory MPs were happy to criticise openly in the Commons Conservative policy.

In cabinet the problem of division was just as apparent and was, perhaps, more of an issue. In 1993, collective cabinet responsibility seemed to have collapsed completely as members of the cabinet leaked information from a meeting in an attempt to undermine the prime minister. In a public relations disaster, Major was overheard calling three of his own cabinet members 'bastards' in response to the leaking of information. The ministers were not named but Major's anger was almost certainly aimed at Michael Howard, Peter Lilley and Michael Portillo.[6] In an attempt to quell rebellion within the party, John Major resigned as Tory leader to trigger a leadership contest which he went on to win but his successful campaign did not tame the party. Faith in the Tories was further eroded with the increasing problem of 'sleaze' in the Conservative Party, as repeated revelations in the press about ministers' extramarital affairs made laughable their policy of 'back to basics' which promoted strong family values. Divisions and policy failure, along with the breakdown in trust as a result of Tory sleaze, eventually sealed the fate of Major's government.

The ascendancy of Euroscepticism under Hague

Between 1993 and 2005, the Tories failed to rise higher than the low thirties in opinion polls and, following general election failure in 1997, Major was replaced as leader of the party by William Hague.[7] The popularity of the Conservative Party under Hague continued to decline in opinion polls to 31 per cent. The party that Hague had become leader of was deeply divided. In an attempt the renew the party, Hague introduce a set of policies that he claimed would give a 'fresh start' to the Conservatives and revive fortunes, and he began a campaign of consultation with the public which he called 'listening to Britain'. As a consequence of trying to 'get in touch' with the voters, there were some new policy initiatives and some opposition to New Labour policies but there was considerable level of agreement with the government. The Tories accepted the minimum wage in an attempt to appear to be 'compassionate Conservatives'. They also accepted some changes to economic management since 1997, such as the granting of independence of the Bank of England.

The Conservatives continued with their tough line on Europe and seemed to reap some reward with the policy including a successful campaign in the European elections in 1999, gaining thirty-six MEPs compared to Labour's twenty-nine. A willingness to support the Conservatives at European elections, however, did not translate into general election success, and the anti-European policy failed to come top of the agenda for most British voters in national elections. In the run up to the 2001 General Election, Hague abandoned the 'fresh start' idea in favour of safe Tory ground. His speech at conference signalled the hardening of attitudes, with a strong stance on immigration and criticism of multiculturalism, referring to the United Kingdom as becoming a 'foreign land'. The change in tack was complete with the publication of the 2001 Conservative election manifesto that committed the party to cutting fuel and business taxes as well as deregulating industry. The Tories also encouraged traditional family values, promising to reward families and married couples through the tax system. The traditional Tory programme included tough law-and-order policies that promised harsher sentencing and an increase in police numbers.[8]

Despite the lack of success of party policy, Hague did set in motion significant changes to the structure of the Conservative Party which would be vital in achieving the eventual return to power for the Tories in 2010 – but not with Hague as leader. In an astute move, William Hague combined his bid to become leader of the Conservative Party – which included a promise to reform the leadership – with a vote against the single currency, something that would win favour with the many **Eurosceptics** in the party. Hague's reform of the leadership election process was an important step towards increasing internal democracy within the Conservative Party.

The Conservatives in Opposition under Iain Duncan Smith and Michael Howard
Iain Duncan Smith was the first Conservative leader to be elected using the new voting system designed by Hague. In the early stages of the contest, Iain Duncan Smith had been behind some of the more established candidates, including Michael Portillo who had originally been the favourite. In a what was a surprise to many, the candidates to go through to final round of voting involving the extraparliamentary party were Ken Clarke, who had previously been in third place but eventually had come first in the final vote by MPs, and Iain Duncan Smith who had not managed to secure more than a third of the votes in the parliamentary party in any of the previous rounds. As a right winger, Iain Duncan Smith proved more popular in the wider party than the Europhile moderate, Ken Clarke, and consequently Smith came out on top.

Under Iain Duncan Smith the party was based firmly on the right from the start, championing a strong stance against the Euro alongside a morally conservative social policy which caused one member of his front bench, John Bercow, to resign over the party's attitude towards the adoption of gay rights. Under Iain Duncan Smith's leadership the party was plagued by internal divisions, especially over Europe. The most significant development under Iain Duncan Smith was the establishment of a policy review; this did not report, however, as Iain Duncan Smith was removed as leader before it could do so, and he would have to leave it to his successor to drive forward a new policy direction. There was pressure on Iain Duncan Smith to resign for much of 2003, with some calls coming from members of his own shadow cabinet as well as from big donors to the Tory Party. Later that year, Iain Duncan Smith was removed as leader as a result of a challenge to his leadership mounted at conference where his opponents managed to secure enough signatures to activate a no-confidence vote. The call for another leadership election, and the resulting vote of no confidence which Iain Duncan Smith narrowly lost, meant that he was the first Conservative leader since Austen Chamberlain not to fight an election.

Exhausted by continuous infighting and fearful of another divisive leadership contest, the Tories, in November 2003, put before the parliamentary party the single candidature of Michael Howard as an 'emergency candidate'. Rather than go through another leadership election in which the whole Conservative Party would be consulted, Michael Howard was installed as leader to avoid risking again rejection of the candidate favoured by MPs. The rapid replacement of Iain Duncan Smith revealed that the Conservative Party was not as attached to their new, more democratic procedure, as some reformers had hoped, giving a 'resounding vote of no confidence in their own selection rules' (Quinn).[9]

Howard led a less divided party whose members were tired of infighting and less confrontational than in previous years. The Conservatives under Howard remained firmly on the Right and the 2005 election manifesto was aimed largely at gaining the core Tory vote. Policies were traditional and, among those who had helped to draw up the manifesto, was the little-known MP, David Cameron, whose contribution to the 2005 General Election would bear little resemblance to his proposals when running for the Conservative leadership later the same year. The manifesto proposed £4 billion in tax cuts and a reduction of government spending to be achieved by reducing the role of the state and by cutting bureaucracy. Proposals to reinstall traditional standards of discipline at all levels of society meant that law-and-order policy was more right wing than in 2001. Crime policy incorporated promises to reduce crime figures by increasing bobbies on the beat by 40,000 as well as increasing the number of prisons.

This theme of discipline was continued in education policy, with promises of more powers to teachers in schools to impose harsher punishments . In addition, further school places were to be created to give parents more choice. Order was also going to be restored to hospitals, with the promise of giving powers to matrons to ensure higher standards of cleanliness. An equally hard line was set on immigration, calling for strict controls to net immigration in addition to offshore processing centres. During the 2005 election the Conservatives did gain thirty-three more seats but, overall, the campaign was criticised for having focused too heavily on traditional Conservative policies that failed to win back voters. After the defeat, Howard announced that he would not be leader by the time of the next election and in, his final shadow cabinet, Howard would bring in young blood, with George Osborne and David Cameron gaining places on the front bench for the first time. Later in 2005 Howard stood down, triggering a new leadership contest which would eventually see the election of the first moderate candidate under the new rules.

After thirteen years in Opposition, Cameron successfully brought the Conservatives back into office but only as part of a coalition. Since becoming leader of the Conservatives, Cameron's ability to reinvigorate the party was helped by a number of factors: firstly, by largely regaining public trust; secondly, by recapturing the centre ground as a 'catch-all' party; and thirdly, by presenting the Conservatives as a modern 'in-touch' party. Cameron spent his years in Opposition seeking ways to distinguish himself from his predecessors: he placed greater emphasis on environmental policy; he emphasised that the benefits of growth would be shared between tax cuts and increased public spending; he accepted Blair's academies in preference to grammar schools; and he also offered a softer line on law and order. The very flexibility of Conservative ideology, however, made it hard to find a 'Clause IV' moment, and each move to the Left angered traditionalists, such as journalists Peter Hitchens and Melanie Phillips, who saw the Tories' political function being abandoned. Party benefactor and treasurer Michael Ashcroft, on the other hand, felt that Cameron had not gone far enough in rebranding the Conservatives.[10]

Ideology

This section will explore the ideology, or lack of it, within Conservatism and suggest core values that can be found throughout the history of the Conservative Party. As the name suggests, the aim of Conservatism is to preserve the status quo; this has been interpreted in different ways, however, with some Conservatives being purely reactionary whereas others have chosen to embrace moderate change where necessary. For many, Conservatism cannot be pinned down to ideological characteristics. Most famously, the rejection of ideology was captured by Lord Hailsham when he described Conservatism as an 'approach rather than an ideology'. The idea of the absence of key content has led Conservatives such as Anthony Quinton to argue that it is better to understand Conservatism as broad attitudes rather than as specific principles. In his book, the *Politics of Imperfection* (1978), Quinton identifies three key attitudes, traditionalism, **organicism** and scepticism, that run through all Conservative beliefs.

Traditionalism

Traditionalism can be defined as a preference for the protection of existing institutions and values. Traditionalism is important to Conservatives because it provides stability and reinforces existing hierarchy and moral values. Traditionalism can be seen in the support for traditional social institutions, such as the family, state authority and social hierarchy. Conservatives believe that the heart of traditionalism is found in the family. It is in the family where children learn the traditional domestic structure, as well as traditional expectations for interpersonal relationships with the man as the head of the household and main breadwinner. Conservative traditionalism promotes the preference for the nuclear family over extended or reconstituted families, as well as favouring marriage before having children rather than cohabitation which has become increasingly common in today's Britain. The Conservative Party's support for marriage can be seen in its proposal of tax breaks for married couples.

This preference for the traditional family has brought the Conservative Party into confrontation with the public and has also led to controversy among party members. The softening of the Conservative Party's stance on homosexual relationships, with the leadership accepting the standing of homosexual couples as equal in the eyes of the state to that of heterosexual couples, has challenged traditional Conservative beliefs. Not all party members share the same view and, in 2010, Conservative MP Chris Grayling was recorded defending the actions of Christian bed-and-breakfast accommodation owners who had turned away gay couples.

Hierarchy

Traditionalism is also valued because it maintains hierarchy within the state and society. Conservatives value hierarchy because it allows order to be maintained, ensuring that traditional elites remain dominant, but also creates security for the people who, they believe, draw comfort from being guided by natural leaders. Conservatives had traditionally believed in hierarchy within society and stressed the importance of leaving politics to the 'natural rulers' who were members of the Conservative Party which could be seen as the natural party of government.

Conservative thinkers, such as Disraeli, argued that society was not equal and that some people were superior to others. He proposed that there was a natural hierarchy within society and that any political system had to reflect this social order, with each section of society having a distinct role to play in preserving the state. Owing to these assigned social roles, Disraeli maintained that the traditional ruling class needed to be maintained as the government. He realised, however, that to do this, it was essential that the ruling class acted in a paternalistic way towards the rest of society to ensure that the traditional hierarchy would not be overthrown by social upheaval.

Though members of the Conservative Party today do not talk about 'natural inequality', the preservation of hierarchy is still ensured by Conservatives' desire to maintain aspects of the political system. Preservation of traditional hierarchy includes a preference for executive dominance to allow for strong leadership. Tories continue to support ideas such as having an unwritten constitution and a first-past-the-post voting system which is more likely to return a majority government. With the decision to go into coalition, the current Conservative-led government is not an all-powerful executive. In this case, the Conservatives have had to be pragmatic and to accept shared power rather than have none at all. Despite the lack of Conservative dominance, hierarchy within the coalition's executive can still be seen. Much of the decision-making within the coalition's executive lies with a **kitchen cabinet** of Cameron, Osborne, Clegg and Alexander.

Paternalism

Paternalism is the exercise of power over someone to protect that person's well-being. For Conservatives the state must exercise power over the public to protect their interests. A paternalistic approach is rather like the unequal but caring relationship between a father and child, in that it provides security but also ensures dominance. The hierarchical relationship between the state and the people is much like a parent–child relationship because the father (the government) is very much in control but also has a nurturing role towards the child (the people).

Disraeli proposed that it was necessary to manage the move to democracy in a paternalistic way to avoid any possible danger of revolution. By controlling, but also protecting and nurturing, the people, traditional elites could protect their own positions while preserving the national interest. Disraeli warned that, as part of the development of a capitalist society, Britain had become divided. He predicted that, if inequalities and deprivation continued to grow, Britain would be fixed as two nations, one rich and one poor. If the gap between rich and poor was not altered, poorer members of society would seek redress by violent means, causing chaos and the breakdown of social order. To prevent the slide into two nations, Disraeli championed 'one-nation Conservatism' that would lead to an elite-led democracy. To encourage support for his idea, Disraeli argued that 'one-nation Conservatism ' should include reforms to alleviate suffering but also encourage a strong sense of nationalism and pride in the Empire to muster unity and attachment to the state. 'One-nation Conservatism' also drew on the idea of *noblesse oblige* (from the French, meaning 'privilege entails responsibility') that gives rise to a feudal responsibility of the ruling class to look after those on their land. For Disraeli, this obligation of care by the government applied to all British subjects. Paternalism is essential because, as leaders, the government owes a duty of care to the public but acting in a paternalistic manner is necessary to remain in government and therefore have the power to ensure values are preserved, as well as the ability to oversee organic change.

Private property

Another traditional institution Conservatives have sought to protect is private property because property ownership can be seen both as an individual right but also as a way of assuring order and hierarchy in society. The importance of property lies in the role it has in developing individual responsibility, in upholding standards, and in offering a stake in the preservation of the status quo. Traditionally, thinkers such as Edmund Burke proposed that not everyone in society was capable of property ownership and that property could not be shared by all. Instead, Burke argued that there was a need to keep property in the hands of those with experience, namely, those such as the landed elite. Ownership of property did not come without responsibility, however, and Burke argued that it was essential that those who had the privilege of property should protect the security of the whole of society, including those without property.

The belief that not everyone can own property is no longer advocated by Conservative Party but property ownership remains essential because it allows for individual expression and, for today's Tories, it is a basic right for everyone to be able to own property and accumulate wealth. Conservatives are critical of socialist ideas which demand that the state should own large sections of the economy, and commentators, such as Roger Scruton, maintain that 'Public ownership destroys incentive'. Conservatives have also emphasised the sense of duty and public pride that can be found in owning property. Lord Hailsham linked property to order and to the stability found in traditional institutions, insisting that property ownership was an individual right, offers protection for the family, and creates a good community because it provides an incentive to work. The theory of stability coming from private ownership of property was a key motivation for Thatcher in introducing the 'right to buy' in the Housing Act, 1980 that gave people the opportunity to buy their council houses.

Organicism

Conservatives believe that society is like a living organism which is too complicated to be understood just from a human perspective and should not therefore be tampered with unnecessarily. Conservatives also support organicism firstly because of a preference, if change is to occur, for gradual not radical alteration and, secondly, because organic change encourages pragmatism over a fixed ideological path. In some cases, organicism can also have religious meaning in the sense that humans cannot, and should not, assume the functions of the Creator, seeing attempts to 'play God' as sacrilegious.

The Conservative theorist Michael Oakshott said that possibilities which arise from change are 'boundless and bottomless' so human beings cannot have the complete answer. Karl Popper criticised ideologies for naively thinking that any individual has the formula for a perfect society, maintaining that any revolutionary idea which proposed to abandon the existing order merely wished to make, 'a blank canvas of society, on which to scrawl his own prejudices'. Conservatives criticised radical changes as always destined to cause problems in the future because individuals were unable to foresee the consequences of their actions and therefore could not propose a successful solution. In this sense, radical change is more likely to be destructive rather than constructive. Historical examples can be used to illustrate this principle in practice: for instance, the power vacuum left by the very 'un-organic' removal of Charles I as king of England. The execution of Charles left politicians trying, without success, to find an alternative form of government and, eventually, England was returned to the stability of monarchy by the Restoration. Individuals' inability to predict the consequences of change illustrates Oakeshott's point that 'Careful cure is not worse than the disease'.

Conservatives support organicism because it ensures that change, when it does happen, is gradual. Sir Robert Peel was concerned that the Conservatism of the eighteenth and early nineteenth centuries was in danger of being purely reactionary. Consequently, he proposed that, rather than being opposed to all change, Conservatism should embrace reforms if those reforms were thought to be desirable or unavoidable. In his Tamworth Manifesto, 1834, he proposed that, sometimes, it was necessary to 'reform in order to preserve' and that, by being in control of what was inevitable change, it could be moderated and traditional forms of authority could be combined with democratic features thereby preserving the position of the traditional elites.[11]

Pragmatic rather than ideological

Organicism is also fundamental to Conservatives because they believe in a pragmatic, rather than an ideological, approach to government. By the middle of the twentieth century, Michael Oakeshott proposed that fixed ideologies had revealed their frailties. Oakeshott also proposed that following abstract principles or ideologies did not allow flexibility to adapt to new situations. Instead, proponents of ideologies, such as socialism, doggedly follow ideological guidelines and fail to react to problems within society and the political system. Taking a pragmatic approach, that reacted to the conditions of the time, allowed for natural balance and avoided conflict. Oakeshott suggested, too, that politics should not be about forcing others to live by your ideological principles but about discussion and compromise with political discourse – 'a conversation rather than an argument'.[12] The goal of a government should not be to preserve ideological principles but to act in the best interests of the country. Rather than introduce radical change, the government should 'steer' the country as if it were a ship. Organicism in action can be seen during Macmillan's premiership (1957–63) where the government accepted the nationalisation which had occurred under the previous Labour government and ran the country as a mixed economy, allowing for political consensus.

Scepticism

Key to Conservatism are belief in the limitations of humankind and scepticism about human nature. Early Conservative thinkers, such as Edmund Burke in his work *Reflections on the Revolution in France*, maintained that humans are not rational creatures but are driven by instinct and emotions. Because humans are irrational rather than rational, Burke proposed that it was necessary to reject the liberal ideas of the Enlightenment which encouraged individual choice. Burke agued that, because people would always react in a selfish manner, it was unwise to give too much power to an individual and then expect him or her to make logical choices. This led Burke to reject the principle of democracy on the grounds that people do not always know what is best.

To counter the personal failings of individuals, Conservatives propose that there is a need to seek guidance from traditional figures of authority. Burke maintained that traditional authority would act on the principles that have proved successful over generations, using the 'prejudices of the past' to guide politics rather than the will of the people. The idea of learning from the past was taken further in the work of G. K. Chesterton who called for people to study the 'wisdom of previous generations'. He called this theory the 'democracy of the dead'.

A sceptical view of human nature has also led Conservatives to favour strong social controls. Because of people's innate moral and intellectual imperfections, it was essential that the population experience strong discipline and was provided with clear guidance. This was true, Conservatives thought, in the private sphere, where children must be disciplined, but they also applied the idea to the public sphere where there was the need to keep an imperfect population in check through the use of strong law and order. Therefore, control could be ensured by superior force from above using the authoritative organs of the state such as the police and the legal system. Strong sources of social control are not only important to maintain order, they are also essential because the frailties of human nature are such that control and guidance are sought by the population who found the imposition of order comforting. Order and security were maintained through continuity of traditions and through tried and tested practices and respect for traditional institutions.

As well as believing that the frailty of humans requires order to be imposed, because of their scepticism about human capabilities, Conservatives have also proposed that politics should play a limited role in any individual's life. Conservatives see humans as psychologically limited and dependent creatures, and argue that people like 'knowing their place' and desire what is 'safe' and familiar. Conservatives place emphasis on the belief that the majority of social relations should occur in the private sphere and that *politics* has only limited relevance to human affairs because it should not be the main focus of a person's life. Owing to identified frailties in human nature, Conservatives assert that the lack of focus on political interaction will be welcomed because people desire direction and do not want to be deeply involved in political affairs.

Authority of the state
The protection provided by the authority of the state is a necessary part of the relationship between government and the governed, with the importance of state authority sitting alongside the rule of law that protects individual rights. Lord Hugh Cecil called this balance providing the, 'appropriate amount of freedom for the progressive

development of human character'.[13] Conservatives favour a strong state but warn against a large controlling state (desired by socialists) that would limit individual choice and property rights that comprise a cornerstone of stability.

The authority of the state is given legitimacy in the modern British system through elections, with the assumption that, once elected, the government has the authority to make decisions in the public interest. As the state has authority, the public trusts its judgement without being involved in decision-making. Traditionally, the inner workings of government have not been considered to be the business of the public and, historically, Conservatives have restricted access to those workings to ensure a strong state. This paternal idea of state authority is reflected in decisions to keep the actions of government secret, which explains the Conservative opposition to the Freedom of Information Act, 2000. Nevertheless, the current Conservative-led coalition has discarded traditional closed government and made a number of moves to improve openness, such as the transparency website launched by the Conservatives in 2010 which allows the public access to data from government departments. The encouragement of openness under Cameron reflects the coalition's belief in the importance of preserving liberty and the avoidance of a tyrannical or over-interfering state.

Nationalism

Nationalism and the glorification of British history and culture are vitally important to Conservatives who stress the necessity of protecting distinct traditions and promoting unity. Historically, patriotism has been used by Conservative governments to win over support and, in particular, has been turned to as a way of securing the working-class vote. The encouragement by the state of nationalist sentiment can be seen in Disraeli's glorification of Empire in the nineteenth century and under Thatcher, too, who managed to win an election in 1983 despite economic hardship, because of the popularity of the successful war in the Falklands Islands Equally, the current Conservative government has prioritised the glorification of Britain's triumphant past with Education Secretary, Michael Gove, announcing that no pupil should leave school without knowing 'narrative British history', seeing the teaching of history as a celebration of British accomplishment.

Linked to the celebration of national identity is the preservation of British individuality and the protection of the nation state. Protecting the nation state involves securing British sovereignty. Conservatives see sovereignty as being increasingly under threat through globalisation and the spread of new cultural influences but also through membership of the European Union. Conservatives assert that European integration and the pooling of decision-making at an international level challenge the authority of the state. For Conservatives, the issue of Europe has become such a tense one that it split the party between Eurosceptics and Europhiles in the 1990s, and the internal wrangling over Europe was a significant factor in keeping the party in Opposition for thirteen years. Although the Conservative Party has become more united under Cameron, it remains Eurosceptic; this has been shown in the decision to leave the alliance of the other moderate conservative parties in the European Parliament to create the more radically Eurosceptic European Conservatives and Reformists (ECR). Nationalism has also led Conservatives historically to favour a hawkish foreign policy to uphold Britain's position in the world, with the Conservative Party supporting recent conflicts in Afghanistan and Iraq. To sustain the position of the United Kingdom in the international scene, Conservatives have traditionally favoured high defence spending and, consequently, the cuts to the defence budget by the current Conservative-led coalition have proved very controversial within the party, causing tensions in the cabinet with Defence Secretary, Liam Fox, openly criticising reduction of spending.

Support

Patterns of support and traditional Conservative vote

The Conservative Party has been the most successful British political party of recent times, in office for more than two-thirds of the twentieth century and, though out of office for thirteen years after 1997, the party is now back in government, albeit as part of a coalition. The Conservatives have also managed to gain the backing of significant factions within Britain, including the press, business, the city, and the rural vote. Undoubtedly, among the reasons for this success is the party's ability to attract a broad range of voters as well as being able to evolve with the times to remain electorally viable. Traditionally a party of the landed classes, the Conservatives developed over the nineteenth and twentieth centuries to become one with a base of support among the middle classes, historically winning four-fifths of the middle-class vote. The party evolved further during the second half of the twentieth century to win a considerable chunk of the working-class vote, too, appealing to many voters with the promise of social advancement as well as its traditional moral values and emphasis on social responsibility.

The Conservatives and the working-class vote

Historically, patriotism has been used by Conservative governments to win over working-class support. As well as making the appeal to working-class patriotism described above, Thatcher was also perhaps the most successful Conservative leader in encouraging working-class voters by providing support and encouragement for self-help and social progression. The selling off of council houses allowed many working-class people to move up the social hierarchy through the acquisition of property. The Conservatives under Cameron have tried to appeal to working-class voters by playing on the 'honest working man/women's' anger at the abuse of benefits. The introduction of the universal benefit has been used by the current government to win support by ensuring that people in work are better off. Tax breaks have also traditionally been used by the Tories to win over working-class voters and have been used by the current Conservative government to appeal to lower wage-earners with the promise to raise the income tax threshold to £10,000.

The Conservative Party and ethnic minorities

Despite many advances in the breadth of Conservative support, there remain some sections of society that the Conservatives fail to attract, the most significant being ethnic-minority voters. The traditional explanation for this lies in the fact that the majority of Asian groups and the black population have favoured Labour because ethnic minorities are disproportionately represented in poorly paid manual jobs. Even though many ethnic minority voters chose not to vote for Labour in 2005, their votes did not go to the Tories; instead, smaller parties benefited from their anger over Labour policy in 'the war on terror'. A continuing failure by the Conservatives to win over ethnic-minority voters was seen in the 2010 General Election with a reduction of the ethnic vote by 0.229 per cent.[14]

The absence of representation of ethnic minorities within the Conservative Party has also been seen as a factor for low ethnic-minority support. To combat this, the Conservative Party has aimed to increase the number of ethnic-minority members at Westminster. By increasing the number of ethnic-minority MPs, it is hoped that ethnic minorities will find it easier to identify with the party, rather than being turned off because Conservative candidates appear so different from themselves.

At a national level, the Conservative Party has failed to win over the ethnic-minority community en masse in part because of an absence of trust felt towards the Conservatives' traditional hard line on immigration, especially among members of the ethnic-minority community who arrived in Britain in the 1960s and 1970s. With some ethnic-minority communities Tory rhetoric of traditional values also fails to appeal, especially in areas with a high concentration of ethnic minorities, such as London, where the population generally has a more modern set of values. The policy of the Conservative mayor, Boris Johnson, contrasts with that taken nationwide, with his initiatives in office revealing some understanding of how to appeal to ethnic-minority voters by, for example, promoting the representation of ethnic minorities within London councils.

There are many emerging patterns, however, which could bring about the gradual disappearance of ethnic minorities' reluctance to vote Conservative. In recent years about a quarter of Asians have voted Conservative. The growing wealth in parts of the Asian community, especially the British Indian community, as well as the appeal of Tory middle-class values, help to explain this phenomenon. The increase in the numbers of high-profile ethnic-minority representatives within the Conservatives, such as the chairperson, Baroness Warsi, has broken new ground and has the potential to win support if moves to create a more ethnically balanced party are consolidated. At present, the extent to which the appointment of Warsi represents a landmark in Tory development is debatable.

The significance of age and gender on the Conservative vote

Historically, the typical Conservative voter has been an older person, explained on the assumption that, as people grow older, they become more conservative morally and tradition also becomes more important. This trend is not as strong as it once was, however, with many people who became eligible to vote in the post-war period, especially those living through the reforming Labour governments such as that of Attlee (1945–51) and that of Wilson (1964–70), favouring Labour because of the identity established in these years.[15] Therefore, the link between growing older and voting Conservative is not as firm as it was in previous generations, and explaining the impact of age on Conservative support is no longer clear.

Historically, too, women have been more likely to vote Conservative; this has often been explained by the fact that, in the past, women were less likely to be in paid employment (and, therefore, were not members of trade unions and identified less with Labour) and that they identified more closely with Conservative values, such as the importance of family. It has also been suggested that women tended to be more deferential so that they were more likely to accept the importance Conservatives place on authority. The tendency towards women voting Conservative has become less strong, however, especially in recent elections. By 2005, MORI polls revealed that women were more likely to vote Labour than Conservative (though this was also part of a general trend away from the Tories). Young women are, on balance, more likely to vote Labour although, in the run-up to the 2010 General Election MORI polls showed that issues such as the Iraq War threatened to discourage women from voting Labour.

The Conservative campaign of 2010 placed a particular emphasis on attracting women voters. To some extent, the drive was successful and there was an increase in the women's vote in all age categories, the highest being in the age eighteen to twenty-four category in which the Tory vote increased by 8 per cent; overall, however, 36 per cent of women voted Conservative compared to 38 per cent of men, leading to a complex picture in which not just older women were being attracted to the Conservatives.[16] Conventionally, middle-class mothers who represent 'middle Britain' were targets for Tory campaigners but recently, because of some policy decisions, such as the announcement that higher-rate taxpayers would not receive child benefit, the Conservatives have missed this target demographic. The Secretary of State for Work and Pensions, Iain Duncan Smith, said it was 'bonkers' for people earning £50,000 to be receiving lots of benefits. Right-wing newspapers failed to agree, however, and openly criticised the Conservative Party: *The Daily Telegraph*, for example, described the proposed child-benefit change as 'crude and unfair to stay-at-home mums'.

Support in the General Election, 2010

The Conservatives' support increased significantly during the 2010 General Election, and although they failed to gain an outright majority, the result showed that the party had successfully won over traditionally Conservative sections of the electorate. Within a year of Cameron becoming leader in 2005, the Conservatives were ahead in the polls and, despite a small blip when the Labour leadership passed from Blair to Brown, the Tories have remained on top. The peak of support for the Conservatives was in the summer of 2008 with some impressive midterm by-elections wins, such as Crewe and Nantwich and Norwich North. The Conservative Party was also the party most represented at a local level in the 2009 elections, holding 48 per cent of council seats.

In the run-up to the general election, however, the Tory lead diminished, with some fear, albeit brief, of the impact of 'Cleggmania' (the popularity of the Liberal Democrat leader, Nick Clegg). After the first televised debate, the percentage of Conservative support fell, though not below that for the other parties. During the election campaign the Conservatives looked nervy, with the pressure of expectation of success weighing heavily on them. During the televised debates between 15 and 29 April 2010, Cameron looked anxious and failed to assert his dominance, undermined in part by the success of Clegg.

Fears about the Conservative Party's chances of winning were largely unfounded, however, and the Conservatives won, though not by as much as had been hoped. The Conservative Party became the biggest party in the Commons, but without the majority they desired, winning 36.1 per cent of the vote which translated into 307 seats compared to 258 for the Labour Party. The 307 seats represented an increase of ninety-five seats from the Conservatives' performance in the previous election in 2005.

The Conservative Party was the most successful party in retaining its core vote and it lost fewer votes to the Lib Dems than had been feared. The Conservatives' share of the vote went up in all regions, picking up a considerable number of their traditional supporters in the east and south-east but, more significantly, winning a larger share of the vote in places in which, historically, the party had fared less well, such as the north-east and Humberside, gaining their biggest increase, of 4.5 per cent, in the West Midlands, an area hit especially hard by the recession. The Tories even increased their proportion of the vote in Scotland, a region that had been traditionally hostile to the Conservatives. Where the Conservatives did lose seats, it was more often to the Liberal Democrats and therefore not as damaging as losing seats to their nearest rivals, Labour. In addition, there was no significant loss of Conservative support to minor parties, such as UKIP, which was a fear after Cameron repositioned the party on to the centre ground.

Funding

Traditionally, the funding available to the Conservative Party has been greater than that of its opponents. Consequently, the party has been able to fund more candidates, a factor that was vital to Conservative success. The wider availability of funds for candidates has allowed the Tories to distribute material more widely and to reach more voters. Historically, the Conservatives have used their financial muscle to get ahead of the other parties by using newly available methods, such as cinema, which they pioneered in the post-war period and which was closely associated with Stanley Baldwin who made use of this medium for election broadcasts when no other party did. The advantages of funding can be seen today. In the 2011 referendum on the voting system the Conservative-backed 'no' campaign's literature far outweighed the resources available to the 'yes' campaign.

Big donors and 'non-doms'

The Conservatives have tended to rely more heavily on big donors to fund the party, with business and individuals choosing to give money to the Tories when they are in government. What has proved to be more difficult for them is to maintain funding levels when they are in Opposition, so that the thirteen years following their defeat in 1997 were particularly hard for them. Big injections of money, including large donations made by Lord Ashcroft, the party's former deputy chairman, have proved controversial in a number of ways. Some concern was raised about the input and influence that Lord Ashcroft had but equally controversial was the fact that he was a 'non-dom' so that he did not pay United Kingdom tax, raising questions about the suitability of his donations. During the run-up to the 2010 General Election considerable funds, seemingly from big donor Lord Ashcroft, were put into supporting target seats. The cash injection had a considerable impact, with the Conservative Party doing better in seats where they had extra funding compared with their performance in other seats around the country. Twenty potentially at-risk seats were successfully defended along with twenty-seven of those held as marginals in 2005. In addition, seventy-seven potential gains earmarked by the party for extra support were given a considerable boost by extra cash coming from private donations.[17] The future role of large individual donations looks uncertain, with the Conservatives supporting a cap of £50,000 on donations and limits on the amount that can be spent during election campaigns. The target set for general elections was £15 million but the Conservatives spent £16,682,874 on the last election campaign, more than double the amount spent by Labour.

Conservative Party fundraising

Instead of turning to big donations, it is likely that, in future, the Conservatives will have to rely more heavily on other methods of fundraising. One source that the Conservatives could use is money raised by the constituencies which have, in the past, been better than Labour's constituencies at raising money. Constituency fundraising is not as lucrative as big-money donors have been and has been seriously damaged by falling membership. The decline in the Conservative Party's membership mirrors the general trend in the fall in membership of political parties since 1945. Despite an early rise in members shortly after Cameron's election as leader in December 2005, since 2006, party membership has fallen to a lower level than when Cameron became leader, with around 290,000 members. One possible alternative source of funding is the Conservative Party Foundation which aims to secure long-term funding for the party.[18]

Structure and organisation

The leader

In the past, the leader of the Conservative Party has enjoyed more power than leaders of other parties; this is largely because the leader of the Conservative Parliamentary Party has a dominant policy-making role and has no defined scope laid down in a constitution. The control of policy-making gives the Conservative leader substantial power. The leader has the authority to form policy, in discussion with the cabinet, and may also use other agencies, such as think tanks or special advisers, at his or her discretion. Historically, Conservative Party leaders were appointed by 'backstairs intrigue' with leading members within the party and the monarch making the choice. The aim of selecting the leader behind closed doors was to sort out differences in the party in private, rather than airing them in public. This informal practice was stopped, however, as part of a number of internal reforms in an attempt to democratise the inner workings of the Conservative Party. As a result, the engineering by Macmillan and close associates in 1962 to appoint Sir Alec Douglas Home, overlooking party heavyweights such as R. A. Butler and Lord Hailsham, was the last unelected appointment.[19]

Powers of the Conservative Party leader

The power of the Conservative Party leader is significantly enhanced by the fact that his or her powers are not restricted by a party constitution so that, in theory, the power is limitless. Because there is no formal authority, control and discipline have been preserved by deference to the hierarchical structures within the political party. The leader also has no official powers over the wider party outside Parliament, with convention stating that the leader's power is exercised through inherent respect for his or her position of authority. The extent of the power of the leader can be seen as a key feature of the party, and one that has been identified by political scientists, with R. T. McKenzie going so far as to argue that the strength of the leader is 'the most striking feature of the Conservative Party organisation'.[20] There are some merits to McKenzie's claim; the centralisation of the party is an important strength, as are the powers to choose members and the ultimate control of Central Office. Moreover, the degree of clout of the Tory leader can be successfully gauged by comparing the considerable powers enjoyed by the Conservative leader to those lesser powers of his/her Labour counterpart. The Conservative leader has the power to appoint the front bench and there is no obligation to share power, as is demonstrated by the fact that there is no requirement at all for a deputy leader. The considerable power of the Tory leader over appointments is in contrast to the ballot system used to choose Labour's front bench as well as the requirement for an independently elected deputy leader. The Conservative leader has the power to select the party chairperson, and consequently, has a considerable role in choosing the direction of the party.

Democratisation of the party

Moves to democratise the party and to alter its political culture mean that the power relationship between leader and party is evolving. The power of the Conservative leader has always been fluid, altering according to the political climate and depending on the character of and support for the incumbent. Up to 1998, the selection of the leader was purely the jurisdiction of Conservative MPs; consequently, challenges to the leadership happened more often in the Conservative Party than in Labour with its reformed procedures. In practice, the traditional method of using a ballot of Conservative MPs to choose the leader made dissent easier. The simplicity of the leadership challenge procedure is more of an issue when considered alongside the shift in political culture. The decline in emphasis on deference has led to considerable boldness in confronting the leader. Increased pressure on the leader can be illustrated by the fact that the incumbent leader of the Conservative Party was challenged three times between 1989 and 1995.

Appointment of the leader

Since 1998, selection of the leader of the Conservative Party takes place in two parts, with the first stage involving the parliamentary party and the second stage including all party members. A leadership race can take place under specific circumstances: the leader may offer his/her resignation to the **1922 Committee** which, in exceptional situations, may enable the leader to call for a leadership contest to reaffirm his/her own position, as happened with John Major, or the leader may lose a 'vote of no confidence' among MPs which can be triggered by 15 per cent of MPs writing anonymously to the chairperson of the 1922 Committee. If a vote of no confidence is called, the incumbent leader must secure a simple majority to maintain his/her position. If he or she is unable to do this, that leader must stand aside and allow a leadership contest to take place. During a leadership race, nominations are taken by the 1922 Committee and the first ballot takes place with votes being cast by MPs. The two leading candidates will then go forward to an election involving the whole party on a one-member-one-vote system.

Despite Conservative traditions of respect for authority and acceptance of natural hierarchy, the role of the leader has not always been an easy one. Leaders have often found the party hard to manage: Conservative leader Stanley Baldwin said that trying to lead the Tories was like driving pigs to market. Indeed, many leaders have found the party difficult to work with: thus, the mistrust felt by Churchill, the stab in the back experienced by Thatcher, or the lack of loyalty or appreciation felt by Major.[21]

Perhaps more than that of any other mainstream party, the fate of the Conservative Party rests upon the success and popularity of its leader. During the 2010 election campaign the power of, and focus on, the leader were greater than ever, with the campaign hinging on his personality and appeal. Cameron had won over party members at the 2005 party conference at the height of campaigning for the leadership. Cameron's 'without notes' speech delivered passionately while walking around the platform proved to be a big hit and contrasted starkly with the poorly delivered speech of David Davis who had been ahead after the first ballot, with sixty-two votes compared to Cameron's fifty-six.[22]

The power of the leader can also be seen in his or her ability to shape policy. With Cameron the Conservative Party has been pulled to the electoral centre ground. With his 'change to win' slogan Cameron, managed to draw the party away from the right, the position from which it had fought the 2005 election. Though it must be acknowledged that Cameron was the candidate who had the least opposition, the popular Conservative focus on Europe and tough law-and-order stance had been abandoned in favour of 'one nation' ideas (Box 2.2). In 2010 Cameron was, for the first time, the most popular member of the Conservative party largely because of the perception of him as a strong prime minister.

Box 2.2 A comparison of Conservative leadership styles

Margaret Thatcher was notorious for her authoritarian approach, favouring driving through her own policy initiative, in a prime ministerial style of leadership, rather than collectively formulating policy in cabinet. Thatcher trusted heavily in the counsel of a few key advisers, such as her Chief Press Secretary Bernard Ingham, and often came into conflict with colleagues who criticised her strategy. Consequently, her cabinets became dominated with 'yes men' as potential political rivals within the party hierarchy, including Geoffrey Howe and Nigel Lawson, left. Power was also centralised under Thatcher and this came through in policy decisions like the abolition of the Greater London Council in 1986 which strengthened Britain as a unitary state. The centralisation of power within the Thatcher administration was also clear in her dealings with the party in Parliament, with her lack of consultation and failure to listen to the mood of the cabinet or parliamentary party leading to her eventual downfall.

John Major had a consensual style of leadership, favouring cabinet government. After the turmoil and internal conflict under Thatcher, Major was determined to hold the party together through inclusive leadership, along with open discussion and input on policy decisions. For some inside and outside the party the consensual approach was seen as weakness, causing internal defiance within his cabinet and open criticism of Major in Parliament. In response to accusations of his weak leadership, Major resigned as leader in 1993 triggering a leadership contest that invited opponents to stand up and be counted. Major won the contest but the victory had a limited effect on asserting his authority, with the party remaining heavily divided between the 'wets' and the 'dries'.

David Cameron was elected leader on the promise of reforming the party, but also as the moderate, conciliatory candidate. As leader he has kept decision-making among a limited number of trusted advisers .and key ministers such as friends like George Osborne.

In government, Cameron's leadership style has been influenced by the fact that the Conservatives are part of a coalition but the level of combined decision-making has been limited, with the Tories remaining very much the dominant partner. There is also evidence of Cameron adopting the **spatial leadership** style, distancing himself from controversial decisions, including denying any knowledge of the dealings of his former communications chief, Andy Coulson. Similarly, Cameron has tried to detach himself from unpopular policy. After the widespread criticism of the Health and Social Care Bill, Cameron promised to keep a close eye on the formulation of policy, inferring that his minister, Andrew Lansley, had made errors of judgement.

The parliamentary party

The inherent dominance of the Conservative Parliamentary Party over the consistency party is shown in the historical roots of the organisation. Conservative governments existed in 1834 but an extra-parliamentary party was not introduced until 1867 when Conservative politics in constituencies was fashioned by Conservative MPs with the purpose of serving their interests at a local level. This historical dominance meant that, traditionally, there has been little consultation between the Conservative Party in Parliament and its grass roots. This assumption, that the MPs and peers would dominate, was encapsulated in Balfour's comment that he would sooner take advice from his valet than from Conservative conference. This minor role played by the Conservative Party conference contrasts starkly with the traditionally strong role of conference within the Labour Party. Thus, the distance between the leadership and the constituency was still evident up to the 1970s; for instance, until Ted Heath became leader of the party, the practice of the leader attending conference had not been the case. Without the party leader present, therefore, there was almost no chance of conference influencing policy.

Traditional Tory values of respect for authority and hierarchy meant that the extra-parliamentary party was expected to be subordinate and loyal to their MPs; this concept has been widely challenged in recent times with the agenda of the Conservative Parliamentary Party tested to check that it is not out of step with Conservative opinion on the ground.

Just as in other political parties, Conservative candidates tended to be male and were likely to be middle-aged; indeed, until the early 1990s the average age of candidates had been increasing. MPs and candidates also tend to be Caucasian. It was not until 1992 that the first non-white Conservative MP was elected. In addition, it was not until 2010 that the Conservatives had their first non-white cabinet member, party chairperson Baroness Warsi. Central to Cameron's aim of reforming the Conservative Party was to alter the make-up of the parliamentary party, nine out of ten of whom were white males when Cameron became leader. Since 2001 there has been a conscious move to 'headhunt' a new type of candidate in an effort to amend this problem. Rather than just paying lip-service to the centrists, Conservative Campaign Headquarters (CCHQ) would aim to get this new style of candidate elected offering the perspective candidates places on the leadership's approved party list. This, of course, meant that candidates still had to overcome the traditionally more conservative constituency parties that would make the final selections but, if the constituency chose a list candidate, then there would be the possibility of extra funding from CCHQ. Chris Philp maintains that this move towards a new type of candidate was seen by some as 'the Party's clause IV' which would recast how the Conservatives were viewed by the voters.[23] This was a radical move for a party that was so attached to a basic principle of equality of opportunity. It faced considerable opposition from many quarters, and at every level, of the party, including those on the Right and on the Left. Nevertheless, the decision to change was seen by Cameron as a cornerstone of his philosophy as a moderate leader of the Conservative Party. Estimates suggested that, if the Conservatives continued to rely on simple equality of opportunity, it would take 400 years to even out the gender imbalance within the party.

Despite the attempts to have more women candidates, the parliamentary party failed to become more representative because women often found themselves in constituencies where they were in third place or where the party required a swing of 10 per cent or more to be elected. Therefore, the move to improve women's representation is incomplete despite the introduction of a radical policy to accelerate change. There was a failure to push through preferences for women candidates and controversy was avoided by not placing enough women in winnable seats.

Conservative Campaign Headquarters (CCHQ)

Conservative Campaign headquarters (CCHQ), formerly known as Conservative Central Office (CCO), is the central base of the Conservative Party. The tasks of CCHQ are to raise funds, to form policy alongside the leader, to co-ordinate Conservative activity, including election campaigns, and to ensure that the parliamentary party stays in touch with concerns in the constituencies. A central headquarters was established in 1870 and was set up primarily, as famously described by H. C. Raikes MP, as the 'handmaid' to the parliamentary party.[24]

Conservative Campaign Headquarters leads financing, manages elections and outlines policy. Raising funding for the party is one of the essential roles performed by head office and, as other political parties have also found, raising money has proved difficult and, at times, a controversial task. This has become even more evident in recent years. A key role of CCHQ is to manage elections under the guidance of the party leadership. Traditionally, CCHQ has had access to more money than the other parties because the Conservative Party's annual income is around £20 million, with considerable sums coming in from individual donors. In 2010, the lines of authority were blurred and this led to tension and some confusion about whose role was what. George Osborne was tasked with leading the election campaign for the Tories as general election campaign manager; this overlapped, however, with the role of Eric Pickles (then chairman) and that of Andy Coulson as chief of communications. The situation became even more confused and controversial over the influence of Lord Ashcroft whose generous donations were essential in providing considerable funding for campaigns in target seats.

Another strategic move by CCHQ was to look for a different

style of candidate in an attempt to improve election success. CCHQ approached business owners as well as members of groups that, traditionally, had not been widely represented among candidates, including ethnic minorities and women (supporting findings in the Hansard Society's report, 'Women at the Top').[25] As part of the strategy to improve performance, there was an acknowledgment of the undesirable dominance of men in Parliament and particular emphasis was placed on trying to recruit successful women by asking them if they would be interested in becoming Conservative MPs. Another motivating factor of the CCHQ was to win back the female vote that had departed from the Tories in 1997, by providing a selection of women candidates with whom they could identify.

The board of the Conservative Party
The board is the final decision-making body at the top of the Conservative Party. The board directs aspects of the Conservative operation, including the selection of candidates, raising funds, and the membership of the party. The board is elected from all parts of the party, including voluntary and political members, and finalises all matters concerning the Conservative Party, working closely with CCHQ, MPs, MEPs and councillors, as well as with the voluntary membership. The board meets once a month and has a number of subcommittees to examine ideas before coming to a final decision. Within the board, elections are held to select vice presidents, the chairperson and the president's position on the National Convention; all other officers are elected unopposed.

The constituency party
The organisation of the Conservative Party, particularly the grass roots at constituency level, has been one of its strengths and fundamental to its domination of the political landscape. The organisational framework of constituencies has firm foundations in rural and suburban areas, as well as in small towns, creating a base for support and also financial backing. As with the parliamentary party, most constituency members tend to be middle class and white, and, in the past, older than members of the other major parties, though the average age of constituency members is going down. To convey the grass-roots opinion to the leadership representatives of constituency

parties meet at local and at national levels, including at conference. Though the constituency parties have this opportunity to present ideas to the leadership, there is no mechanism in place to force the leadership to take note of constituency feeling. That said, leaders who ignore constituency opinion or try to force decisions on constituency parties have often run into difficulty. The power of the constituency has grown in recent years as all Conservative members are now involved in electing the leader. The opinion and politics in the constituencies are often less moderate than those of the parliamentary party, which may go some way to explaining the surprise election of right winger, Iain Duncan Smith, as leader of the party in 2001 on the back of grass-roots votes.

Policy under Cameron

In the Conservative Party power to control policy rests ultimately with the leader and, unlike those that exist in some other parties, there are no constitutional limits on the leader's policy-making powers. The leader is assisted in policy-making by the Conservative Campaign Headquarters, and there is an increasing use of think tanks. Once policy decisions have been made, the leader puts those decisions to the Conservative board for final approval but the steering of policy remains the remit of the leader.

Just like the attempt to rebrand and offer new polices that occurred with Labour under Blair, the Conservatives went through a similar rebranding under Cameron. When asked about the Conservatives in Opposition, 66 per cent of voters agreed that the Conservative Party was 'out of touch'.[26] Under Cameron, there was a change of image symbolised by a change in the party logo, and there was also a noticeable alteration of policy away from the low-tax, anti-Europe stance to a more pragmatic one. There was a more practical approach to economic policy, prioritisation of the NHS – a policy usually associated with their opponents – and there were new issues for the Conservatives, such as the environment. After winning the election, the Conservatives were forced to seek support from the Liberal Democrats to enable them to form a government. As part of a coalition, Conservative power and direction over policy have unquestionably been altered but not to the extent that some commentators predicted or some Conservatives feared.

The economy

The trust in their handling of the economy that the Conservatives had always enjoyed was lost during the Major government primarily as a result of the poor handling of the financial crisis leading up to, during, and as a result of, Black Wednesday in 1992. During the 2010 election campaign, the Tories returned to traditional position on the limited role of the state but also emphasised the need for economic competence which they would offer by reducing the deficit.

The Conservative Party has begun to cut public expenditure with the deficit managed through a reduction in public services to enable the government to service the debt. The ratio of spending cuts to increased taxes proposed by the Conservatives was four to one, compared with two to one for the Labour Party. In power, the Conservatives have made much of the notion that harsh measures were necessary because of the wastefulness of Labour and the mess that they left behind. The outgoing administration did not help their case by, in jest, leaving a note that read 'Good Luck. There is no money left.' The author of the note was Liam Byrne, Chief Secretary to the Treasury, and with relish, the coalition jumped on his joke as 'evidence' of the complacency of Labour.[27] The coalition has returned to a small-state stance, unpicking some of the interventionist policies of their Labour predecessors, including ending the £80 million loan to Forgemasters in Sheffield who had been saved under Labour. Despite these harsh cuts, the Conservatives were not punished at the ballot box, and there was no significant change in their percentage of the vote in the local elections of 2011. The absence of a backlash can be explained by the fact that traditional Conservative voters have supported the cuts and those who opposed the cuts chose either not to vote or decided to punish the Liberal Democrats who were the real losers in the 2011 local elections.

The Conservatives' economic policy as set out by Chancellor of the Exchequer, George Osborne, in 2010 was considerably different from the proposals put in place by the outgoing Labour government. The biggest differences were in the speed and depth of the cuts. Within less than a month of becoming chancellor, Osborne revealed 6.2 billion pounds of cuts followed by an emergency budget to deal with the severe and pressing problems left by the Labour administration. Under the coalition economic policy, the budget of each department would have to be cut by one-fifth, with all departments told that they would need to review their spending plans, leading to conflict between ministries over how much each was to receive. Some ministers chose to fight dirty, like defence minister, Liam Fox, who leaked information about the military's concerns for cuts in order to get a much better settlement for the Ministry of Defence.

Cameron set out a large programme of cuts that are destined to continue over the next four years. In addition to cuts, tax rises have been announced and this contrasts sharply with Conservative instinct to keep tax low. Such moves brought criticism from within the party, though the policy did gain praise from the Bank of England as being the correct course even though that inflation has risen in recent months to 4.4 per cent, double the target set by the Bank of England. In return, the coalition has pledged that the Bank of England will be given overall control of financial regulation, revealing a working relationship between the government and the Bank of England that is much warmer than it was when Alistair Darling was chancellor.

It is not possible fully to judge the success of the economic policy at such an early stage. The announcement by the coalition that the Britain was no longer in danger of losing its triple-A rating would, on the face of it, seem like a considerable success, though the threat that the country was going to lose that rating was rather overstated by Labour's opponents in the run-up to the 2010 election. Therefore, securing the triple-A rating, presented as a milestone by the coalition, may not be the great success that it claimed. In fact, there is little proof that the Conservatives' economic policy is having a positive affect. Rather than conclusive evidence of improvement, there has been a mixture of encouraging signs and worrying ones: for instance, towards the end of 2011 the British economy contracted leading the chancellor to downgrade growth prospects, only for the economy to pick up again with growth of 2.1 per cent in the new year.[28] The performance of the coalition's economic policy needs to be assessed over a much longer period to draw any conclusions.

In Opposition, the Conservatives had proposed a tax system to encourage traditional moral values but, on entering office, have not introduced the tax breaks for married couples which were going to be part of its flagship policy. The reasons for the moderation, now that they are in power, can largely be explained by the fact that they are in a coalition with the Liberal Democrats who are ideologically opposed to any policy that favours one lifestyle choice over another. The Conservatives in government have also experienced criticism from within the party on their failure to fulfil manifesto promises. Iain Duncan Smith's influential think tank, The Centre for Social Justice, has condemned the government for failing to introduce a tax system that seemed to have fallen 'off the radar'.[29]

Health reform

By and large, planned Conservative health reforms have been poorly received. The public seems to be fearful that the Conservatives' intention in its proposals is to privatise the NHS rather than reform healthcare provision. Health was the only area in which the Conservatives had committed themselves to increase spending but, in government, they have found their policy on health problematic rather than popular. In the Conservatives' Health and Social Care Bill, from 2013 all 151 primary care trusts (PCTs) and strategic health authorities will have been removed, giving GPs control of 80 per cent of the healthcare budget. It is planned that GPs will then have the responsibility of buying the healthcare appropriate to the needs of the communities they serve.

The reform of healthcare is an example of the 'big society' idea in action. The plans have come up against political pressure as well as criticism from professionals and the public, however, with concerns that the huge role to be played by the private sector will open up the NHS to any willing provider. Even before the plans have been put in place, there is evidence of their cool reception by the public. In a MORI poll there was strong evidence of fears that a postcode lottery would be created by the new legislation. Of those questioned, 81 per cent stated that they thought that NHS services should be the same throughout the country. The variety that would be created by GPs choosing what to spend the budget on could lead to regional discrepancies. Cameron has been fiercely criticised by the Opposition for being 'arrogant' in thinking he could continue with the policy in the face of the disagreement from all the healthcare unions. The prime minister has also experienced opposition from within his own government with the Liberal Democrats looking to stall the bill. As a result of worries raised by political, professional and public feedback,

Cameron has decided to shelve health plans for the time being until a solution is reached that tackles the problems identified by critics. It is most important to ensure that health professionals are at one with the government. Thus, when the final bill comes before the house, it may have many significant amendments from the original plan set out by Health Secretary, Andrew Lansley.

Social policy and the 'big society'

Under Cameron, the Conservative Party has favoured a one-nation approach to social policy. As part of the rejuvenation of the Tory brand, emphasis on the duty of the government to care for citizens runs alongside traditional ideas of encouraging people to help themselves. When Cameron was asked about how the Conservatives under his leadership were going to manage the issue of social deprivation, he maintained that providing money for deprived sections of society is not enough. There is a need, he felt, to tackle the 'causes of poverty'. Cameron went on to argue that the Conservatives had the same objectives as Labour but would not use 'top-down government' to solve the problem. For Cameron, 'top-down government' is to be avoided by promoting the 'big society'. The 'big society' is one of Cameron's flagship policies, using private companies and charitable organisations to provide services rather than overreliance on the state to provide welfare.

As part of managing the budget, less money will be available to deal with poverty so, to meet the gap left by a decrease in public money for welfare, Cameron has proposed that other organisations come in to share the burden as part of the 'big society' project. Therefore the aim of the 'big society' was to mend 'broken Britain' and to make up the shortfall in public spending and reduce the size of the state. Thus, the idea of the 'big society' is intended to encompass the best of Tory beliefs: small state, public duty and social responsibility. In Cameron's words, 'a society where the leading force for progress is social responsibility, not state control'.[30] The 'big society' was supposed to work in practice with an increase in volunteering; the message of the big society, however, has failed to be successfully communicated to the voters. Because of this lack of excitement from the public, the 'big society' that was the flagship of Cameron's administration has been less of a priority, with Cameron himself admitting in an interview with the *Evening Standard* that the idea would be difficult to sell.

Welfare-reform proposals that had been set out before the general election had intended to take a tough line on benefit claimants to ensure that claimants are not rewarded better for being out of work than they would be if they were in employment. The aim of government reform was to create a universal credit that would entice people, including the long-term unemployed, back into work. In government the coalition has put this policy into practice. To ensure that benefits are fair the universal benefit has been capped at £26,000, so that those on benefit do not receive more than those in work; thus, the Thatcherite principle of self-help comes into play.

The universal benefit has faced a number of criticisms: for failing to be flexible enough; for not simplifying the tax system; and there have also been concerns over fairness. Critics are worried that the claims that universal benefits are cost-effective and uncomplicated are not realised in practice. Sceptics predict that the scheme may suffer in the same way that previous streamlining proposals have done, fearing that the universal benefit may have difficulty in its one-size-fits-all form. The universal benefit has also been come under fire on the grounds that the work-capability assessment leads to unfairness. The job of deciding who qualifies for the benefit has been assigned to the private company, ATOS. ATOS has already incurred £21 million worth of costs in appeals because of inaccurate assessments and has been criticised by the Work and Pensions Select Committee for its poor judgement on who is 'fit to work'. Benefit reforms have also been condemned by women's organisations, such as the Women's Budget Group, who argue that the universal benefit will inhibit progress towards gender equality; these groups fear that the benefit will reduce women's access to the household budget.

Education
In practice, the 'big society' project has led to substantial changes in education policy, though the impact of these changes remains unfulfilled. The Labour policy of academies has continued and has been broadened leading to an increase in the number of academies, with academy status available to those high-achieving schools that want to escape regulation rather than just being a project to benefit

failing schools. The theory behind the increase in academies has been influenced by Thatcherite ideas in that new academies have greater control over how they organise and deliver services. Many schools have opted for academy status and there has been considerable take-up by well-performing schools so that, initially at least, the project has proved to be popular, though the long-term impact of academies cannot be assessed yet.

As well as academies, education reform has included the increased opportunity for private individuals to chose to opt out of local-authority control and set up free schools. The free schools project has had little take-up. Critics within the Conservative Party have blamed the failure on the fact that schools are not allowed to make a profit under the current scheme so, they claim, there is little incentive to allow the market to function effectively.

Other core Conservative values are evident in education policy, including the reinforcement of discipline in schools. Conservative policy proposes to give more power to teachers to assert their authority, including the right to search pupils and confiscate banned items. The government has also promised to protect teachers' right to use reasonable force or physical restraint to control unruly children. The ability to punish bad behaviour has been simplified and supported by removing the requirement to give twenty-fours' notice for detention, thereby freeing teachers from some of the red tape.

Higher-education policy has also proved to be very controversial and, in December 2010, there were widespread student protests. The reforms to higher-education funding mean that students will have to pay fees of up to £9,000 a year and they will have to start repaying student loans once as soon as they have graduated and are earning more £21,000 per annum. The policy aims to increase access to university for less well-off students by removing up-front tuition costs and providing grants, with the poorest quarter of students having to pay less in total than under the previous system.

The reforms have been led by universities minister, David Willetts, on the basis of the recommendations made in the Browne report set up by the previous government. Despite widespread criticism, especially from Labour and Liberal Democrat backbenchers, it seems likely that there would have been similar reform of higher education even if the Labour Party had remained in power. Though the system has been set up to increase equality of opportunity, difficulties are likely to arise in practice. Even though £9,000 a year is the upper limit for tuition fees, many universities have chosen to charge the maximum amount. Oxford and Cambridge, as well as the Russell Group, have opted to charge £9,000, and Exeter is the first former polytechnic to confirm that it will also be charging the full amount. The level of tuition fees has become a de facto indicator of the quality of the university, and many have argued that this should have been predicted by the government. It is questionable whether the policy really will lead to equality of opportunity because university will still be denied to many who lack the means to subsidise their lives as students, even if they do qualify for the grant as well as the loan, with the true costs of living at university not covered by the amount put aside by the government.

The Conservatives have backtracked over some of the more controversial aspects of policy detail. In 2010, David Willetts announced premium-rate university places so that more places would be available which for richer students who could pay more. The plan was quickly withdrawn, however, because of criticism that the policy would cement privilege. Willetts presented the policy as an application of market forces to university education, by providing places if the demand was there. In reality, creating premium-rate places projected an image that the party under Cameron has tried to dispel, and the government moved quickly to abandon an idea which suggested that those with money could pay to get on.

The structure of government
Returning to the centre ground has also meant reinforcing traditional Conservative values of a 'Tory democracy' as well as respecting important checks and balances laid out in the constitution that had been neglected under dominant prime ministers such as Thatcher and later Blair of New Labour. As part of Cameron's rebranding, he set out to show that, under the modern Conservatives, things would be different, and that they would take a more open approach which would reinvigorate the democratic credentials of the Conservative Party. The Conservatives' democratic task force was headed by Ken Clarke who condoned 'sofa government' in which decisions were made in an informal discussion among a policy-making elite.[31]

Evidence of a commitment to more open government can be seen in the publishing-transparency website introduced by Home Secretary, Theresa May, in 2010 to allow the public access to data from government departments.

Despite this talk of openness, one year into Cameron's premiership, this commitment to open and inclusive government seems less of a reality, with the kitchen cabinet of Cameron, Osborne, Clegg and Alexander (collectively known as 'the quad' by the Civil Service) reportedly dominating decision-making. Revelations over the Conservative government's links with Rupert Murdoch's News Corporation have also caused fresh controversy about who has access to government, with Murdoch stating in his recent select committee hearing that he was 'invited within days to have a cup of tea and to be thanked by Mr. Cameron', signifying that he had a close working relationship with the prime minister.[32] It has been suggested that News International has been frequently consulted, and Cameron alone has had twenty-one meetings with Mr Murdoch or other News Corporation executives since entering government. This shows that the media corporation, an unelected organisation, has had the opportunity to exert influence on policy direction. Ironically, the only reason that the meetings with Murdoch's corporation have come to light is because of the greater openness of government, with information about meetings available on the government website. Moreover, the Conservatives do not seem to have been alone in their connections with the News Corporation, and previous Labour administrations and the Labour leader have also had meetings with the organisation.

Law and order
A tough attitude on law and order has always been an important aspect of Conservative Party policy, and draws on fundamental aspects of the Conservative approach which aims to 'conserve' society's stability and support state authority. New Labour, however, took its tough law-and-order platform from the Conservatives with the promise to be 'tough on crime' and, despite the best efforts of Cameron's Conservatives to reclaim the policy, it remains an area of policy in which the party has not fully asserted itself. There is pressure within the party to adopt a more hard-line agenda on law and order,

with former chairman, Lord Ashcroft, announcing that crime had become the Tories' 'biggest vulnerability' with opinion polls revealing that the public no longer believes that the Conservatives will take a tough stance. The fear over the party's loss of identity on crime policy caused Cameron to enforce Justice Secretary, Ken Clarke, to adopt a different approach. Initially, Clarke had proposed a 50 per cent reduction in length of sentence for those making early pleas Under pressure from inside and outside the party, however, the prime minister persuaded the Justice Secretary to drop the controversial plans.

A more traditional stance on law and order was clear from the Conservatives' condemnation of the early release of Lockerbie bomber, Abdelbaset Mohmed Ali al-Megrahi, saying his release went against 'natural justice'. Yet overall, most crime policy is based on the **libertarian** principle of reducing the bureaucracy of the state rather than an emphasis on punishment. As part of the Police Reform and Social Responsibility Bill, 2011, policies include a commitment to reducing the size of police bureaucracy with the concomitant threats to police numbers and changes to pay. To make the police more accountable, the bill also includes legislation to remove police authorities and introduce locally elected police commissioners. Other moves to increase accountability include a government website with 'crime maps' so members of the public can monitor crime in their local area. Overall, in a time of austerity, Tory crime policy has concentrated more on streamlining the bodies that deal with crime rather than on expensive crime initiatives that emphasise retribution. This said, the change of direction on sentencing policy could signal a new trend in the Conservatives' efforts to re-establish their image on crime policy.

Conclusion

In government, Cameron's policy-making power has been restricted by being in coalition, though not to the extent that many predicted. As regards policy, Thatcher remains an inspiration for many of the economic measures of the current Conservative administration. The influence of Thatcherism can be seen in Cameron's reduction in public spending and in his preference for limited government. This said, Cameron's Conservatives have been 'softer' than Thatcher,

Box 2.3 Cameron's modernisation

Change	Continuity
Image: increasing representation for women and ethnic minorities among Conservative MPs; change of logo, slogans and leadership style.	Most of the Conservative leadership team is still drawn from senior public schools and Oxbridge backgrounds.
Domestic policy: Cameron has emphasised the priority of environmental aims, softened tone on law and order, and supported academies rather than grammar schools.	Foreign policy: Cameron moved his MEPs into a new anti-federalist block in the European Parliament, and opposed the Eurozone recovery plan in December 2011.
Economics: even before the recession, Cameron reduced expectations of tax cuts which, he said, would have to share the proceeds of growth with increased public expenditure.	Recession: George Osborne has reduced public spending dramatically and reformed public services, including the NHS; also free schools have been introduced, and there is a cap on benefit entitlements.
Coalition: Cameron took the opportunity to work with the Liberal Democrats when some in his party argued that this would dilute Conservative policy.	Constitutional reform: Cameron fiercely resisted the introduction of AV, opposes Scottish independence, and has called for the Human Rights Act to be repealed.

Question: How much has the Conservative Party changed under the leadership of David Cameron?

intervening when absolutely necessary and ensuring more regulation of the banking and finance sectors, in particular, rather than giving them free reign. In wider policy decisions, the rules of the market have been applied but there has been a concerted effort by Cameron to appear to be a 'compassionate Conservative'. 'One-nation' compassion can be seen in the promised support for the National Health Service and in the government's modernising moral attitudes to encourage greater equality of opportunity and to suggest to the public that it is more caring. Hints of an ideological motivation for many economic reforms seem to have shaped policy up to now but the true nature of Cameron's Conservatives cannot yet be fully gauged, having had only just over a year in office. The direction of policy will depend on circumstances, such as the economic conditions in the country, and on political relationships within the coalition.

. . . .

✓ What you should have learnt from reading this chapter

- The reason for the continued success of the Conservative Party has been its ability to develop gradually. Evolutionary change has taken the party from an organisation of the ruling class to become a party with cross-class appeal, successfully establishing itself as the trusted party of government. Throughout its history the party has taking a pragmatic approach, though the direction of the party was change permanently under Margaret Thatcher's premiership with a distinctively ideological policy, the influence of which can still be seen today.

- Despite the wide variation of approaches taken by the Conservatives in the party's 177-year history, key ideas have remained constant. The preservation of traditional institutions and values, including the importance of upholding moral values, has been most consistently followed. Organic change has also occurred throughout, so that desired characteristics have been retained while the Conservatives have also remained responsive to society's needs and wants. The sceptical attitude of Conservatives has encouraged caution and a negative view of human nature that have led the party to advocate strong discipline in the public and private spheres.

- The Conservative Party is a 'top-down' organisation and has a powerful leadership that is not confined by constitutional restraints. There have been some moves to encourage internal democracy, such as reforms to the election of the leader and moves by CCHQ to gauge opinion in the constituencies, but policy is formulated and directed by the leadership and by CCHQ. Policy under Cameron shows hints at ideological motivation, borrowing key ideas from Thatcherism, but a key difference has been his rebranding of the party, taking a much 'softer' line than many previous leaders have done.

Glossary of key terms

Cabinet government A style of government in which the prime minister acts as a 'first among equals' in cabinet where there is collective decision-making on policy. Cabinet government was identified by A. V. Dicey as one of the key conventions of the British constitution.

Eurosceptic A person who is sceptical of European integration and the transfer of decision-making powers to the European Union (EU). Eurosceptics believe that British identity and sovereignty have been lost by being part of the EU. Eurosceptics advocate a reduction in the powers of the EU or complete withdrawal from the EU.

Kitchen cabinet A close-knit group of ministers or advisers involved in decision-making at the head of government.

Libertarianism A political ideology that prioritises individual liberty, especially freedom of action and property rights. Libertarian ideas have had a powerful influence on the New Right in Britain and the United States.

Monetarism An approach to the economy, promoted by economists such as Milton Friedman, that emphasises the role of government in controlling inflation by monitoring money supply.

1922 Committee A group of Conservative backbench MPs that meets once a week to determine their view on key issues independently of the front bench. The 1922 Committee gets its name from the first meeting of Conservative MPs at the Carlton Club in 1922 to determine the direction of the Conservative Party. At the meeting MPs decided to leave the coalition led by Lloyd George. The 1922 Committee must be consulted when a leadership election is called and, though its powers are determined by convention, leaders ignore the opinion of the 1922 Committee at their peril.

Organicism Favouring an organic or 'natural' approach that promotes gradual change rather than radical or revolutionary change.

Poll tax A tax levied on people rather than on property. In 1990 Margaret Thatcher introduced a poll tax (also known as the community charge) that was set at the same rate for everyone rather than having variable rates according to the property that individuals owned. The tax was very unpopular and caused rioting, with many people refusing to pay. The tax was controversial because the flat rate meant the amount many people had to pay, especially poorer members of society, increased significantly.

Privatisation The process of removing something from the remit of the state into the hands of private companies or individuals.

Spatial leadership A style of leadership adopted by some prime ministers where he or she distances himself/herself from the political turmoil to appear to be above the problems of the government. Michael Foley argued that prime ministers such as Blair and Thatcher have used this tactic during their time in office and indicated that the office of the prime minister was becoming more presidential in character.

❓ Likely examination questions

Does David Cameron's brand of Conservatism represent a break from previous conservative administrations?

To what extent has reform of the leadership procedures improved the internal democracy of the Conservative Party?

'The leader of the Conservative Party has complete control over policy-making.' How far do you agree with this statement?

'The modern Conservative Party is a "catch-all" party which draws support from all sections of society.' To what extent do you agree with this judgement?

To what extent has the ability of the Conservative Party to evolve and adapt been crucial to the Party's continued electoral success?

'The modern Conservative Party is pragmatic rather than ideological.' Discuss.

'Under Cameron the Conservative Party has become a centrist party.' Discuss.

Helpful websites

www.conservatives.com/ is the main website of the Conservative Party.

www.conservativehome.blogs.com/ is the main discussion site for Conservatives about current issues.

www.conservativehistory.org.uk/ is the website of the main academic study group focusing on the development of the Conservative Party.

www.theconservativefoundation.co.uk/ Information on the role of the Conservative Foundation.

Suggestions for further reading

Bale, T., *The Conservative Party from Thatcher to Cameron* (Polity Press, 2011).

Ball, S., *The Conservative Party and British Politics 1902–1951* (Longman, 1995).

Clark, A., *The Tories* (Phoenix, 1998).

Denham, A. and O'Hara, K., *Democratising Conservative Leadership: From Grey Suits to Grass Roots* (Manchester University Press, 2008).

Garnett, M., and Hickson, K., *Conservative Thinkers* (Manchester University Press, 2009).

Greer, S., *Why Vote Conservative* (Biteback, 2010).

Griffiths, S., and Hickson, K., *British Party Politics and Ideology after New Labour* (Palgrave Macmillan, 2010).

Hickson, K. (ed.), *The Political Thought of the Conservative Party Since 1945* (Palgrave Macmillan, 2005).

Philp, C., *Conservative Revival: Blueprint for a Better Britain* (Politico's Publishing, 2006).

PART II

THE MINOR PARTIES

The Liberal Democrats

Contents

Overview

The Liberal Democrats, Britain's newest party, have progressed from near-oblivion to national government in a generation. This chapter will explain the traditions of the liberal ideas that shape the party's values, and the development of the parties that were their predecessors. It will explore the debate about whether Liberal Democrat support is a volatile protest vote or whether it is a gradually growing, positive base. It will also consider whether national government places the least strong of Britain's three largest parties under intolerable pressure.

Key issues to be covered in this chapter

- What do Liberal Democrats believe in?
- How did the Liberal Democrat Party come to be formed?
- Why has Liberal Democrat support grown?
- How democratic is the Liberal Democrat organisation?

History

At less than twenty-five years old, the Liberal Democrat Party is Britain's newest major party, and has had an apparently spectacular rise from the periphery of the political process to participation in national government. The party represents a British political tradition that is centuries old, however, and the apparently sudden rise in support is in some ways misleading.

Origins and development

The Liberal Democrat Party was founded in 1988 but Liberal Democrats claim a heritage stretching back three centuries. Their origins lie in the challenge by parliamentarians to monarchical power in the Glorious Revolution of 1688–9, when the Whigs emerged as the party of reform. In the eighteenth century Whigs, such as John Wilkes and Charles James Fox, were the defenders of free speech and the rule of law against overbearing British governments, particularly during the wars against France from 1793 onwards and amid the social upheaval brought about by the Industrial Revolution. In the nineteenth century, under prime ministers Earl Grey, Lord John Russell and then Gladstone, Whigs pressed for the extension of the franchise to working men, as well as for universal education, reform of the House of Lords and finally for Scottish and Welsh devolution. Many of these principles have remained part of the Liberal Democrats' profile.

At almost the same time as the Conservatives, the Liberal Party emerged as a formal group in Parliament and as a national campaigning organisation. The 1859 government of Lord Palmerston was supported by a combination made up mostly of Whigs, who wanted to strengthen Parliament against the monarchy, together with former supporters of Robert Peel who believed in free trade, as well as a small number of radicals, such as the philosopher John Stuart Mill, who wanted the enfranchisement of workers and women. Like the Conservatives, this broad grouping of politicians had considerable potential for division and was even described by one of its historians as merely 'a coalition of convenience'. Though united in their desire for individual liberty and for restraining the aristocracy, they differed on important questions, such as how far the franchise should be extended, and later, on how far the state should go in providing for public welfare. To support this group at general elections, the Liberal Registration Association and then the National Liberal Federation were founded by Joseph Chamberlain in the 1860s and 1870s, and these became the organs of the extraparliamentary Liberal Party.

It was partly through the Liberal Federation that the party began to develop more radical policies as the twentieth century approached. Chamberlain's 'unauthorised programme' of 1886 and the 'Newcastle programme' voted for by the 1891 party conference moved the Liberals away from the laissez-faire approach to economic and social policy associated with Gladstone, advocating state-funded benefits such as pensions and unemployment benefit. These proposals chimed with the theory of 'New Liberalism' being developed by T. H. Green and L. T. Hobhouse, and were put into effect by the Liberal governments of 1906 and 1910, which also restricted the power of the House of Lords and tried to bring home rule to Ireland. The tensions between the 'old' and 'new' interpretations of Liberal principles were expressed in Chamberlain's comparison of Gladstone with Rip Van Winkle, and are still evident in the debate between 'social' and 'economic' Liberal Democrats today.

Over the next two decades, the party suffered two blows: its support, already weakening by 1910, drained away to the Labour Party after the introduction of a franchise in which, after 1918, class was no longer a significant factor. At the same time, the Liberals split into two factions as a result of Lloyd George replacing Asquith as prime minister in 1916. Lloyd George's faction, allied to the Conservatives, remained in office until 1922 when Tory support was withdrawn; Asquith's, opposed by both Labour and the Tories, suffered at the polls. A combination of internal division and external threat – the relative significance of these elements is a matter of fierce dispute among historians – caused the Liberals' membership in the House of Commons to be reduced from nearly 400 seats, and almost half of the vote, in 1906 to twenty seats and 7 per cent of the vote by 1936. Whether what remained of the Liberal Party has any connection with the Liberals after the war, let alone the Liberal Democrats, is the subject of heated controversy between the Liberal Democrats and their opponents. The former claim an unbroken and noble line exists from early radicals through Gladstone and Lloyd George to the present day; the latter argue that the modern Liberals and Liberal Democrats are a catch-all, opportunist group which bears only the name of a party that outlived its usefulness two generations ago.

Post-war survival and revival: 1945–79

During the two decades following World War II, the Liberal Party was in serious danger of disappearing altogether. By the 1950s, it was reduced to six MPs and less than 3 per cent of the vote at general elections; it fought barely 100 seats and, in some parts of the country, survived only by making local electoral pacts, usually with the Conservatives. Divisions between Liberals committed to thoroughgoing free-market policies and those in the Radical Reform Group who supported the newly established welfare state gave some leading figures like Lloyd George's son Gwilym and daughter Megan the opportunity to defect to the main parties (in the Lloyd Georges' cases, to the Tories and Labour respectively).

The survival of the Liberal Party, however, demonstrates the resilience of parties as organisations. The party retained a national headquarters and regional offices, and had a network of support-ers in Nonconformist churches, Liberal clubs and the local press in various parts of the country. As the Conservative government became less popular under Eden and Macmillan, a new Liberal leader, Jo Grimond, had the charisma and dynamism to exploit television communication to the party's benefit. From 1955 on, membership grew, and the Liberals had a number of notable by-election successes, gaining seats at Torrington (1958) and Orpington (1962). The latter of these was a previously safe Conservative seat, and its capture seemed to indicate that the Liberals had not only survived but that they might become a major party once more. It was hoped that by appealing to 'Orpington men' – socially mobile, young suburban voters – the Liberals might realign British party politics by becoming a radical, non-socialist alternative to Labour. This potential was explored in a protracted and uneven pattern over the next four decades, and the two main parties proved stubbornly resistant to displacement. One of Grimond's problems, which became a perennial dilemma for Liberals, was that, while he sought to replace Labour, his most promising target seats were mostly Conservative, and the Liberals prospered best under weakening Conservative administrations.

Grimond's strategy was undone by the elections of 1964 and 1966 which saw a Labour government returned to office. Even with a slim majority after the first of these contests, the Labour Prime Minister, Harold Wilson, would not enter into formal negotiations with Grimond, and the Conservative Party reasserted itself as the alternative to Labour. In 1967 Grimond retired from the Liberal leadership to be replaced by Jeremy Thorpe. The party's vulnerability under Labour governments was illustrated by the 1970 election at which its number of MPs was halved to six – and three of these could have lost their seats with a switch of less than 2,000 votes between them. The party was also financially weak.

It was with the turn of public opinion against a new Conservative government that the Liberals thrived again. A string of five by-election gains between 1972 and 1974 was followed by the Liberals' capture of nearly a fifth of the vote at both of the 1974 general elections. After the first of these, at which no party gained an overall majority in the Commons, Jeremy Thorpe was invited by Prime Minister, Edward Heath, to take part in a coalition government. Following vocal opposition from among the fourteen Liberal MPs and from Liberal activists and supporters, he declined. Later in the decade, however, the Liberals supported the Labour government of James Callaghan in exchange for consultation over policy in the Lib–Lab Pact of 1977–8. The causes of this arrangement were largely negative, though the outcomes for the Liberals were not entirely so. Neither Labour nor the Liberals were eager to face a third election in three years: the Liberals had just replaced Thorpe with David Steel as leader, following allegations of conspiracy to murder for which Thorpe was tried and acquitted in 1979. The unravelling of the Thorpe affair, and the bitterness of the leadership election which followed, drained the party's morale and undermined its electoral support. The pact with Labour bought time and gave an impression of seriousness to a damaged party but it brought little change in policy – there was no electoral reform, for example – and it blunted the party's appeal in seats where it was fighting Labour.

The 1970s saw the development of a new strategy, known as 'community politics', for competing in urban environments where Labour was strong. This approach, set out in a resolution passed by the 1970 Liberal Assembly, emphasised the need to focus upon

localised and practical issues to give voters faith in the idea that the
Liberals could solve problems, and to engage them in broader political debate. Pioneered in Liverpool, Manchester and Leeds, it was
associated with success in local government. Whereas there had been
no Liberal MPs from former Labour seats in the 1970 Parliament,
there were five in 1983.

Alliance and merger: 1980–9

In 1979, when another period of Conservative government opened
up, the Liberals retained eleven MPs. This time, however, the
distinctive qualities of Thatcherism, changes in the Labour Party
and the development of a new party close to the Liberals made this
a period of greater success for the Liberal Democrats' forebears
than any since the 1920s. The harsh effects of Margaret Thatcher's
economic policies, including high interest rates and high unemployment with its attendant social problems, alienated some traditional
Conservative voters, while the Labour Party's movement to the Left
on public ownership, defence and Europe caused the split described
in Part I of this book.

The vacuum created by the polarisation of the main parties was
not exploited immediately by the Liberal Party but by a former
chancellor, home secretary and deputy leader of the Labour Party
who had gone on to be president of the European Commission. In
November 1979, Roy Jenkins gave a televised lecture in which he
argued that the two main parties were no longer capable of function-
ing as vehicles of popular opinion, and that a new organisation was
needed to promote the ideas of the 'radical centre'. He had already
discussed this with David Steel who had encouraged Jenkins to start
a new party as a means of drawing new support on to the ground
shared with the Liberals, with the long-term idea of bringing these
forces together. Other Liberals were less positive about the notion of
a new centre party: Rochdale MP, Cyril Smith, told an audience on
the BBC's *Question Time* programme that it should be 'strangled at
birth', and Steel's opponent in the leadership contest, John Pardoe,
later argued that Jenkins should have been urged to join the Liberal
Party itself.

Despite these misgivings, the Social Democratic Party (SDP) was
launched in March 1981 amid great publicity, and attracted thirty

MPs (all but one Labour) and 60,000 members (mostly not previously in any party) to join it. The leadership of the SDP included people with senior ministerial experience which the Liberals had been unable to claim for generations, and Liberal MPs had worked with some of these figures during the Lib–Lab Pact. It was widely assumed that the Liberal Party would join in an alliance with the SDP, whereby they would avoid contesting elections against one another, and, at general elections, would agree a joint programme for government. This unusual arrangement was endorsed by a vote of sixteen to one at the Liberals' Llandudno assembly, during which Steel told his delegates to 'go back to your constituencies and prepare for government'.

The SDP–Liberal Alliance fought the 1983 and 1987 general elections, the 1984 European elections, and the intervening local elections under this arrangement. During this period, the Liberals won a larger number of seats than they had held at any time since World War II, and the SDP added half a dozen more. Most significantly, the alliance parties won between them a larger share of the vote than the Liberals had held at any time since 1923, a share which they have not achieved since.

The Alliance was a wasting asset, however. Its constituent parts were easily divided over leadership and over certain policies but, most significantly, they were divided over their own future. The parties decided not to choose a joint leader but, during the 1983 election, media pressure prompted the identification of the SDP leader, Roy Jenkins, as 'prime minister designate' in the event of an alliance government. This caused less difficulty between the parties than did the relationship between Steel and Jenkins's successor, David Owen. Owen was younger than Jenkins, had a reputation for bombast and self-assuredness, and reflected the SDP's strong commitment to nuclear weapons which were opposed on principle by a large contingent of Liberals. Owen was also less resistant to Thatcherism than Steel was, and was hostile to attempts to merge the two parties. The tensions between the two leaders were an open secret, mocked on the weekly satirical television programme, *Spitting Image*, which portrayed Steel as a naive and suggestible figure of symbolically diminutive stature compared to Owen.

When the results of the 1987 election suggested that the alliance had peaked at the previous contest, pressure emerged for a merger of the two parties, and Steel's call for a decision to be made about this initiated another period of dismal fortune and tenuous existence for Britain's third party. The proposal that the Liberals and Social Democrats should merge split both parties into pro- and anti-merger camps. In the Liberal Party, the larger and better established of the two, the anti-merger group was small and had relatively little impact on the Social and Liberal Democratic Party after its foundation in March 1988; the SDP, however, was more evenly split, and its leader, David Owen, tried to continue the Party despite the fact that most Social Democrats who voted in the party's ballot wanted to support merger. The result was two years of acrimonious argument within the Liberal Democrats (as they came to be called after two name changes) and bitter battles at the polls with former colleagues who had not joined (see Part III). During this time, the Liberal Democrats, under their new leader Paddy Ashdown, suffered the ignominy of coming fourth after the Greens at the 1989 European elections. It was only with the disappearance of the rival SDP in 1990 that the Liberal Democrats began to win by-elections in their traditional way.

The rise and fall of 'the project': 1990–9

The 1992 election saw the Liberal Democrats' vote drop below 18 per cent of the poll but the party kept its bridgehead of twenty MPs and, after the election of Tony Blair as Labour leader in 1994, Ashdown set a new strategic course – or rather a new version of a familiar one – **realignment** of the Left. Ashdown sought to respond to the offer, which Blair appeared to be making, of a closer relationship between the two Opposition parties. This development, known as 'the project', involved seeking out common ground on constitutional issues, and targeting each party's electoral efforts in those constituencies where they had the better prospect of defeating the Conservatives, thereby avoiding splitting the anti-Conservative vote as the alliance had done. This gave birth to a formal agreement between Robin Cook and Robert Maclennan on constitutional reform, and brought the devastating 1997 defeat for the Conservatives in which they were reduced to 165 MPs while the Liberal Democrats – with a smaller share of the vote than in 1992 – more than doubled their number of MPs to forty-six.

After the election, Blair tried to arrange Ashdown's appointment to the cabinet but was blocked by John Prescott, Jack Straw and Gordon Brown. The Liberal Democrats did, however, join a cabinet committee on constitutional affairs, and Ashdown's relationship with the Labour leadership bore some fruit: from a Liberal Democrat point of view, however, each achievement was marred by imperfections. Proportional representation – though not the sort the Liberal Democrats would have preferred – was used for elections to the European Parliament; a Freedom of Information Act was introduced but Jack Straw inserted a national security defence into its terms which limited its impact; the Human Rights Act came close to the Bill of Rights in a written constitution which Lib Dems wanted but was not compulsorily enforceable by US-style judicial review; and the devolved institutions in Scotland and Wales had fewer powers than Liberals had traditionally hoped for. Even the most sceptical, purist Liberal Democrat, however, had to acknowledge that Liberal policies, which a generation before had seemed like a pipe dream, were being put into effect, albeit imperfectly.

The project's honeymoon period was just over a year during which time most of the reforms described above were initiated. The project foundered on the Liberal Democrats' greatest priority, electoral reform of the House of Commons. The Labour manifesto of 1997 promised a referendum in which the public could choose whether or not to introduce proportional representation (PR), and acted quickly to propose an alternative to the current system through a commission under SDP founder and now Liberal Democrat leader in the Lords, Roy Jenkins. When the Jenkins Commission reported in October 1998, it soon became clear that the Labour government would not hold the promised referendum before the next election, if at all. Paddy Ashdown, already under criticism for keeping his enlarged parliamentary party in the dark about relations with Blair, realised that his leadership was discredited and, within months, announced his resignation.

Fighting on two fronts and within: 1999–2010
Under the new leader, Charles Kennedy, relations with Labour quickly cooled, reflecting both party resentments over the outcomes of the project and Kennedy's greater personal distance from

Blair. The Liberal Democrats' joint cabinet committee meetings with Labour ministers came to an end. As well as delivering only half measures on constitutional reform, Labour had disappointed Liberal Democrats by sticking to Tory spending limits for two years, introducing university tuition fees, and pursuing an authoritarian law-and-order agenda. In Blair's second term, this hostility grew with the failures to reform the House of Lords and to devolve the English regions, as well as the introductions of university top-up fees and foundation hospitals, and, most visibly of all, the invasion of Iraq and the 'war on terror'. On these issues, the Liberal Democrats outflanked Labour on the Left, and often found themselves voting with 'old' Labour rebels in the division lobbies over civil liberties and social policy. For the first time in many elections, they were fighting hard on both fronts and, for the first time ever under a Labour government, they were gaining ground. The 2005 General Election saw the largest third party contingent returned to the Commons since 1923, and the Liberal Democrats gained more seats from Labour than from the Tories. Kennedy was at the forefront of these achievements, occupying 75 per cent of the spotlight in the 2005 Liberal Democrat campaign.

But Kennedy's achievements masked growing disquiet in the party about his personal performance. His obvious strengths as a television campaigner – he was nicknamed 'Chatshow Charlie' for his appearances on light-entertainment shows such as *Have I Got News for You* – were for some Liberal Democrats always outweighed by his weaknesses in organisation, his grasp of policy detail and his reluctance to make decisions (Kennedy resisted making appointments to his shadow cabinet or to the Lords until the last minute, for example). Some resented what they regarded as Ashdown's manoeuvring of Kennedy into office; and many felt that the 2005 campaign had failed to exploit to the full the unique opportunity presented by simultaneous Labour weakness over Iraq and continued Tory division and extremism. These failings were set in the context of persistent rumours about Kennedy's alcohol dependency which became the subject of open discussion in his interview with Jeremy Paxman for the 2005 election campaign. Following a string of absences from, and poor performances at, keynote public events, Kennedy was forced out of office by public votes of no confidence from most of his shadow cabinet team. Kennedy finally acknowledged his problems with alcohol and, in December 2005, he became the shortest-lived Liberal or Lib Dem Leader since 1935.

Neither of Kennedy's successors has yet outlasted him: the Liberal Democrat Party was plagued by uncertain leadership for three years from 2005 but, curiously, this has had little impact upon its fortunes. Menzies Campbell had the misfortune to win a leadership contest marred by the withdrawal of an opponent who had been revealed to have been using the services of a male prostitute. He then presided over the party's gradual decline in the polls. Though Campbell could not be blamed for the first of these developments, his responsibility for the latter was, at the least, arguable for, while his reputation as Lib Dem shadow foreign secretary had been elevated by journalists and fellow parliamentarians alike, his performance as leader lacked bite. While criticism of his age was unfair, the fact that it arose was nonetheless damaging. Though not put in place as a caretaker leader, Campbell became one and, after less than two years, he was persuaded to resign. So sour was the atmosphere around his departure that he declined even to attend the press conference at which his resignation was announced.

Nick Clegg won the leadership contest which followed by a margin of only 500 votes out of a party membership of 60,000. The campaign, described by *The Sun* as 'the dirtiest leadership contest in British Politics', involved the coining by Clegg's opponents of the tag 'Calamity Clegg' to accompany a dossier of his alleged gaffes. The nickname stuck as, during his first year in charge, Clegg proceeded to deny the existence of God, wrongly estimate, in a radio phone-in, the level of the state pension at £30 a week, and claim in an interview with *GQ* magazine that he had had as many as thirty lovers. There was a major rebellion by a quarter of Liberal Democrat MPs against Clegg's whips over the question of a referendum on the Lisbon Treaty. More significantly still, the Liberal Democrats have struggled to project their political identity in the face of a 'modernised' Conservative Party and a Labour Party divested of the unpopularity of Tony Blair.

In local elections, however, the Liberal Democrats have held their ground, relatively advanced compared to their position a generation ago, and ground that would have been inconceivable to Liberals in the 1950s. The Liberal Democrats even gained a parliamentary seat at a by-election that was held between the resignation of Charles Kennedy and the election of Menzies Campbell, indicating that Liberalism is a force in British politics greater than any one leader or issue, and one that is dismissed by its opponents at their peril as a purely negative protest. The next election campaign was to demonstrate the potential of that force more fully than it had for a century.

2010 onwards: in government

The Liberal Democrats began their 2010 election campaign in unfavourable circumstances: the rising party, the Conservatives, was the one they were challenging in most of their target seats, and the one chasing them in their own most marginal ones; the issue of Iraq, which Kennedy had exploited to some effect in 2005, had gone; and their new Leader, Nick Clegg, had failed to make an impression with the public (polls showed that more voters recognised the name of Kauto Star, the Derby-winning horse than his, and almost half of the public mistook a picture of Clegg for Peter Jones, the star of *Dragon's Den*).

It was Clegg, however, who transformed the party's fortunes in the early stages of the campaign, using an unexpectedly striking performance in the first television debate between party leaders to present himself as the outsider, the unknown politician challenging a political system widely regarded as at best ineffective and at worst corrupt. Following this debate, the Liberal Democrat poll rating doubled and Clegg himself was rated as the most popular party leader in polling history except for Winston Churchill. The following three weeks saw this advance clawed back by the Conservatives, helped by lurid attacks on Clegg in the right-wing press and public nervousness about the economic crisis in Europe, but the Conservatives never recovered enough support to win a parliamentary majority and David Cameron was forced to offer the Liberal Democrats a coalition partnership.

Most Liberal Democrats were ideologically closer to Labour than to the Conservatives but they were left with little alternative other than to take up a coalition with the Tories because, even in combination with Labour, they would not quite have formed a parliamentary majority. In addition, several leading Labour figures, such as

David Blunkett and John Reid, had stated publicly that they would not support a deal with the Liberal Democrats. It was, nonetheless, suspected by some that the decision to work with the Conservatives was easier for relatively free-market Liberals, such as Clegg and David Laws, than it might have been for Paddy Ashdown or Ming Campbell.

The tension between different elements of the party has been evident, as time has gone on, in the pressure on Nick Clegg to differentiate himself more clearly from the Conservatives. A third of Liberal Democrat MPs defied their whip over university tuition fees, and Clegg put up a vigorous rearguard action against reforms of the NHS which it was feared would lead to privatisation of the service. The 2012 Budget brought forward fulfilment of the Liberal Democrats' policy of raising the threshold for payment of income tax. The increasing success of the previous five decades had finally brought the third party into power but the pressures of office, as the junior partner in a coalition, were testing its discipline and unity more severely than ever.

Organisation and finance

Organisation

The Liberal Democrats often claim to have a more democratic structure than the Conservatives and Labour, citing the following:

- The party structure is federal so that the organisations in Wales and Scotland control their policy and strategy more independently from their UK leadership than is the case in the main parties.
- The Liberal Party was the first to elect its leader by vote of the extraparliamentary party, and the SDP adopted a one-member, one-vote postal-ballot system before any other party. This system is used by the Liberal Democrats to elect their leader and the president of the party, using the alternative vote method.
- Party policy is made by the twice-yearly party conference whereas, for Labour and the Conservatives, policy control has been removed to policy forums or councils under the influence of the leadership.

- Decisions on whether or not to enter government have to have the support of the party in the country thanks to a system known as the 'triple lock' – unless enough MPs and members of the federal executive support coalition, the issue has to be put to a full party conference and, potentially, to a postal ballot of members.

The powers of the Liberal Democrat party conference appear on paper to be greater than those of the main parties' conferences, and there is a good deal of continuity between conference decisions and manifesto commitments – a good example would be the decision to raise the proposed threshold of any 'mansion tax' from the £1 million Vince Cable initially proposed to £2 million following protests from conference delegates. Russell and Fieldhouse's study of the Liberal Democrats, however, noted as early as 2001 that the party's increased representation in the Commons and in the Scottish and Welsh devolved legislatures was giving Liberal Democrat MPs, MSPs and AMs a greater sense of their independent authority and creating potentially dangerous tensions between the extraparliamentary and parliamentary parties.[1] Entry into national government has exacerbated this problem, entailing the abandonment of key policies such as opposition to higher-education tuition fees. Nick Clegg's decision to resist health reforms after their criticism at the Liberal Democrat spring conference of 2011 suggests that the conference still has an important role though it is a more indirect one over Liberal Democrat policy in government than it has had over party commitments at elections – and the line between the two may be harder to draw than when the Liberal Democrats were constantly in opposition.

Finance
The Liberal Democrats, with 60,000 members, can rely only on something between a third and a quarter of the revenue from subscriptions of the other parties, and have never had any significant corporate income, such as the trade-union affiliation fees of the Labour Party or the business support enjoyed by the Conservatives. Accordingly, their headquarters and election campaigns run on smaller budgets than those of the main parties: in the year leading up to the 2010 election, the Conservatives received £45 million in

donations; Labour £24 million; the Liberal Democrats £7.3 million. At the election of that year, the Liberal Democrats spent £4.8 million, compared to Labour's £8 million and the Conservatives' £16.7 million. Like other parties, the Liberal Democrats have come to rely more heavily than in the past on large donations from individual benefactors, though their number of benefactors is larger (but the total of their donations smaller) than Labour's. Nonetheless, the Liberal Democrats have not escaped the accusation of impropriety which has affected all the parties because of such donations. Michael Brown, an entrepreneur who gave £2.4 million to the party in 2005, was later convicted of fraud and his donation was returned.

Electoral support

There are features of the third-party vote which are beyond question, including its growth over time and its broad social composition; the details of the latter, however, and the causes of both are the subjects of some dispute.

There can be no argument that the number of votes for the Liberal Party and its successors has grown significantly over the last fifty years. From below 10 per cent until 1964, it stayed between 10 per cent and 20 per cent at every election but one from then until 1983; and, since that election, it has always been over 15 per cent, more often than not above 20 per cent. From its low point to its highest, the third-party vote has risen from 2.5 per cent to 25 per cent during the post-war era. Part of the explanation for this is the increased number of candidates. The Liberals fought only a third of seats in the 1950s, and did not put up a full slate of candidates consistently until the 1980s. The average vote for each Liberal candidate grew from 12 per cent in 1950 to over 20 per cent by the 1980s, however, and the explanations for this can be divided into the positive and the negative.

The negative explanation was summed up by John Major's assessment that 'The Liberals have no identifiable persona: they ebb and flow as the temporary repository for discontented voters' (*The Spectator*, 1 January 2000, p. 10). Critics note that the third party prospers when other parties leave an 'open goal' by having unpopular leaders, extreme policies or a reputation for poor government (as with Labour in 1983, the Conservatives in 1997, or both parties in 1974). This particularly accounts for their success at by-elections where voters leave their usual party to send a temporary signal of dissatisfaction to it by voting for the Liberal Democrats. This might explain the third party's high voter turnover rate between general elections. At every election except one between 1974 and 2001, they retained fewer of their votes from the previous election, and recruited more new voters, than either of the other parties (Labour lost more voters than the alliance in the rout of 1983). At some elections, the turnover neared 50 per cent.[2]

There is, however, a core of third-party support which has identifiable characteristics and which is more stable than the analysis above suggests. The Liberal vote has historically been strongest in the 'Celtic fringes' of the Scottish borders, mid-Wales and the West Country and, in the 1960s, began to develop among the suburban middle classes. Liberal Democrat voters are drawn more equally from across social classes than are the voters of the two main parties although their makeup is closer to the Conservatives' than to Labour's electorate, 'a paler reflection' of Conservative support, in the assessment of one study of the 2010 General Election.[3] In contrast to the Conservatives, however, Liberal Democrat support has recently been higher where there are more young voters, especially students, and the middle-class support they have is disproportionately from the public sector. The Liberal Democrats also have a good record of building up support through activism and success in local government, and of spreading support into neighbouring seats to the ones they hold, in a syndrome which has been labelled 'creeping Liberalism' or 'yellow fever'.[4] The Liberal Democrats can therefore claim a record of sustained support among certain groups and in specified locations, even if a good proportion of their support is short term and negative in motivation.

One feature of the Liberal Democrat appeal, which places the party in a different position from its competitors, is its need to deal with varying competitors. Where the main parties can either ignore the Liberal Democrats or subsume them in the same critical comment as their chief opponent, the Liberal Democrats have to fight on two fronts, trying to unseat Labour in the urban north and the Conservatives in the south. This leads to different – critics would say contrary – signals coming from Liberal Democrat candidates in these different circumstances, making the party 'all things to all people'. Their critics would also say that this was a reflection of the Liberal Democrats' lack of an ideological compass.

Box 3.1 Strands of Liberal Democrat thought

Source A: David Laws in *The Orange Book* (2004).

We must reject 'nanny-state liberalism'. We must reject the assumption that because we are internationalist we must always be in favour of 'internationalist' solutions that are offered to any problem, regardless of our decentralising beliefs. We must continue to reclaim **economic liberalism**; and marry economic liberalism to our **social liberalism**, in order to deliver more opportunity and freedom to all of our citizens – particularly those on lower incomes who cannot opt out of failing state services. We must reclaim Liberalism in all its forms and with all its mutually reinforcing strengths, and continue to resist nanny-state Liberalism or 'Liberalism à la carte', which would be no more than a philosophy of good intentions, bobbing about unanchored in the muddled middle of British politics. If we can reclaim our Liberal heritage, we will not only increase our chances of exercising power in British politics, but, much more importantly, we will ensure we are exercising power with passion, purpose and effect.

Source B: Duncan Brack, Richard S. Grayson and David Howarth, *Reinventing the State* (2007).

The goal of this book's contributors is to enable the individual to make the most of his or her life. This will not happen if the state stands idly by. Nor will it happen if the state steps in to control. But it will happen if the state enables, if the state hands power back, and if the state tames the power of the market. To achieve these aims requires the reinvention of the British state. The country's current structures of government and society do not work, and the ideologies – if one can call them that – of Labour and Conservatives do not provide a solution. Given the challenges that the UK now faces – the external threats of climate change, terrorism and unchecked globalisation, the internal ones of an unequal and unparticipative society – but also given the basic values and tremendous capabilities of Britain's people, when treated as the responsible and intelligent people they mostly are, social liberalism's combination of political freedom, social justice and democracy are needed now more than ever.

Source C: Andrew Rawnsley, 'The Lib Dems need to be more than just the people who say no', *The Observer*, 18 September 2011.

The philosophical tensions within the [Liberal Democrat] party between its social democrats, social liberals and classical liberals are pretty plain. The biggest risk that they took when they went into the coalition was to nail their prospects and Britain's future to George Osborne's economic judgement. The best that can be said of that gamble is that it looks bigger than ever. Since the spring, Mr Clegg has made an increasingly aggressive effort to reassert his differences with the Conservatives. The list of public differences between him and David Cameron has now grown to include clashes over the correct response to the summer riots, human rights legislation, the EU, health, free schools, taxation of the wealthy and how to deal with Islamic extremists. A more assertive approach to coalition has helped to bind some of the party's wounds, but it has yet to have any palpable effect on voters. Over the longer term, the Lib Dems will want and need to have more to show for being in government than just claiming they constrained the Tories, an essentially negative achievement. They will have to convince the country that some good things wouldn't have happened without them either.

Question: How has the Liberal Democrats' participation in the coalition affected the balance between the ideological traditions in the party?

Policy and ideology[5]

The policy of the Liberal Democrats has sometimes been the subject of ridicule by critics, sometimes of ignorance. As a party out of office and free from public scrutiny for many years, and with a less clear social constituency to guide their deliberations, it is unsurprising that, sometimes, divergences between Liberals were evident. Worse still, they were accused of 'sogginess', 'splitting the difference' or even of having no consistent policy at all. Tony Blair condemned them as guilty of 'opportunism'. There are, however, identifiable long-term beliefs linked to Liberal political philosophy – rationalism, civil liberties and voluntarism, for instance – which illustrate the continuities as well as the repeated divisions in Liberal Democrat policy.

Liberalism conceives of the purpose of the state as being to protect natural, or some would express it as civil, **rights**. In Liberal political theory, this is the explanation given for our establishing and agreeing to obey legal precepts. Different Liberals have always interpreted the idea of rights in different ways, however: some think of rights as 'negative', requiring inaction by the government (such as freedom of speech or the right to protest or to trade freely); other Liberals say these rights are of little use without 'positive' rights (such as rights to an education, to health care or to social security). A century ago, this debate split 'old' Liberals, such as William Gladstone, from 'new' Liberals, including Joseph Chamberlain and later Lloyd George; in the 1950s the argument was between 'free traders' and the 'Radical Reform Group'; and, today, these two camps in the Liberal Democrats are characterised as 'economic' and 'social' Liberals. Their contrasting approaches were reflected in two books to which Liberal Democrat MPs and supporters contributed, *The Orange Book* and *Reinventing the State*.[6]

Constitutional reform

Liberal Democrats have a consistent record of supporting changes to our system of government to disperse power geographically and between branches and levels of government, and to make its use more accountable. They want:

- Parliamentary reform: to replace the House of Lords with a chamber elected for staggered twelve-year terms.
- Devolution: to establish regional elected assemblies in England to parallel the ones they demanded for a century in Scotland and Wales.
- Judicial reform: to give the courts the right to strike down laws breaking a Bill of Rights, which would be set in a written constitution.
- Electoral reform: to use proportional systems of election (preferably the single transferable vote) for all elections in the United Kingdom.

This agenda has had greater impact in the last ten years than Liberals of earlier generations could have hoped for, with Labour and then the Conservatives introducing: proportional representation in some elections; devolution; the Human Rights Act; and the Fixed Term Parliament Act of 2011. But government measures in these areas have nonetheless been less than Liberal Democrats would have liked. Their demands for a written constitution to entrench civil liberties against government or against Parliament have distinguished them from the Labour government's 'war on terror'; and the defeat of AV in the referendum of 2011 set back the cause of electoral reform for the Commons for a generation.

Foreign policy
The Liberal Democrats have maintained a distinctive position on foreign-policy questions which has given greater priority to international co-operation than the policies of the Conservatives and Labour. There is also historically an antimilitarist and particularly antinuclear tradition within British Liberalism which can influence policy. Other elements in the party, and short-term circumstances, can, however, modify the policies these principles suggest.

The Liberal Party opposed peacetime national service after World War II, was outspoken in its opposition to the British intervention in Suez in the 1950s, and called for the withdrawal of British troops from East of Suez before the main parties accepted the need for it in 1968. Most recently, the Liberal Democrats opposed Britain's involvement in the American-led invasion of Iraq in 2003, and, at the 2010 General Election opposed the replacement of Britain's Trident nuclear missile system.

The Liberal Democrats' opposition to the war in Iraq highlights their commitment to international co-operation and law because they argued against an attack on the grounds that no United Nations resolution authorising it had been agreed. Similarly they have been the party keenest to welcome European integration and to join in the development of the European Union: the Liberals supported membership of the European Economic Community almost from its beginning in the 1950s, and remain the only one of the three largest parties in favour in principle of British membership of the Eurozone.

The Liberals' alliance and merger with the SDP introduced a

strongly pro-nuclear element into the party, however, and muted any doubts Liberals might have had about the Falklands conflict in 1982; Liberal leaders have always been aware, too, of the relatively hawkish and Eurosceptic balance of public opinion and have therefore sought to restrain the impact of the antimilitarist and integrationist traditions of the party (as David Steel signally failed to do at the Liberals' 1986 assembly). These factors have, at times, moderated the distinctiveness of the Liberal Democrats' foreign-policy position, and may have played a part in their recent abandonment of the commitment to join the Euro immediately and their conciliation with the Conservatives over the replacement of Trident.

Economic policy
This is the area of greatest potential disagreement among Liberal Democrats, and the area in which the Liberal tradition has moved most dramatically over time from the laissez-faire of Adam Smith to the interventionism of John Maynard Keynes.

Liberal Democrats have championed specific government measures to redistribute wealth by taking the lower paid out of taxation and taxing high, especially unearned, incomes. The raising of the income tax threshold to £10,000 a year and the introduction of a 'mansion tax' on properties worth over £2 million are examples of their redistributive instincts. The macroeconomic commitment to spending on welfare was strengthened by the addition of the Social Democrats to the third party in 1981–88. The Liberal Democrats proposed an increase in the base rate of income tax of a penny in the pound at the general elections from 1992 to 2005 to pay for expanded state spending, especially on education.

Liberal Democrats have always, however, resisted the extension of public ownership (as they did during the Lib–Lab Pact of 1977) and remain committed in principle to the ideas of capitalism and free enterprise as the bases of the economy. Though they fought the 2010 General Election on a policy of waiting at least a year before cutting public spending, the Liberal Democrats then participated in the largest programme of immediate cuts in the history of the public sector in Britain – £6 billion – and a plan for a further £80 billion in cuts over the whole Parliament. Vince Cable and others presented this as a regrettable necessity caused by the threat to confidence triggered by the collapse of the Greek economy and Labour's extravagance as symbolised by the note left to David Laws by his Labour predecessor as Chief Secretary to the Treasury, Liam Byrne, reading 'I'm afraid to tell you there's no money left'. Critics, however, saw this as a reflection of the 'limited state' tradition of Liberal thinking.

One distinctive aspect of Liberal Democrat thinking on economics is their belief in profit-sharing and in worker participation in industry. This is a policy they pursued during the Lib–Lab Pact, gaining worker representation on the Post Office board, and which they again championed with the privatisation of elements of the Royal Mail service after 2010, pressing for the distribution of shares to employees.

Social policy

The Liberal Party has a long heritage of introducing major social reforms, from David Lloyd George's advocacy of old age pensions and national insurance to Keynes's plans to relieve interwar unemployment and William Beveridge's report proposing the NHS which, as a Liberal MP, he promoted during the war. In elections from 1992 to 2005, the Liberal Democrats have reflected this commitment by their promises to invest more heavily in education and health than either the Conservatives or New Labour plawnned, specifically rejecting in 2005 and 2010 the idea of charging students fees for higher-education tuition. As a Liberal peer, however, Beveridge expressed concern at the decline of voluntary provision of social services after the war, and there has always been a tradition in the party willing to contemplate the New Right agenda of greater consumer choice in public services – education vouchers were proposed in *The Unservile State*, a book published with the co-operation of party leader Jo Grimond in 1957 – and the introduction of an American-style social insurance system in place of the NHS was contemplated by David Laws in *The Orange Book* in 2004.

In office, the Liberal Democrats conceded the raising of tuition fees (but limited the rise) and supported the development of 'free schools' under Conservative education secretary, Michael Gove. At the same time, they insisted, as part of the coalition agreement, on the 'pupil premium', a supplementary payment to schools for each child on their registers entitled to free school meals. They also resisted

Box 3.2 Liberal Democrat support and prospects

Source A: Liberal (Democrat) share of vote and MPs, 1970–2010

General Election	Liberal (Democrat) % of vote	No. of Liberal (Democrat) MPs
1970	7.5	6
1974 (Feb.)	19.3	14
1974 (Oct.)	18.3	13
1979	13.8	11
1983	25.4*	23*
1987	22.6*	22*
1992	17.8	20
1997	16.8	46
2001	18.3	52
2005	22.0	62
2010	23.0	57

*Including votes and MPs of the SDP

Source B: Mark Stuart in *The Cameron–Clegg Government: Coalition Government in an Age of Austerity* (edited by Simon Lee and Matt Beech, 2011).

Thus far, by entering into the coalition with the Conservatives, the Liberal Democrats have borne the brunt of the blame from the voters for the failings of the new government. No amount of effort on the part of Liberal Democrat ministers to bolt 'fairness' artificially on to each and every cut in public expenditure seems to be working with the electorate. The Liberal Democrats now face a slow and painful death at the hands of the voters, beginning with the local and devolved elections in 2011. Despite such electoral pressure, the parliamentary party will probably cling even tighter to their coalition partners at a national level, while locally they are forced to watch as the Liberal Democrat membership and support crumble before their eyes.

Question: What has been the driving force behind Liberal Democrat fortunes, and can it survive the coalition?

Andrew Lansley's health reforms as representing a policy too close to privatisation. The social policy of the Liberal Democrats therefore accepts the existence of a 'mixed economy' of welfare and the potential value of consumer choice to drive up standards; it also calls for heavy public funding of state provision, and the disproportionate weighting of that expenditure towards the poorest.

The future

In the last thirty years the Liberal Democrats have gone from being a party of protest to a party of power at all levels of the political system. Their dramatic rise in representation and office-holding disguises a relatively stable level of support when the limited resources available to them before the 1970s are taken into account. Similarly constant are the challenges to the third party in deciding which direction to take within their own ideological tradition, and which voters to seek and which other parties to work with. These are questions which will not go away.

. . . .

✔ What you should have learnt from reading this chapter

- The Liberal Democrats' achievement in joining the government in 2010 was the culmination of a growth in their support and representation at all levels since the 1960s, during which time the Liberals merged with the SDP.

- There is debate about whether their support arises from the long-term positive appeal of their policies and leaders, or a short-term negative rejection of the main parties' performances.

- Liberal Democrats are identified at various points on the spectrum from left to right, giving greater priority to public spending or reduction of the role of the state, and being more or less hostile to Labour or the Conservatives.

- Liberal Democrats have worked with both main parties in recent years and can be divided about how closely to co-operate with others.

- Some Liberal Democrat policies on European integration and constitutional reform have been accepted by the main parties.

Glossary of key terms

Economic liberalism Liberalism giving priority to free markets and, at its purest, laissez-faire; identified with Adam Smith, Gladstone and, in recent years, with the *Orange Book*.

Realignment The strategy of most Liberal Leaders since Jo Grimond, and seen in the Lib–Lab Pact, the SDP–Liberal Alliance, and Paddy Ashdown's 'project', of positioning themselves on the Left, either to work with or replace Labour.

Rights theory The belief, found in Locke and Mill, and reflected in the Human Rights Act, that the function of the state is to protect individual rights rather than tradition, or to promote equality of outcome per se.

Social liberalism The belief that Liberalism requires state action to reduce inequality of opportunity by higher spending on education, health and housing; identified with Lloyd George's 'New Liberalism', J. M. Keynes and William Beveridge, and recently expressed in *Reinventing the State*.

Likely examination questions

Identify and explain three distinctive policies of the Liberal Democrats.

Account for the rise of the Liberals and Liberal Democrats in recent years.

What has been the impact of the Liberal and Liberal Democrat parties on British politics?

To what extent does the Liberal Democrat Party promote liberalism?

Helpful websites

The Liberal Democrat History Group website (www.liberalhistory.org.uk/) gives an outline history of the Liberal and Liberal Democrat parties as well as details of publications, discussion meetings and research supported by the group.

Liberal Democrat Voice (www.libdemvoice.org/) is the main discussion forum of Liberal Democrats, and gives an insight into the reactions of different elements of the party to current events.

Suggestions for further reading

The following are recent histories of the Liberals and Liberal Democrats:

Cook, C., *A Short History of the Liberal Party: the Road Back to Power* (Palgrave Macmillan, 2010).

Douglas, R., *Liberals: the History of the Liberal and Liberal Democrat Parties* (Continuum, 2005).

Dutton, D., *A History of the Liberal Party in the Twentieth Century* (Palgrave, 2004).

Ingham, R., and Brack, D. (eds), *Peace, Reform and Liberation: a History of Liberal Politics in Britain 1679–2011* (Biteback, 2011).

This gives a thorough survey of ideological debate in the party in the last few decades:

Hickson, K. (ed.), *The Political Thought of the Liberals and Liberal Democrats since 1945* (Manchester University Press, 2009).

The recent debate among Liberal Democrats can be explored in detail through: Marshall, P. and Laws, D. (eds), *The Orange Book: Reclaiming Liberalism* (Profile, 2004); Astle, J. et al. (eds), *Britain After Blair: a Liberal Agenda* (Profile, 2006); and Brack, D., Grayson, R. and Howarth, D. (eds), *Reinventing the State: Social Liberalism for the 21st Century* (Politico's Publishing, 2007).

The first two titles analyse Liberal Democrat support, the third the party's membership:

Cutts, D., Fieldhouse, E. and Russell, A., 'The Campaign that Changed Everything and Still Did Not Matter? The Liberal Democrat Campaign and Performance' in Geddes, A. and Tonge, J., *Britain Votes 2010* (Hansard Society and Oxford University Press, 2010).

Russell, A. and Fieldhouse, E., *Neither Left nor Right? The Liberal Democrats and the Electorate* (Manchester University Press, 2005).

Whiteley, P., Seyd, P. and Billinghurst, A., *Third Force Politics: Liberal Democrats at the Grassroots* (Oxford University Press, 2006).

CHAPTER 4

Scottish, Welsh and Northern Irish Parties

Contents

Overview

For the last forty years the support and impact of nationalist parties in Scotland, Wales and Northern Ireland have grown from those of irrelevant eccentrics to the status of assumed governing parties in their own territories. This chapters examines what factors led to this, what the impact of the nationalists' advance has been on national political life, what issues remain to be addressed by them, and what ideological and tactical divisions inhibit them.

Key issues to be covered in this chapter

- Why did support for nationalism grow in the 1960s?
- What questions of policy and strategy divide nationalist movements internally?
- How have nationalist parties responded to the development of devolution?

Origins

Three territories of the United Kingdom have their own party systems reflecting the distinctive identities and demands of each region's population. This is partly reflected in the differences between the Scottish or Welsh sections of the Conservative, Labour and Liberal Democrat parties and their respective British leaderships, but it has also given rise to completely separate parties in Scotland, Wales and Northern Ireland, and these have come to play a major role in the electoral politics and government of their regions and sometimes in the government of the United Kingdom.

In all three territories, the party system remained much as it was in England until the 1960s. Though the Welsh nationalist party, Plaid Cymru, the Scottish National Party and the nationalist and unionist parties of Northern Ireland were founded between the world wars, neither the Welsh nor Scottish parties fought as many as two dozen constituencies at any general election before 1970, and they always lost. The nationalists in Northern Ireland, Sinn Fein, found it difficult to win seats because of gerrymandered constituency boundaries, were opposed to taking up seats in the British House of Commons, and, even when elected, were sometimes disqualified. The Unionists were allied to the Conservatives in Great Britain. Circumstances of the late 1960s, however, of economic decline coupled with national self-determination and civil rights campaigns elsewhere in the world, made fertile ground on which to develop the appeal of parties demanding the right to these territories and elements of their populations to greater self-government citing arguments for **separatism** and **cultural nationalism**. All such parties, however, suffer from divisions between 'gradualists', who will accept piecemeal movement towards their objectives and will negotiate with United Kingdom parties for concessions, and 'fundamentalists' most committed to direct action and least willing to accept partial measures.

Though the aims, fortunes and impact of the parties specific to these three territories vary considerably, in their roles within the British party system there is sufficient common ground to identify three periods of development: emergence in the 1960s and 1970s; opposition in the 1980s and most of the 1990s; and government under **devolution** after 1997.

Emergence: 1966–79

Plaid Cymru ('the Party of Wales') was formed in 1925, its initial emphasis being on the protection of the Welsh language rather than on Welsh self-government which became a key policy in the 1930s. The Scottish National Party was founded nine years later and was similarly associated with lobbying and propaganda activity as much as electoral politics but their demands for self-government were bolder, embracing the idea of complete independence from England. By the 1960s each party regularly won 4 or 5 per cent of the Welsh and Scottish vote at general elections but did not win a seat in Parliament until 1966: that year a by-election at Carmarthen was won by Gwynfor Evans, the broadcaster, lawyer and market gardener who had been Plaid Cymru's president and mainstay since 1945. His victory built upon his own personal profile, on loyalty to the Welsh language (used by more than half of the population in this and all of the five parliamentary seats ever won by Plaid Cymru but, significantly, in no others) and upon economic hardships, notably the running down of coal production by the Wilson government and the effects of the rail closures initiated by the Beeching Report three years earlier. This formula, and the demand for Welsh self-government arising from it, became the basis of Plaid Cymru's growing success over the next four decades.

In Scotland the SNP's breakthrough came with a by-election victory at Hamilton in 1967, after which the party established a sizeable presence in Scottish local government, and always had representation in the Commons, winning eleven seats and over 30 per cent of the Scottish vote in October 1974.

Although Gwynfor Evans lost his seat in 1970, Plaid established itself with over a tenth of the Welsh vote, and won three seats in 1974. When the Labour government lost its parliamentary majority in 1976, it brought forward proposals for devolved government which, though more limited than Plaid Cymru and the SNP wanted, were supported by them in a referendum on St David's Day 1979. The idea of devolution had been seriously examined by British governments since the Kilbrandon Commission of 1969–73. The proposals were defeated 4–1 by Welsh voters, delivering a sharp reminder that Welsh nationalism has a more varied population to which to appeal than its Scottish counterpart: very popular in West Wales, where Welsh cultural identity is strong, it has a weak appeal in southern, border constituencies, such as Monmouth, where much of the population is of English origin and many people even work in England. One measure of the different structure of nationalist support in Scotland and Wales is that in October 1974 the SNP lost no deposits (to retain a deposit one eighth of the vote was required) in seventy-one seats, whereas twenty-six of Plaid Cymru's thirty-six candidates lost theirs. A number of political analysts have described Wales as having three identities – Denis Balsom identified them as the Welsh-speaking heartland of the north and west *Y Fro Gymraeg*; a consciously Welsh – but not Welsh-speaking – 'Welsh Wales' in the South Wales valleys; and a more ambivalent 'British Wales' making up the remainder, largely in the east and along the south coast.[1] It was to be Plaid's task to reach beyond the first of these to the second.

The SNP had been offered a more powerful body in the devolution referendum, and it was supported by 52 per cent of voters, but a clause in the referendum regulations required that the measure have the support of 40 per cent of the electorate, which had not been achieved. There had been division within the SNP over whether to accept limited devolution, and both Welsh and Scottish nationalists were left by 1979 in a mood of frustration and resentment, and with a Conservative government heavily rejected by their nations' voters.

Northern Ireland also experimented with new forms of self-government in the 1970s: nationalists there (who wanted the north to be governed as part of a united Ireland, not part of the United Kingdom) gained representation in a power-sharing assembly and executive as a result of the Sunningdale agreement in 1974. They had gained seats in the Commons first through the 'Unity' movement which brought together republican and moderate nationalist opinion and won a by-election in 1969 and two seats in 1970; and then through a new constitutional nationalist party, the Social Democratic and Labour Party. As in Scotland and Wales, the nationalists had risen electorally alongside campaigns of street protest and direct action though, in Northern Ireland, this included a paramilitary element not present in the other two movements. The Sunningdale agreement was brought down by unionist opposition after only five months of the assembly's operation and, after a failed political convention of all parties in 1975, the nationalist movement was, as in Scotland and Wales, left conscious of its political potential but, for the time being, empty-handed.

Opposition: 1979–97

Under Margaret Thatcher's premiership, the nationalists suffered electorally (at first) and in terms of influence over policy. The SNP and Plaid Cymru were reduced from fourteen to four MPs, and the Thatcher governments were wholly opposed to any constitutional change such as devolution. Nationalists had to satisfy themselves with occasional grudging concessions from a firmly unionist government: the Conservatives' promise of a Welsh-language television channel, S4C, was kept in 1982 only following a campaign of civil disobedience including a threat of hunger strike by Gwynfor Evans. In the same year, Margaret Thatcher was persuaded by Northern Ireland secretary James Prior to experiment with 'rolling devolution' but this power-sharing scheme petered out in four years because of abstention by most parties.

Over the next decade, nationalist parties in all three territories refocused their agendas and strategies to challenge the political establishment. In Scotland and Wales they were helped in this by the particular resentment of their territories' population towards the Conservative governments of the period. By 1997 the Conservatives were unable to win a single parliamentary seat in Scotland or Wales. The SNP declared formally that its policy was for Scottish independence rather than devolution, and both they and Plaid Cymru outflanked Labour on the left of the political spectrum, calling for higher public expenditure and resisting Conservative changes in industry and welfare. In 1981, Plaid Cymru specifically adopted a policy of 'community socialism' and the election as president of Dafydd Elis-Thomas in 1984 emphasised the party's shift to the left. The SNP raised its profile by its strident campaign against the poll tax in Scotland in 1988 and, in 1990, chose Alex Salmond, who had been suspended from the party in 1979 as a member of the leftist '79' group, as its leader.

The SNP and Plaid Cymru won ten seats in the 1997 Parliament but their greater achievement had been to put pressure on the

Labour Party to commit itself to devolution in Scotland and Wales. Previously divided on the issue, Labour now agreed with the Liberal Democrats a programme of reforms aimed at giving the two nations limited self-government and thereby puncturing the nationalist threat to their vote.

In Northern Ireland the nationalist movement was represented by two separate parties after Sinn Fein, the political wing of the republican movement which also embraced the Provisional IRA, began contesting elections against the SDLP. The two parties agreed in the early 1990s a set of proposals for the government of the north of Ireland, and this set of demands emerged alongside the announcement of the IRA ceasefire in 1994 and the beginning of the Peace Process. For the first time in twenty years nationalists were in serious negotiations about sharing power, and this time they brought with them the prospect of peace.

Box 4.1 Features of nationalist parties

Parties	SNP	Plaid Cymru	Irish nationalists
Aims	Independence for Scotland within the European Union	Self-government for Wales within the United Kingdom	Reunification of Northern Ireland with the Irish Republic
Methods	Electoral contests, with rare civil disobedience	Electoral contests, with rare civil disobedience	Divided until recently between electoral and armed strategies
Support	Evenly spread 20–50% of the Scottish vote	10% base in North and West Wales; up to 30% including southern areas	Mainly Catholic 30–40% of the vote, divided between SDLP and Sinn Fein

Question: What are the similarities and differences between the nationalist parties in Scotland, Wales and Northern Ireland, and what accounts for them?

Government: 1997 onwards

The devolution of power from Westminster to the parliament in Scotland and the assemblies in Wales and Northern Ireland transformed the status of the nationalist parties in all three areas because – far from losing momentum as some in the main parties had hoped – they did better in elections specific to Scotland and Wales than in elections to the House of Commons and, in all three sets of institutions, they became parties of government. The parliament and assemblies were endorsed in referendums in 1997 and 1998, and first elected in 1998 and 1999.

In Northern Ireland, for reasons explored in another title in this series of books, it was 2007 before the province's parties could agree to work together so that the machinery of devolved government worked consistently.[2] By the time that this occurred, nationalists were voting mainly for Sinn Fein, the more uncompromising republican party; on the unionist side, the old, moderate Ulster Unionists had been replaced by the Democratic Unionists as the chief representative party; both these parties (and all others), however, worked together in the power-sharing bodies set up in 1998, exercising powers previously reserved for Westminster and Whitehall and, therefore, for the main parties only.

Plaid Cymru immediately demonstrated that devolution gave them the platform to function as a party of leftist objection to Blair's Labour government at the end of two years during which the British government had stuck to Conservative spending plans. They gained an unprecedented 28 per cent of the vote in the first elections to the Welsh Assembly, claiming many safe Labour seats in industrial South Wales where they had struggled to make an impact before 1997. This new combination of support, as Alan Sandry has shown,[3] embraced appeals to strands of liberal, green and socialist thought as well as to Plaid Cymru's traditional base, and proved difficult to sustain. In Scotland the SNP also became the official Opposition as the second largest party. Both parties slipped back slightly in 2003 but, at the third devolved elections in 2007, both formed the government of their nation, either – in Plaid Cymru's case – in coalition with Labour, or – for the SNP as the largest Scottish party – as a minority administration. Plaid Cymru had the satisfaction in 2011 of seeing the powers of the Welsh Assembly – only narrowly approved in the 1997 public vote – extended following another referendum.

The nationalists had benefited from the gratitude of their publics for the introduction of devolution, and from the shorter-term unpopularity of the main party in their territories, Labour. These competing explanations form the basis of a debate on the success of the SNP in which Murray Pittock takes the longer-term social and cultural, inevitable view of increasing Scottish self-government,[4] and where Vernon Bogdanor argues that nationalist success in Scotland is dependent upon the right economic and political conditions.[5]

These views were put to the test after 2010 when the role of outflanking Labour in power was taken from the nationalists by the formation of the Lib Dem–Conservative coalition government. The fates of the two parties were very different:

- The SNP had its best results ever in 2011, and formed Scotland's first majority government. The Scottish executive will hold a referendum on independence for Scotland before the end of the parliament.
- Plaid Cymru's result in 2011 was their worst result since the establishment of the Welsh Assembly, falling below 20 per cent of the vote for the first time. The group's deputy leader lost her seat and leader Ieuan Wyn Jones promised to step down within the first half of the assembly's term.

The implication of this early evidence seems to be that the SNP is prospering under a Conservative-led government whereas Plaid Cymru is not. The reasons for this include: the performance of Alex Salmond as SNP Leader and the SNP's very effective organisation and campaign; the broader appeal which the SNP has always exercised compared to that of Plaid Cymru; the greater powers with which the SNP is able to express a distinctive Scottish agenda; and the further prospect of independence which the SNP can hold out against an unpopular British government. Nationalists in all parts of the United Kingdom (and unionists, too, as separate parties from the Conservatives in Northern Ireland) are here to stay, and make a multiparty system even harder for Britain-wide parties to wish away. How they influence developments in the future remains to be seen.

What you should have learnt from reading this chapter

- Nationalist parties existed in three territories of the United Kingdom from the 1920s onwards but emerged as political forces only in the atmosphere of social and economic change of the 1960s and 1970s.

- Nationalist parties all represent minority opinions in their own territories, based upon different appeals to cultural identity or economic interest as well as on nationalist ideology.

- All nationalist parties have at times encompassed a range of opinions about whether or not to participate in concessionary devolution, and also about the use of civil disobedience.

- Strategic changes towards the Left in Scottish and Welsh nationalism and towards electoral, rather than paramilitary, methods in Northern Ireland occurred in the 1980s and 1990s.

- Devolution of power to the three territories since 1997 has brought the nationalists into government.

 Glossary of key terms

Cultural nationalism The demand for self-government as a means of protecting the language, religion and way of life distinctive to a territory or community.
Devolution The transfer of power to a territory within the United Kingdom without surrendering British sovereignty.
Separatism The belief that a territory should become a separate state with its own currency, foreign policy and representation at international level.

 Likely examination questions

Account for the success of nationalist parties in the United Kingdom in recent years.

Identify the similarities and differences between Scottish, Welsh and Northern Irish nationalists.

Does nationalist support arise from cultural or from economic factors?

Does nationalism in Scotland, Wales and Northern Ireland threaten the United Kingdom?

Helpful websites

These are the websites of the four main nationalist parties:

www.snp.org/

www.plaidcymru.org/

www.sdlp.ie/

www.sinnfein.ie/

The links to Scotland, Wales and Northern Ireland on the BBC News and Politics page (www.bbc.co.uk/news/politics/) are the best source of coverage of recent events involving nationalist parties.

Suggestions for further reading

McAllister, L., *Plaid Cymru: the Emergence of a Political Party* (Seren, 2001).

McEvoy, J., *The Politics of Northern Ireland* (Edinburgh University Press, 2008).

Mitchell, J., Bennie, L. and Johns, R., *The Scottish National Party: Transition to Power* (Oxford University Press, 2011).

Murray, G. and Tonge, J., *Sinn Fein and the SDLP: From Alienation to Participation* (C. Hurst & Co., 2005).

Pittock, M., *The Road to Independence: Scotland since the Sixties* (Reaktion Books, 2008).

Sandry, A., *Plaid Cymru: an Ideological Analysis* (Welsh Academic Press, 2011).

PART III

PERIPHERAL PARTIES

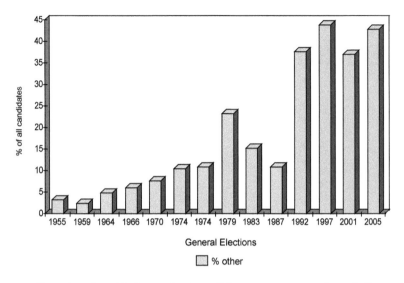

Peripheral and independent candidates as a proportion of all candidates in general elections, 1955–2005

Introduction

The following two chapters deal with the parties which are active in British political life, have public recognition and, in recent years, have gained representation outside Parliament or briefly within it. They are usually limited geographically in their activity and in their electoral potential, and are also characterised by tightly focused policy agendas, preoccupied with single issues or themes around which policies are based. Part III also examines the phenomenon of the independent candidate in British politics.

The role of parties other than the Conservatives, Labour, the Liberal Democrats and the nationalists is frequently the subject of criticism or levity. It is sometimes argued that the ideological breadth and flexibility of the main parties enable them to assimilate extreme elements in British politics, leaving only the most irresponsible and unrealistic on the periphery. Following a satirical sketch on the television programme *Monty Python's Flying Circus* in the 1960s, the 'others' became identified with the 'Monster Raving Loony Party', a comic invention implying that such candidates were, at best, eccentric, at worst, dangerous.

In an example of life imitating art, this party title was adopted by David Sutch – going under his professional name as a rock singer, Screaming Lord Sutch – as the platform on which he stood at a series of by-elections promoting idiosyncratic proposals for government. Sutch became widely recognised for his outlandish dress and lively campaigning manner – 'Vote for insanity: you know it makes sense' – and spawned a generation of copycat impudent candidatures at general elections, usually against high-profile ministers who would, as a result, be flanked on the platform by rival candidates like 'Miss Whiplash', 'Lord Buckethead' and a number of commercial candidatures from businesses keen to secure the £8,000-worth of free postage given to candidates in exchange for their £500 deposit. Eventually, in 1985, the government felt compelled to introduce a higher deposit with a lower threshold of forfeiture as a disincentive to what one minister called 'a tidal wave of clown candidates'.

The publicity surrounding David Sutch, however, overlooked the fact that, at each by-election he contested, his party made a singular policy suggestion. At his first contest in 1963, this had been that the vote should be given to eighteen-year-olds; in subsequent attempts, Sutch called for all-day licensing on Sundays, a national lottery, passports for pets and the licensing of commercial radio before any main party had proposed it. All of these, of course, subsequently came on to the statute book. Others of his proposals, such as the nullification of any election result in which the winner secures fewer votes than the number of non-voters, merit serious consideration. The significance of this is that even the most apparently insubstantial and unpopular of candidates and parties may perform the functions of informing and mobilising the public without winning elections. Other peripheral by-election candidates have called for greater road safety, reform of the law on abortion, the protection of local hospital services, the liberalisation of laws on entertainment and brothel-keeping, and the withdrawal of British troops from Cyprus. Few independent candidates have been elected to the Commons and, as we shall see, the circumstances of their success are distinctive – but the growth in their number and range has been noticeable.

Whilst the impact of individual peripheral candidates may be debateable, there has also been a rise in the number of small parties with limited resources but with a useful function to perform. Moreover, unlike Lord Sutch, they have recently been able to secure representation and to influence the larger parties systematically by their success. The increase in participation by candidates at general elections from outside the major and minor parties can be seen in the figure below: fifty years ago there were only twenty-nine such candidates in mainland Britain, and more than half of these came from the Communist Party; until 1970 such candidates never represented as much as one in ten of the total. Yet from 1974 to 1987 they were between a tenth and a quarter of candidates and after that they were between a third and half of all candidates. In 2010, candidates of the parties represented in more than one previous parliament (the major and minor parties) only just managed to outnumber those of the periphery by 2,092 to 2,060.

Chapters 5 and 6 examine in two broad categories, 'Right' and 'Left', how and why those parties have grown in activity and support.

Right-wing Peripheral Parties

Contents

Overview

For more than fifty years, peripheral candidates have fought British elections on a blend of policies involving defence of national self-government (particularly against the European Union), authoritarian law-and-order policies, hostility to immigration and, in the most extreme cases, to any racial integration. Their impact has been heavily dependent upon the reaction of those outside their ranks, including other parties and the media, and on short-term events and economic conditions rather than on any long-term loyalty. Nevertheless, the twenty-first century has seen the strongest and most sustained progress by far-right parties ever in Britain, and major parties have paid heed.

Key issues to be covered in this chapter

- Which are the key right-wing parties in Britain?
- What support do they enjoy and where does it come from?
- What are the similarities and differences between them?
- What is their impact upon policy?

In the immediate post-war era, those anxious about the break-up of the British Empire and the advance of socialism found powerful incentives to support a weakened Conservative Party, and could be reassured by its leader, Winston Churchill. Outside Tory ranks there existed only the most obscure bodies, such as the League of Empire Loyalists (LEL) which was formed as Churchill's leadership gave way to more liberal Tories in the mid-1950s and which favoured a strong and active monarchy and Church, opposed the United Nations and resisted the end of Empire – including supporting apartheid. The league contested only a handful of elections, and concentrated instead on disrupting diplomatic, church and political meetings, and BBC broadcasts of which it disapproved.

It was not until 1959 that a recognised candidate of the Far Right took on the Conservatives when pre-war British Fascist leader Oswald Moseley stood in Kensington North. Though he secured only 2,800 votes (8 per cent), this was more than three times the margin by which Labour kept the seat from the Conservatives, and it became apparent that an appeal to the supporters of the Far Right might pay dividends, a recognition which was manifested in the shifting climate of party leaders' opinions over race and immigration in the 1960s. At the 1964 General Election, a member of the tiny British National Party won 9 per cent of the vote in Southall, and a Conservative was elected at Smethwick using the slogan 'if you want a nigger for a neighbour, vote Labour'. For its part, the new Labour government abandoned its promise to repeal Conservative immigration controls and, indeed, introduced stricter ones of its own.

The National Front

In 1968, as controversy raged over the attempt by large numbers of Kenyan Asians to enter Britain, the National Front (NF) was formed by the merger of the League of Empire Loyalists with other right-wing bodies, some of them explicitly paramilitary and **neo-fascist**. The Front aimed to give voters in more constituencies the opportunity to vote for compulsory repatriation of certain immigrants and deliberate racial discrimination by the state, and, for a time, came to be a significant electoral force in parts of the country. In 1970, it put forward only ten candidates, none of whom won as much as 6 per cent of the vote but, under the Conservative government of Edward Heath, the NF prospered. Though Heath further tightened immigration controls, he also had a liberal reputation earned from his sacking of Enoch Powell in 1968, and, when he gave special dispensation to admit 50,000 Ugandan Asians into Britain in 1972, the NF took its opportunity. It changed its leader, increased its membership, recruiting some former Conservative officials and candidates, and improved its showing at elections. At a by-election in West Bromwich in 1973, the NF gained 16 per cent of the vote and, in the general election of October 1974, the party fielded ninety candidates, earning a Party Election Broadcast and winning 113,000 votes. Later in the 1970s, the Front achieved substantial votes in local elections, coming third ahead of the Liberals in the 1977 Greater London Council elections. In 1979 the NF made its broadest general election assault, fielding 303 candidates and winning 191,000 votes; all lost their deposits, however, and, within five years, the National Front was effectively moribund.

The scale of the NF's success should not be exaggerated however serious the threat of its potential might have been thought. Its serious support was short-lived, had a high turnover, and was confined to limited geographical areas in the textile towns of the Pennines, manufacturing parts of the Midlands, and certain constituencies in the capital. All of these had experienced high levels of immigration and economic hardship. Partly because of the electoral system, the NF never won any representation at municipal or parliamentary levels (though the breakaway National Party did win two council seats in Blackburn in 1976). The rise and fall of the NF depended on the same factors that have influenced far-right parties throughout the post-war period. The National Front thrived on: unity and organisation within its own ranks; weakness and division in the main parties (particularly the Conservatives, as when Heath sacked Powell who refused to speak on behalf of the Conservative candidate at West Bromwich); and a high profile for favourable issues in the media (notably immigration but, more generally, a perception of national economic and social decline). The NF's brief success came to an end because of a serious split among the leadership in 1975 between **'populists'** (who wanted to tone down the Front's appeal to widen electoral support) and more dogmatic 'elitists'; and because

Margaret Thatcher made hard-line commitments on immigration explicitly directed at winning back those who had defected to the Far Right while those on the Left formed the 'Anti-Nazi League' with the purpose of discrediting the NF to potential young recruits. Some of the lessons of this were learned by the NF's successors.

The years of the Thatcher premiership were hard for the Far Right whose strategy of presenting themselves as the people who would act where the Tories lacked courage was severely restricted, and whose organisation collapsed to the point where the final split involved, in one member's account, 'ten people going one way and forty going another'. The Far Right's reputation was further damaged by the public attention given to racist direct-action groups such as 'Combat 18' who became increasingly important in a shrinking community of activists. In 1982, John Tyndall, a former NF leader, re-established the British National Party and the two far-right groups contested the 1983 election, gaining only 41,000 votes between them. With the higher cost of lost deposits and scarce resources, and with Tyndall in prison for inciting racial hatred, neither party stood candidates in 1987. The NF was eventually wound up in 1992.

The British National Party

It was the British National Party (BNP) that was to be the beneficiary of the next wave of support for the Far Right. It is no coincidence that this occurred following the replacement of Margaret Thatcher by John Major as prime minister. Major took public pride in his upbringing in multicultural Brixton and rejected attempts by his own backbenchers to goad him into discussing race issues in 1997. In 1992 the BNP gained a fifth of the vote in a council by-election in Tower Hamlets, and the following year the party won the seat representing the Isle of Dogs on the same council. Though this seat was lost the following year, the BNP gained publicity when its head-quarters in Welling was besieged by anti-Nazi protestors who clashed with the police, and media interest was beginning to grow on the subject of asylum seekers, increasing numbers of whom were seeking refuge in Britain from conflicts around the world and against whose entry the government was tightening controls.

The BNP was unable to take advantage of these conditions until the next century, however. Even with a new leader, Nick Griffin, and under a Labour government associated by critics with 'political correctness', and with increasing attention given to asylum seekers in the tabloid press in 2001, the BNP offered no more than thirty-five general election candidates who gained only 47,000 votes between them. It was events at the local and international levels which put the BNP on the road to unprecedented success.

In the summer of 2001, there were riots in the northern towns of Oldham, Burnley and Bradford in which large numbers of Asian youths clashed with police. The explanations for these riots advanced in official reports emphasised the way in which white and ethnic-minority communities had become segregated from one another at work, in schools and in housing; some observers noted that the BNP had been active in those towns in the run-up to the riots and had stirred up racial tension. These tensions were exacerbated by the events of 11 September, after which the role of Muslims in Britain became a major question of public debate. Whatever the BNP's activities beforehand, in 2002 they were able to win three council seats in Burnley, and went on in the following year to become the official Opposition to Labour on the council. They achieved the same status on Barking and Dagenham council and, over the next six years, built up a total of over fifty councillors, including a member of the Greater London Authority elected in 2008. At the 2005 General Election, the BNP exceeded the National Front's 1979 total vote, winning 192,000 supporters – this time with only 119 candidates and on a lower turnout. It succeeded in gaining over a tenth of the vote in a number of constituencies. In 2009 the BNP gained a county council seat for the first time, and its greatest electoral prize to date: two seats in the European Parliament – one held by Nick Griffin, and the other by Andrew Brons, a veteran of the National Front.

Compared with earlier far-right parties there are three distinctive features of the BNP's revival: firstly, its scale is considerably greater than that of the NF in the 1970s; secondly, it is more sustained, and is characterised in places by the retention of seats and the consolidation of strength on councils, as well as incremental growth over six years; and lastly, the BNP has reached new types of voter, winning council seats outside the traditional hunting ground of the Far Right in disaffected, disadvantaged, urban white communities. Some BNP councillors now represented relatively prosperous suburban areas, such as Solihull in the West Midlands.

There are both short-term and long-term causes of the Far Right's sudden surge. There has always been a seam in British public opinion strongly attached to images of traditional national identity and hostile to change in the population and its culture; usually, this has been contained within the boundaries of the main parties. The Conservatives, suffering from a public image of extremism, however, have felt reluctant to follow Thatcher's strategy of reaching out to the Far Right's voters. To this have been added local tensions exacerbated by poverty and segregation, and the effective leadership of Nick Griffin, the Cambridge graduate and rabble-rouser, who has been adept at achieving publicity when unsuccessfully prosecuted for incitement to racial hatred, barracked at the Oxford Union or prevented from speaking at the hustings. There has been a modest rebranding of the BNP to avoid the use of overtly racist language in favour of taking up local issues and the more anonymous use of the first person plural to appeal to voters. At the same time, the increasing anxiety of the press about asylum and immigration has added superficial respectability to the BNP's agenda. All of this explains the inception, scale and scope of the BNP's success but not its timing. This must be attributed to the **Islamophobic** impact of the 'war on terror' since 2001, and again since the London bombings of 2005. The BNP gained its first councillors since 1993 in the year after 11 September; its biggest increase – more than doubling its number of seats – came in the year after July 2005.

The impact of the BNP's revival on the political agenda is difficult to deny: government minister Margaret Hodge went as far as to claim that most white voters in her constituency of Barking and Dagenham were ready to vote for the party, and called for length of residence in the United Kingdom to be taken into account when allocating council housing. The Conservatives made demands for strict controls on immigration and raised asylum as a key theme in their 2005 campaign. The Labour government responded to this pressure by introducing such controls and by boasting about the numbers of asylum applicants who had been removed from the country.

The reasons for the success of the BNP also place limits on its prospects, and there is evidence that the party has achieved the maximum benefit available from these circumstances. The attention of the media from 2008 onwards has been on the economy rather than on immigration; the BNP has suffered splits among its leadership, leading to the formation of the English Democratic Party, and over a dozen of its councillors – including its lone London Assembly member – have resigned from the party, some following criminal proceedings. The prospects of a Conservative general election victory galvanised 'soft' BNP supporters to reconsider their long-term loyalties. Though the BNP has retained some seats, most BNP councillors lose their seats on presenting themselves for re-election. The European election victories of 2009 did not represent an increase in BNP support but arose because of the reluctance of Labour voters to turn out at a time of deep division in the Brown cabinet.

Nick Griffin's appearance on BBC television's *Question Time* in October 2009 proved to be a high watermark of BNP success and a pyrrhic victory, robbing him of his 'outsider' status and fuelling doubts within the BNP about whether he is radical enough. At the 2010 General Election, the BNP nominated 337 candidates but only increased its vote by 2 per cent to a total of just over half a million. Griffin himself lost vote share in a high-profile contest against Margaret Hodge in Barking where the BNP had been within a few votes of second place in 2005. Twenty-six BNP councillors standing that year were defeated. Griffin later announced that he would step down as leader in 2013 though this did not prevent his fellow-MEP, Andrew Brons, from challenging his leadership in a bitter contest in 2011 which Griffin won by less than 1 per cent of the votes cast. The BNP has achieved more electoral success than any far-right party but this has relied upon modification of its appeal and seems to be temporary. Its high watermark may be further up the beach than that of its forebears but the tide has receded.

Anti-EU parties

Where the anti-immigration element of the Far Right is reflected in the appeal of the BNP, opposition to the United Kingdom's assimilation into Europe (**anti-Europeanism**) is expressed by the UK Independence Party. UKIP was founded in 1993 by Dr Alan Sked, an historian with a long-established hostility to the development of a

Box 5.1 The rise and fall of the Far Right

Source A: *The Daily Telegraph*, 9 June 2009

The British National Party is in line for a £4 million cash boost as its European election breakthrough was widely condemned as 'shaming' for Britain. The far-right group won its first two seats in the European Parliament as the Labour vote collapsed, sending shock waves through Westminster and the country. Leader Nick Griffin, one of the successful MEPs, said it meant a 'huge change in British politics'. Mr Griffin said: 'It is a historic breakthrough. It is a great moment for democracy. Labour has helped to turn this country into a crime-ridden slum with no industry left.' He said his party's success was due in part to the indigenous white population of Britain being treated as 'second-class citizens' in their own country. 'In this country, it is the indigenous majority who are the second-class citizens in every possible sphere, not as a consequence of the immigrants themselves, but because our ruling elite has made us second-class citizens and that is one reason why we got such a huge vote in the north of England.' Speaking after his victory, Mr Brons said: 'I regard this as the first step to the UK getting freedom from the EU dictatorship. Despite the headlines, despite the money, despite the misrepresentation we have managed to win through.' Andy Burnham, the health secretary, said it was the 'ultimate protest vote, a two-fingered vote and largely a comment on Westminster politics'.

Source B: *The Guardian*, 20 May 2011

The British National party's dominance of far-right politics in the UK is under threat for the first time in a decade after a string of poor election results and a growing rebellion against its leader, Nick Griffin. The BNP chairman, who has led the party since 1999, is facing a second leadership challenge in less than twelve months, a mass defection of key organisers and the prospect of a new 'popular front' made up of other far-right groups and former BNP activists. This week Richard Barnbrook, who was the BNP's sole representative on the London Assembly until he was expelled from the party last year, said it was time for a realignment in 'nationalist politics' in the UK. Barnbrook, who now sits as an independent on the London Assembly, has written to leaders of four other far-right or nationalist organisations – including the English Defence League and the English Democrats – calling for the creation of 'one strong, united, cohesive force'. Griffin is also facing an increasingly emboldened rebellion inside the party. Richard Edmonds, seen as a 'BNP hard-liner', has launched a formal leadership challenge and although it is unlikely he will win, his defeat is expected to trigger another wave of defections. Andrew Brons, the BNP's second MEP and an increasingly significant figure, has distanced himself from Griffin and this week appeared to back the leadership challenge, prompting speculation that he is preparing to lead a breakaway group.

Question: Does the sudden collapse of BNP support show that the Far Right is not a substantial element in British politics?

federal European Union, and is committed to withdrawal of Britain from the EU. As with the re-emergence of the BNP, it is significant that this coincided with the leadership of John Major and his support of the Maastricht Treaty paving the way for European economic and monetary union and sparking internal warfare in the Conservative Party. UKIP attracted considerable interest in the 1990s, holding 1,000-strong conferences and putting up candidates at most parliamentary by-elections. Only at one of these, in April 1996, was their deposit narrowly saved. At the European Assembly elections of 1994, UKIP contested twenty-two of the eighty-four mainland British seats but won no more than 5.4 per cent in any of them.

In its early stages, UKIP was inhibited by the temporary intervention of a rival, the Referendum Party, the aim of which was to pressurise the main parties – particularly John Major's Conservatives – into promising a referendum on British membership of the European Union by standing against their more pro-European MPs and candidates. The Referendum Party was founded in November 1995 by multimillionaire, Sir James Goldsmith, and benefited from two advantages over UKIP. First was Goldsmith's backing who, from the outset, promised over £10 million for election expenditure and who – as a competent platform speaker and the father-in-law of international cricketer, Imran Khan – attracted considerably greater media interest than Dr Sked. This meant that the Referendum Party could afford to field 546 candidates against UKIP's 194 at the 1997 General Election, and use campaigning techniques such as mass delivery of propaganda videos to voters. Secondly, the Referendum

Party could cast a wider net by demanding not withdrawal from the EU (although this was without doubt the aim of most of the party's supporters) but rather the holding of a referendum on the issue of membership. By comparison, UKIP looked the weaker, and more inflexible, cousin. In all but two of the 165 contests involving both Eurosceptic parties, Goldsmith's party won more votes. Forty-two Referendum Party candidates saved their deposits whereas only one UKIP candidate did so. Neither party gained as much as 10 per cent of the vote in any seat.

Analysis of the election showed that no more than six Conservative seats were lost because of a peripheral Eurosceptic – and two of these faced UKIP rather than the Referendum Party. The intervention of these candidates, however, had raised the issue of Europe at a general election in an explicit way which splits within, and consensus between, the major parties had made difficult in the past. When shortly after the 1997 election James Goldsmith died, it was UKIP which inherited the Eurosceptic legacy.

Under the Blair governments, Europe remained an issue capable of generating controversy and a small number of votes: firstly, over Britain's possible entry into the single currency and, later, because of the arguments over the European Constitution and Lisbon Treaty. The successful campaign by the *Daily Mail* and other newspapers to secure a government promise to hold a referendum on the constitution in 2004 helped to create an atmosphere of intensified anxiety among Eurosceptics which gave an ideal platform to UKIP at that year's European elections. UKIP had shown in 1999 that, using the proportional list system to its advantage, it could turn these contests into something of a 'home fixture' at which concerned voters, normally loyal to the main parties, could protest at European integration. On that occasion, they gained 7 per cent of the vote and three seats in the European Assembly; five years later they won 16.1 per cent of the vote, pushing the Liberal Democrats into third place nationally, and gained twelve seats. This success rested partly upon the brief association of the party with television presenter and former Labour MP, Robert Kilroy-Silk, who had been persuaded to join in 2004 by Lord Bradford, and who won a high-profile victory in the European elections. Within nine months, however, he had resigned the party condemning it as 'a joke'. The year 2008 saw UKIP claim its first MP when backbench Conservative Robert Spink defected to the party. And, in the 2009 European elections, UKIP demonstrated its persistence, coming second in the national poll and winning thirteen seats in the European Parliament. In 2010, UKIP won nearly a million votes at the general election though, like Nick Griffin, party leader Nigel Farage failed in a high-profile bid for a seat in the Commons, this time against the Speaker of the House. Like the BNP, though dependent upon circumstances it cannot control, UKIP can not be dismissed as a flash in the pan.

Assessment: the impact of the Right

In evaluating the strength of the peripheral Right, it is first important to note that it does not act as a single bloc and that, in particular, UKIP officials are keen to deny any association with the BNP. The masthead of UKIP's website insists that it is 'non-racist' and reminds those interested that membership of any other political party is prohibited for UKIP members. Roger Knapman, a former Tory whip who has become a UKIP MEP, insists that 'anyone who joins UKIP has to say they are not a member of the BNP or racist groups'. UKIP very firmly rejected an offer of an electoral alliance with the BNP made first by former tennis professional, Buster Mottram, in 2008 and again by the BNP itself at the 2009 European elections. Critics argue, however, that the only significant difference between UKIP and the BNP is one of class and age profile – that UKIP are 'the BNP in blazers'. Alan Sked left the party he founded six years earlier because he was disturbed by some of the support it was attracting: 'there's not much difference in party programmes between them' he concluded, 'the cliché is that the disaffected working class will vote BNP and the disaffected lower middle class will vote UKIP'.[1]

There is clearly some common ground between the parties: both are hostile to current levels of immigration and sceptical of government claims about reductions in the numbers of asylum seekers; both want more effective methods of deportation for failed asylum applicants. Where UKIP's policy is limited to cutting numbers entering, and would operate the policy regardless of ethnic origin, the BNP proposes voluntary repatriation and acknowledges that its measures would be intended to protect the 'white' community. The BNP forbade black and Asian Britons from joining until a recent court case compelled them not to.

Both parties want Britain to withdraw from the European Union and to strengthen British defences and the independence of British foreign policy; both seek traditional, authoritarian approaches to education and to law and order though, while both want stricter sentencing, only the BNP has an explicit policy of restoration of the death penalty. Both parties have a populist approach to constitutional reform, UKIP favouring a partly elected House of Lords, the use of the alternative vote (AV) to elect MPs, and the widespread use of referendums while the BNP made the bold claim in its 2005 manifesto that 'the British people invented modern Parliamentary democracy' and demanded that 'power should be devolved to the lowest level possible so that local communities can make decisions which affect them'. Thus, the preoccupations of the BNP and UKIP are similar; their policies point in the same direction though those of the BNP travel further and are usually expressed in more confrontational terms. On the question of race, there is a clear distinction, at least between their ostensible positions, and there remains a stronger association of the BNP with anticonstitutional and even violent actions which UKIP would regard as entirely improper.

There are also similarities and differences between the two parties' appeals and between their supporters. UKIP's strength is in the south-east outside London and among fishing and agricultural communities; the BNP's core support is in depressed urban constituencies in parts of London, the Midlands and the north where race and immigration are also live issues. The potential for further BNP success in these areas was pointed up by a report in 2008 on politics in Stoke set up by local government minister, John Healey.[2] This complementary trend is also evident in the level of election at which the two parties have their respective strengths: UKIP has made European elections the focus of its greatest success whereas, at local elections, where UKIP has only recently won a dozen seats, the BNP has built up a small but unprecedented cadre of councillors, with substantial representation in a few areas. Neither party has had any real success at parliamentary elections though UKIP has the support of two peers. To win a seat in the House of Commons would be a truly remarkable achievement for either of these parties.

Likewise, neither party is active in Scotland or Wales to anything like the degree it is in England.

It is difficult accurately to gauge the significance of the growth of the peripheral parties on the Right. Their direct exercise of power – the defining feature of political parties, after all – is negligible. They have sixty-two out of 22,000 councillors and control no councils; they win no seats in the Commons and, where elected, can seem ambivalent about their role as representatives. There is a high rate of defection and resignation from the parties, and some spectacular non-attendance by BNP councillors; and Robert Kilroy-Silk announced upon election as a UKIP MEP that his role would be to 'wreck' the European Parliament. Since the fiasco of Nick Griffin's appearance on *Question Time*, the role of the BNP in voicing hostility to Islam in Britain has increasingly been taken by the English Defence League which, as yet, does not stand in elections regularly. It is tempting to dismiss these parties' momentary successes, as *The Independent* did of the BNP's appearance on Burnley Council, as 'minor victories in a small, moderately poor town' rather than as a 'political insurrection'.[3]

The current situation is significantly different, however, from that of fifty years, a generation or even a decade ago. Two parties committed to 'Conservative-plus' approaches to national identity, immigration control, British independence, and traditional social policies have shown a continuing appeal, attracting up to a million voters at general elections and more at European elections. Their membership, activity, representation and media profiles are all more sizeable and sustained than those achieved by the National Front or its predecessors. They rely a great deal upon media concentration on their issues of choice, upon effective leadership and upon strategic weakness in the main parties – but, then, so do other parties. It is their impact upon those main parties, acting as a spur to their Eurosceptic and authoritarian traditions, which is perhaps these parties' most significant effect. The role of immigration as the second most important issue at the 2010 General Election, the controversy over Gordon Brown's description of Gillian Duffy as a 'bigot', and Ed Miliband's subsequent admission that Labour had lost the public's trust on immigration – these events gained their significance partly from the spectre of the far-right parties waiting to claim their vindication.

• •

What you should have learnt from reading this chapter

- A tradition of political thought beyond the right of the Conservatives has existed in Britain since World War II but took the form of competing organisations only with the formation of the National Front and subsequent far-right parties.

- The far-right parties share between themselves and right-wing Conservatives concerns about the decline of British national identity and the effect upon it of mass immigration, European integration and the liberalisation of policies in law and order and education.

- The Far Right is divided about attitudes to race discrimination and about association with direct action or physical protest, with moderate constitutionalists being suspected of betrayal by militant purists.

Glossary of key terms

Anti-Europeanism Opposition to Britain's membership of the European Union rather than wishing for a reassessment of Britain's relationship with it. The distinction divides UKIP from most Conservatives.

Islamophobia Irrational or exaggerated fear of the impact of Islam. First identified in a Runnymede Trust study of 1997, the phenomenon has been seen as part of the cause for the rise of the BNP since 2001.

Neo-fascist Characterisation of the National Front and the British National Party by critics who identify in these parties the same attributes of policy and method as were seen in Nazi Germany and Fascist Italy.

Populists Activists in the National Front who sought to conventionalise the party's image and methods to increase support, a dilemma faced subsequently by the BNP.

Likely examination questions

How do you explain the support for far-right parties in Britain?

Is the British National Party a fascist movement?

How fair is it to treat all far-right parties in Britain as similar?

What has been the impact of far-right parties in Britain?

Helpful websites

The websites of UKIP and the BNP are www.ukip.org/ and www.bnp.org. uk; those wanting an investigative and oppositional insight into the BNP and EDL can go to the websites of Searchlight (www.searchlightmagazine. com/) and Unite Against Fascism (www.uaf.org.uk/).

Suggestions for further reading

The literature on parties of the Far Right is even more run through with partisanship than commentaries on the larger parties. The chapter in the third on post-war British fascism gives the historical background to the BNP up to its recent rise; the first and the last titles are serious but evidently critical accounts of the BNP; the second is a supportive narrative of UKIP's rise.

Copsey, N., *Contemporary British Fascism: The British National Party and the Quest for Legitimacy* (Palgrave Macmillan, 2008).

Daniel, M., *Cranks and Gadflies: the Story of UKIP* (Timewell Press, 2005).

Eatwell, R., *Fascism: A History* (Pimlico, 2003); Chapter 14, 'Neofascism in Britain'.

Goodwin, M. J., *New British Fascism: The Rise of the British National Party* (Routledge, 2011).

Left-wing Peripheral Parties

Contents

Overview

There have always been vehicles for the opinions of those who seek more public ownership and state economic intervention, more progressive taxation and higher public expenditure, and more commitment to disarmament, than the Labour Party is prepared to offer. Whereas peripheral right-wing parties have become stronger in recent years, however, these parties have been weakened by division and strategic uncertainty compared with their post-war forebears – George Thayer identified twelve 'outside-left' groups in Britain in the 1960s. Nevertheless, they have shown a dynamism and potential which make them important in current party competition in the United Kingdom.

Key issues to be covered in this chapter

- Which far-left parties have been active in Britain?
- What levels of support have they attained and why?
- What are the similarities and differences between them?
- Have they had any impact on the political system?

Communist parties

Organised campaigns for the explicit implementation of Marxist ideas have undergone a process of fragmentation and near elimination in Britain since World War II. Between the 1940s and the 1970s, one party could make a legitimate claim to represent this tradition, the Communist Party. Established in 1920, by 1945 it had built up a membership of 50,000, its newspaper, *The Daily Worker*, regularly sold over 120,000 copies, and at the election of that year the Communist Party of Great Britain (CPGB) won over 100,000 votes with only twenty-one candidates, two of whom were elected to the House of Commons. At this point, the party was pro-Stalinist but did not reject electoral politics as a matter of principle and, indeed, saw its function as being to help to radicalise existing institutions – most notably the Labour Party – by participating in constitutional politics.

This, however, was the high point of the Communist Party. It lost both its MPs in 1950 and never won another seat; after 1970 its membership fell to 25,000 and its average vote per candidate at general elections was consistently below one thousand. It also faced stiffer competition from newer, dynamic alternatives, such as the Socialist Workers Party (SWP), the Workers Revolutionary Party (WRP) and the Revolutionary Communist Party (RCP), each of which attracted an activist base of a few thousand people, usually short-term and young members. The SWP, formed in 1976, rejected 'bourgeois' politics and rarely contested elections but the WRP, founded in 1959, fought 114 seats between 1974 and 1992, losing its deposit each time. Though these groups were energetic and at times visible and, like the Communist Party, tried to establish a presence in the trade-union and student movements, their impact upon the exercise of power was limited by their differences of interpretation of Marxism, differences of strategy, and smallness of numbers.

The effect of these groups' activities was indirect and therefore its significance is difficult to ascertain: the Communist Party had a number of supporters in the trade unions, including some leading officials, in the 1960s and 1970s; its magazine, *Marxism Today*, was an important platform for debate about the future of the Left in the 1970s and 1980s, to which noted academics who were not all Communist Party members, such as Stuart Hall, Ivor Crewe and

Eric Hobsbawm, contributed. It can be argued that some of the ideas sustained and developed by these groups found expression on the left of the Labour Party in the 1980s with the success of the Trotskyist 'Militant Tendency' which claimed the support of 8,000 subscribers to its newspapers, most of Liverpool's ruling Labour council group, and two Labour MPs.

All of these groups were experiencing steep decline by the end of the 1980s. Supporters of the Militant Tendency were expelled from Labour for **entryism** following a bravura speech by Neil Kinnock at the 1985 party conference (which was even used in a Labour Party election broadcast in 1987). This echoed the Labour Party's rejection of a **popular front** with the Communist Party in the 1920s and 1930s after it had experienced the effects of '**red scares**' at elections where it had been linked to communism. Two separate factions of the WRP, each publishing a newspaper called *Newsline*, emerged from that party in 1986 and eventually withered to a nominal existence. After years of fierce internal dispute, the Communist Party abandoned Marxism–Leninism and restyled itself as a broad campaigning group, the 'Democratic Left' in 1991. Unlike the situation on the Right, the movement to the centre of the Labour Party did not open up an opportunity for the Far Left; the end of the Cold War and the decline of trade unions and traditional class identity had delivered a blow to all parts of the Left. Of the communist organisations, only the SWP remains. Because it rejects co-operation with, or entry into, major parties and does not itself fight elections, its impact is limited to associating itself with temporary industrial disputes and anti-racist and anti-war campaigns.

Breakaway socialist parties

The capture of Labour's leadership by its modernisers in 1994 led to the breaking away of numerous former Labour figures who sought to represent what they saw to be Labour's traditional and genuine values, particularly around state intervention in industry and the market, and equitable provision of welfare services.

The first of these breakaway parties, the Socialist Labour Party (SLP), was established by the leader of the National Union of Mineworkers, Arthur Scargill, after the decision of the 1995 Special

Labour Conference to rewrite Clause IV of the party's constitution and abandon the commitment in principle to public ownership of industry. Scargill argued that a new vehicle to represent socialism was needed 'when all three political parties support capitalism and support the free market'. The party narrowly saved its deposit in the February 1996 Hemsworth by-election, and did so again in 1997 when Scargill stood at Newport East against Alan Howarth who had defected to New Labour from the Tories. Only one other of the party's fifty-four candidates saved his deposit, however, and Scargill himself did less well in 2001 when he took on Peter Mandelson at Hartlepool. Though the SLP put up 114 candidates in 2001 and enjoyed the benefit of a party election broadcast featuring *Royle Family* actor, Ricky Tomlinson, its candidates gained only an average 1.4 per cent of the poll; by 2005 it had reduced its slate to fifty – only one of whom saved their deposit – and gained only 20,000 votes in total at an average of 0.8 per cent of the vote each. The Socialist Labour Party no longer has any councillors.

Another breakaway from Labour, the Socialist Alliance (SA), emerged a little later, led by Dave Nellist, a former Labour MP and 'Militant Tendency' supporter. Nellist had come within 3.7 per cent of keeping his Coventry seat as an Independent Socialist in 1992 after being expelled from the Labour Party, and he began to form a network of local socialist groups which, by 2000, had fifty-eight branches. In 2001 the SA adopted a new programme and constitution and brought together a number of the tendencies and groups on the Left, including the Communist Party of Great Britain, the International Socialist Group and the SWP. The new party put up ninety-eight candidates and accused New Labour of betraying its supporters on health, education, public transport and pensions in a party election broadcast directed by Ken Loach under the slogan 'there *is* an alternative'. When the war in Iraq began, however, the SWP contingent left the SA to join the Respect coalition, after voting to close the SA down. Nellist contested the 2005 and 2010 elections, gaining 5 per cent and 3 per cent respectively, and abandoning the Socialist Alliance label at the latter contest.

The SA and SLP were joined at the 2001 election by the Scottish Socialist Party (SSP) which had been formed in 1998 by Tommy Sheridan, a flamboyant figure who had cut his teeth in the Anti-Poll

Tax Federation after being expelled from Labour as a Militant sympathiser. The Trotskyite SSP argued for greater state intervention and public expenditure but also for Scottish independence and, within a year of its foundation, Sheridan had won a seat in the first Scottish Parliament. Emboldened by this success, the SSP fought every Scottish seat in the 2001 General Election, winning 3.1 per cent of the Scottish vote. In 2003 the SSP reached the peak of its success, taking six seats and 6.8 per cent of the vote in the Scottish Parliament elections, and Sheridan became something of a minor celebrity, appearing on national television broadcasts, such as *Question Time*, and later hosting his own radio show, *Citizen Tommy*, and appearing at the Edinburgh Festival.

Sheridan, however, was both the SSP's greatest asset and its Achilles heel: when the *News of the World* published allegations of sexual misconduct by Sheridan, he sued for libel and represented himself in court. The case split the SSP because, though four of Sheridan's senior colleagues defended him, eleven testified against him. He resigned the SSP leadership while the trial was on and when, in 2006, he won his case and was awarded £200,000 in compensation, Sheridan began his own party, Solidarity. Sheridan and all of the SSP members lost their seats in the Scottish Parliament in 2007, and his legal problems continued as he was charged in December with having committed perjury during the libel trial. In 2010 he was convicted.

The movement of the Labour Party to the centre ground, then, did not produce any sustained 'refugee' problem for it. The forces of the Far Left, which were stranded by the development of New Labour, were too few and too poorly organised and resourced to mount a serious challenge from without, despite serious misgivings among Labour's own supporters about its record in government. The appetite of the British electorate for theoretical Marxism has never been strong, and the success of peripheral left groups has relied upon links with the trade unions, the Labour Party, or else upon charismatic leadership. The impact of the last of these can be great but rarely lasts, as Scargill, Nellist and Sheridan demonstrate; the value of the first may have gone forever.

The Green Party and Respect

Two peripheral left-wing parties have achieved high profiles and representation at national level where those discussed above have failed: one has arrived at this position over a journey of decades whereas the other has sprung to prominence in a few years; both have relied upon a focus on one issue, rather than on the traditional far-left appeal to class identity and socialist economics, to achieve this.

The Greens

The Green Party represents a relatively small but continuous body of opinion committed to radical action to protect the natural environment, and a larger and more fluctuating number of voters with a general concern about environmental policy. The tension between the 'Dark Greens', who seek dramatic action and are suspicious of conventional political processes, and those who want to exploit their wider appeal in the electoral arena, is part of what has inhibited Green Party progress.

The party emerged from a movement simply called 'People' established in 1970 and, even after it became the Ecology Party in 1973, its work concentrated upon the education of the general public rather than on winning power. With just over 5,000 members, it contested between fifty and 150 seats at the general elections of 1979–87 but secured an average of only 1.0 to 1.5 per cent of the vote in each seat it fought. Henry Drucker's 1980 study of Britain's minor parties, *Multi-Party Britain*, does not even mention the Ecology Party.

By the end of the 1980s, the Ecology Party had become a recognised, if small, player in the political system. In 1985, it formally adopted the name of the Green Party thereby associating itself clearly with the more successful parties of the same name in continental European countries, and it also had their ambitions for power. The Greens also benefited after 1987 from the confusion among the larger parties opposing the Conservatives at the time. With Labour's policy review underway, and the Social Democrats and Liberals embroiled in their merger controversy, it became tempting for leftists with a concern for the environment to look around for a radical vehicle at elections. To this tactical opportunity was added greater media attention to the issues of environmental threat following the disasters at Chernobyl in the Ukraine and Bhopal in India.

Lastly, the Greens won a temporarily valuable supporter in David Icke, the former Coventry City goalkeeper and BBC television sports presenter. Though the Greens rejected the idea of a single leader as a preoccupation of superficial conventional politics, they made Icke their animal rights spokesman and he lent the party a likeable and mainstream image. They also crafted an effective party election broadcast for the 1989 European elections and, in the midst of these favourable circumstances, the Greens achieved an unexpected and unprecedented 15 per cent of the vote, more than double the share achieved by the Liberal Democrats. In the wake of this, their tally of council seats grew, and the Greens in Wales struck up a relationship with Plaid Cymru in which they supported six of the Welsh nationalists' candidates at the 1992 General Election, one of whom was elected.

This was a false dawn but not an insignificant one. Firstly, under the first-past-the-post electoral system, the Greens gained no seats despite having the largest share of the vote of any European green party. At the time, the party was dismissed by Conservative chairman, Norman Tebbit, as 'a dustbin for protest votes' and they have, indeed, been unable to repeat this success at any subsequent national election, and have only recently begun to save deposits in parliamentary contests. They did begin to pick up council seats, however, and they prompted all three main parties to review their environmental programmes. The short-lived nature of the party's success, on the other hand, strengthened the hand of those who were sceptical about taking part in conventional politics and diluting their message; these doubts were multiplied when former electoral asset David Icke announced on the Wogan programme on BBC television that he believed himself to be the son of God, that he had taken to wearing purple as a means of focusing positive energy on himself, and that the Earth is controlled by a race of reptiles. He also predicted widespread natural disasters before the end of that year, 1991. A leading radical ecosocialist, Derek Wall, remembers that:

The right around the Green 2000 faction wanted to make us into a mainstream party with mass appeal, ditch the radicalism, re-engineer the Party constitution and centralise power. We fought them. I remember Sara Parkin talking to *The Independent* about 'socialist parasites' who had been members nearly as long as her. They won and then imploded, when the Party received just a couple of percent at the 1992 General Election. When the 'realists' believe in achieving a Westminster Parliamentary government by 2000 (thus Green 2000), give me fundamentalism.

The Greens considered abandoning electoral activity altogether at their 1995 conference in Wolverhampton but relented and, instead, went on to adopt the 'Green 2000' strategy aimed at relaunching the party's electoral appeal. The Greens gradually consolidated their position so that they now have 140 councillors at all levels of local government, as well as members of the Greater London Assembly and the European Parliament. After becoming the official Opposition on Norwich council in 2008, they claimed to have won enough votes in one of the city's parliamentary seats to be able to win an MP there.

After a vigorous debate within the Green Party, the decision was taken in 2008 by a ballot of all 7,000 members (73 per cent voting 'yes') to choose a single leader in place of the panel of speakers who had represented the party to the media until then. As it had been ten years earlier, it was the electoralist wing of the Greens that won the day by a margin of three to one, and MEP Caroline Lucas became their first leader. Derek Wall told the BBC (23 March 2007) that 'I find the title "leader" embarrassing: it is so patronising, assuming a bunch of people have to be "led", the shepherd label that assumes the members are sheep'. As a concession to the party's continuing suspicion of hierarchy and elites, the Green leader cannot serve more than ten years in office, and the deputy leader must be of the opposite gender to the leader. Lucas supports the Green New Deal Group, a group of politicians, journalists, academics and financial and industrial figures seeking to develop a response to the recession based on creating jobs in renewable energy but which allows for the need for economic growth.

Lucas's most visible achievement was winning the Greens' first parliamentary seat at Brighton Pavilion in 2010. George Monbiot wrote that 'the Green jinx has been lifted', and Lucas herself said that 'the word "historic" fits the bill. All the evidence shows that once

Greens have their foot in the door they are here to stay.' In 2011 the Greens became the largest party on Brighton council. Rupert Read, a Green European candidate and philosophy lecturer, claimed the party would be as 'unstoppable' in its growth as the early Labour Party. At the same election, however, the party saved only a quarter of the deposits it had held in 2005, and its national share of the vote, with over a hundred more candidates, fell. It is possible that the victory of Brighton Pavilion has come at the cost of over-targeting resources and setting back Green campaigning progress more generally. 'Dark Greens' may also wonder whether the cost to Green integrity of presenting themselves as part of the mainstream Left is worth paying for such mixed results. Derek Wall told Naturalchoices. co.uk on 2 September 2010 that for Greens the 2010 election was 'a game of two halves. It was great to get Caroline elected, pushing past 30% is almost unheard of for Green Parties anywhere in the world. However we were mauled in other seats.'

Respect
The latest peripheral party to surface on the left has been the Respect Unity Coalition. This party was formed by the combination of two forces which ultimately could not hold together despite considerable short-term success. The first element was the Stop the War coalition which was started in late 2001 to resist an American military response to the 9/11 attacks and which, in February 2003, organised the largest-ever demonstration in Britain with its rally against the invasion of Iraq. The second element was brought by George Galloway, the flamboyant Labour MP who was expelled from the party in October 2003 for his criticisms of government policy in the Middle East. In January 2004, Respect was founded and immediately attracted a body of support, gaining 12 per cent of the vote at a parliamentary by-election in Leicester and 90,000 votes in London at the European and Greater London Assembly elections. Respect's greatest strength was in urban areas with high Muslim populations and, in the 2005 General Election, the party polled well in Birmingham and Newham, and, spectacularly, George Galloway defeated Labour MP Oona King in Bethnal Green. Galloway was now a nationally recognised political figure, and drew publicity before the election by winning a libel case against *The Daily Telegraph*, and afterwards by an

Box 6.1 Ecology and Green Party election performance

Source A: General Elections, 1979–2010

	Candidates	Total vote	Saved deposits
1979	53	39,918	0
1983	108	54,299	0
1987	133	89,753	0
1992	253	170,368	0
1997	95	63,991	0
2001	145	166,487	10
2005	202	283,477	24
2010	315	285,616	6

Source B: European elections, 1979–2009

	% vote	Seats
1979	<1	0
1984	<1	0
1989	14.9	0
1994	3.2	0
1999	6.3	2
2004	6.3	2
2009	8.6	2

Source C: *Total Politics* 31, 17 December 2010

Caroline Lucas is finding out just how difficult it is to be the first Green MP in Parliament. As leader of a political movement she has been part of for over twenty years, the customs of the Commons are proving frustrating. This is a woman who was arrested for protesting against Trident, who marched down Whitehall with angry students and who started her career with the CND. Now, she has joined the world of morning prayers, PMQs and division bells. As a one-woman parliamentary party, just how much can the pixie-cropped Green Party leader achieve? 'Both before the election and afterwards, I have been asked, "What can a single MP achieve?"' she told the House in her maiden speech in May. 'I am sure that the answer is very clear. A single MP can achieve a great deal.'

But Parliament is not built for 'single MPs'. There is no older, wiser politician to show you the ropes. There is no 'buddy system' whereby you have a partner from the other side of the House to co-operate with. Places on committees are only gained by the grace and favour of other, larger parties. There isn't even a whipping system. 'It makes it really difficult,' Lucas admits. 'You need three MPs in your party to get a whip, to get into the information loops. If you don't have three members, you don't have a whip. Therefore you don't have the information. That is deeply frustrating and deeply undemocratic.'

Source D: *Financial Times*, 28 October 2011

The banner in Caroline Lucas's office is uncompromising: 'Well-behaved women rarely make history'. It seems an odd epithet for this neat, well-spoken fifty-year-old in a sensible grey outfit. But Ms Lucas, the first Green MP in the House of Commons, is not afraid to antagonise ministers as she holds the coalition to account over its environmental promises. This is a tough ambition for a single MP in a Parliament of 650. Yet Ms Lucas has proved herself an adept operator in the Commons, asking sharp questions in committee and chamber. Even the Conservative-leaning *Spectator* magazine placed her as 'Newcomer of the Year' in its annual awards for MPs last year. This is not the same Green party of twenty years ago which denounced economic growth, suffered internal feuding and, at one point, used David Icke as a spokesman.

Under Ms Lucas's leadership the party has sought to shed its lentil-eating reputation in favour of mainstream credibility. It now controls one council, Brighton, and has large groupings in Lancaster and Norwich. At the next general election the Greens plan to target Liberal Democrat seats, in particular in the south-west, in an effort to capitalise on disappointment at their 'betrayal' over tuition fees and spending cuts. Meanwhile Ms Lucas is determined to shine a spotlight on the coalition's failures to make good on their green promises.

Question: Have the Greens traded their radicalism for a higher public profile?

outspoken defence of himself at a Senate Committee hearing in the United States. Respect began to pick up a small number of council seats in Birmingham and Derbyshire as well as on Tower Hamlets council in London where it became the second biggest party. Some mutual support was developed between Respect and Green candidates at local elections.

Galloway's publicity quickly became a liability rather than an asset, however. In January 2006 he took part in reality television show *Celebrity Big Brother* where (as well as being absent from the Commons, where he attended only 8 per cent of votes through the whole parliament) among other activities, he dressed in a leotard and pretended to be a cat. Tensions were also emerging between the ideological outlook of Galloway and his supporters and that of the Stop the War elements, many of whom were associated with the Socialist Workers Party. Galloway publicly criticised the SWP in September 2007 and, by November, the Respect Party had split in two, with two conferences under the party name running separately and simultaneously, and the two factions battling for control of the party headquarters. Respect had no more than 1,500 members and its success appeared to be at an end when Galloway lost his Commons seat at the 2010 General Election, and Salma Yaqoob failed to capture the party's other realistic target, Hall Green in Birmingham (she came second with 25 per cent of the vote).

The persistence of a small far Left tradition in British politics was shown, however, by Galloway's return to Parliament as the victor of the March 2012 by-election at Bradford West. Following a reconciliation within its ranks, Respect won a 10,000-vote majority in a previously safe Labour seat by calling for the immediate withdrawal of British troops in Afghanistan as well as opposing university tuition fees and public sector cuts generally. These beliefs were important, but so was Galloway's legendary campaigning charisma, the high profile of the issues concerned at the time and the ethnic composition of Bradford's electorate. These made a repeat of the victory unlikely. The long-term message of the event was that the main parties had again failed to persuade the public of their legitimacy: it was not merely the result of some voters sharing Galloway's outlook, but of Labour under Ed Miliband having failed to show it could respond to them. Galloway himself said that his supporters were 'very unhappy with the mainstream parties that have caused a kind of alienation among young people.' *The Times* agreed (31 March 2012) that 'in the longer run, Mr Galloway's victory may illustrate a trend away from the two main political tribes . . . The stranglehold of the big parties is slipping and "other parties" are growing.'

Assessment: the impact of the Left

Small parties to the left of Labour have found it difficult to survive, and this was particularly curious during the period in which New Labour had abandoned part of its appeal – based upon class identity, trade unionism, public ownership and equality of outcome – of the post-war era. It would appear from this that these values are no longer sufficient to sustain parties of the Left, and that they must be attached to other issues concerning foreign policy or environmental concerns if they are to make any electoral impact. The suggestion of this pattern is that the language and values of 'old' Labour have lost their efficacy as recruiters in a fundamental, long-term way.

On the other hand, there are other problems which peripheral parties on the Left have faced that are not associated with ideology: they have suffered shortages of resources because they have no wealthy benefactors, and trade unions have been unwilling to break with Labour; the media are relatively unsympathetic to their values and aims; and some have been the victims of unruly and volatile charismatic leaders. Most importantly, however, they are weakened to varying degrees by their strategic doubts about the electoral process itself; the involvement of the Socialist Workers Party, which does not itself fight elections, caused problems for the Socialist Alliance and Respect; elements of the Green Party remain sceptical about what can be achieved through parliamentary politics and conventional leadership.

Prior to the 2010 General Election, twenty trade unionists, party activists, journalists and academics wrote in the national press that:

> There is an alternative to wars, cuts, privatisation and environmental destruction. We believe that the current UK election system does not allow our views to become represented – a truly democratic society requires participation and involvement at all levels – and that the next elections will not lead to major change. However, we do believe

that there are candidates of the left, across several political organisations, who should be supported by everyone who agrees that there is an alternative to Brown, Cameron or Clegg.[1]

Significantly, however, the authors of this appeal represented thirteen very different organisations and endorsed candidates with six very distinct labels. For some on the Far Left, electoral politics is always of only limited legitimacy, and this misgiving is always a potential source of fissure in movements that are already limited in their strength. No far-left party yet seems able to overcome these challenges consistently.

· ·

✔ What you should have learnt from reading this chapter

- The Far Left in Britain has never succeeded in securing sustained electoral support or representation.

- Parties to the left of Labour lack resources and are divided by arguments over methods, by differing focuses on opposing war, protecting the environment and promoting working-class issues, and by volatile leadership.

- The role of Labour has been to soak up the political agenda of the Far Left without giving it any organisational recognition.

⌕ Glossary of key terms

Entryism The strategy of moving a major party such as Labour further to the left by joining and dominating it.
Popular front An alliance of progressive parties to overthrow Conservatism in Britain, first proposed in the 1930s.
Red scare The association by their critics of left-wing groups with the Soviet Union in an attempt to discredit them.

? Likely examination questions

Is there a future for Marxism in Britain?

From where has support for the Far Left in Britain come and why?

What have been the key objectives of far-left parties in Britain?

Helpful websites

The Green Party's website is www.greenparty.org.uk/ and it points the way to numerous other useful sources; the website of the Socialist Alliance, a 'left-unity' network, is www.socialistalliance.org.uk/.

 Suggestions for further reading

Singer, S., *Origins, History and Alliances of the Green Party and Politics* (Lightning Source, 2011).

Wall, D., *The No-Nonsense Guide to Green Politics* (New Internationalist, 2010) gives a 'dark green' or 'radical' view, whereas the writing of Jonathan Porritt, starting with *Seeing Green: the Politics of Ecology Explained* (Wiley-Blackwell 1984), but especially after the 1989 European elections, reflects the electoralist tradition.

On Respect, see Peace, T., 'All I'm Asking, Is For a Little Respect: Assessing the Performance of Britain's most Successful Radical Left Party', *Parliamentary Affairs* online, 12 January 2012: pa.oxfordjournals.org/content/early/2012/01/12/pa.gsr064.full.pdf+html

Ideas and discussions across the left of the political spectrum including green, socialist and feminist thought can be monitored in the magazines *Red Pepper* (www.redpepper.org.uk/) or sometimes in contributions to *New Statesman*; for the non-electoral Far Left, see the *Socialist Worker*.

CHAPTER 7

Other Peripheral Parties and Independent Candidates

Contents

Overview

Very small, sometimes transitory parties and personalities have always been a feature of British politics but, until recently, not one taken seriously by analysts. This chapter assesses the scale and impact of the growth of parties outside the usual political spectrum, and considers whether their limited development is part of a wider pattern of decline in deference in British politics.

Key issues to be covered in this chapter

- How serious has the growth of peripheral parties in British politics been?
- What functions might peripheral and independent candidates perform?
- What factors determine the success of peripheral political parties?

Cases of peripheral parties

There are other parties and candidates on the periphery, including renegades from the larger parties forming **breakaway** organisations or standing as **independents**, **joke candidates** and peripheral parties with a strong local dimension to their identity.

The collapse of the SDP/Liberal Alliance in 1987–8 described in Part II spawned two breakaway parties, the significance of which contrasted between, on the one hand, the short term and minor and, on the other, medium term and negligible.

The 'continuing' SDP was led by the three SDP MPs who refused to accept the merger of their former party with the Liberals, and lasted only from 1988 to 1990. Its membership never reached 10,000 and, in most electoral contests, it performed very poorly despite its high-profile leadership. The continuing Liberal Party was launched in 1989 and, within a year, had appointed a full-time general secretary. It still has over thirty councillors and retains strength in parts of the North West, where in the 2004 elections to the European Parliament, the Liberal Party secured over 96,000 votes, and where in one Liverpool constituency it held third place in 2010. However, the Liberal Party may be regarded as a localised residue of the merger whose handful of councillors and candidates act increasingly as independents, and which will eventually peter out.

Two more-successful examples exist of small parties with highly localised support. Again, one of these is long term and lower profile; the other short term and highly publicised.

Mebyon Kernow ('The Sons of Cornwall')

Mebyon Kernow regards itself as the sister party in Cornwall to the SNP in Scotland and Plaid Cymru in Wales, pressing for greater Cornish self-government. Established in 1951, it has, like Plaid, a strong cultural dimension based around the promotion of the Cornish language (not in everyday use but spoken by about 3,500 people) but also argues for the protection of Cornish jobs, improvement of public transport and rural services such as post offices, and for the development of a Cornish university. The party has two dozen council seats at parish, town and county levels, and won 4.3 per cent of the vote in the first elections to the Cornish unitary authority in 2009 even though it fought fewer than a third of the seats. In the same year the party won nearly 15,000 votes at the European elections. At the 2010 General Election the party contested all Cornwall's six seats, gaining over 2,000 votes in one. Mebyon Kernow also seeks to influence other parties and, until the 1970s, allowed Cornish MPs of all parties – such as Liberal John Pardoe and Conservative David Mudd – to be members.

Mebyon Kernow's membership and representation are likely to remain extremely restricted because, although they start from the level of support enjoyed by the SNP and PC in the 1950s and 1960s, they suffer from the restrictions of Plaid Cymru on a much greater scale: only a small minority of the population of Cornwall is wholly native to the county; its language is entirely artificially revived; and its economy is reliant upon external investment, at least in the short term. The party's ambitions have therefore always been much more muted than those of its opposite numbers in Scotland or even Wales. Nonetheless, it is notable that the Liberal Democrats have taken up the policy of a Cornish university; EU regional funding has been secured for Cornwall (a long-standing MK demand); and, in 2002, Cornish was officially recognised as a regional language by the British government.

Kidderminster Health and Hospital Concern

This organisation began as a campaign to protect hospital services at Kidderminster in Worcestershire but has grown to the position where its representatives have been the largest group on the local council and, in 2001, defeated the sitting Labour MP and junior minister, David Lock, who was accused of reneging on a promise to defend the hospital. The parliamentary seat, Wyre Forest, was won convincingly in 2001, and retained in 2005 by KHHC candidate Dr Richard Taylor who had worked at the hospital. Taylor described his election as 'a tremendous reaction from the people against a very powerful government, against a very powerful political system that overrides the will of the people'. Though the campaign to defend the hospital failed, the success of the KHHC was perhaps the most potent symbol in the 2001 campaign of public disquiet over Labour's failure to deliver on health promises, and added to the pressure which produced Gordon Brown's 1 penny rise in National Insurance contributions to fund increased health expenditure the following November.

The impact of the KHHC is strictly limited to the Wyre Forest area but its novelty lies in its success in translating support at municipal elections, where ratepayers and other local groups have always been able to make inroads into the main parties' votes, into support at a parliamentary – and particularly a general election – contest, where the main parties normally hold sway, thereby affecting their campaigns nationally. It was the blending of local indignation with national resentment over health policy generally that produced this effect and, though it was unusual, it is by no means unrepeatable.

Independent candidates

Lastly, there has been a growth in recent elections of support for independent candidates. The tradition of genuinely independent Members of Parliament died off with the end of university constituencies in 1948; after that, any successes usually arose because of a departure from his or her original party of an MP who is then re-elected by the constituents. Some, like Conservative Donald Robertson (Caithness and Sutherland, 1959–64), were given free runs by their old parties; others, such as former Labour MPs S. O. Davies (Merthyr Tydfil, 1970–2) and Dick Taverne (Lincoln, 1973–4), had to beat their erstwhile comrades to keep their seats. The two most recent cases, however, only ever won as independent members, and one did so against the two main parties: Martin Bell (Tatton, 1997–2001) was elected as an 'anti-sleaze' candidate against Neil Hamilton, the Conservative MP who had been accused of taking cash payments to ask questions in Parliament. Labour and the Liberal Democrats gave a free run to Bell, a former television journalist, who promised not to stand for re-election in Tatton but did unsuccessfully fight the Essex seat of Billericay in 2001. In 2005, Peter Law was elected as independent MP for Blaenau Gwent in South Wales after the Labour Party, of which he was a long-standing member, had imposed an all-female shortlist on the local party choosing its candidate. When Law died in 2006, his successor was another independent who had been a close supporter of Law. Law and his successor faced a full complement of opponents from the other parties but their successes as independent candidates for the Commons are still rare in the extreme, even in days of party dealignment.

There is stronger evidence of a new pattern of representation with the establishment since 2000 of directly elected mayors. Thirteen English districts, including London, have voted to elect their mayors directly and, in six of these, including Ken Livingstone's first victory in 2000, an independent candidate won. The others include former police chief and Middlesbrough's 'Robomayor', Ray Mallon, the citizens' rights' activist, Mike Wolfe in Stoke, and Stuart Drummond, better known as Hartlepool Football Club's mascot 'H'Angus the Monkey'. The success of independents against the main parties in these elections can be attributed in part to the individualistic nature of the elections which, uniquely in British politics, elect a single person rather than a member of a representative body. Independents also benefit from the electoral system used for these contests, however, the supplementary vote (SV), which allows voters to identify a second preference candidate to whom their vote will be transferred if no candidate has half the votes cast, and their own candidate is not one of the top two. In these circumstances, independents are better placed to make an effective appeal to party voters than the candidates of other parties are.

Causes and consequences of peripheral party growth

There have always been peripheral parties in the British political system but their role has now become qualitatively different from the one they occupied in the post-war era. They nominate more candidates, win more attention and more votes than in the past, and crucially they win representation, an achievement that was almost unheard of for any party other than the three major ones and the nationalists before the 1980s. The growth in small-party activity in local government is now the subject of a long-term study being undertaken, with the support of the Leverhulme Trust, at the University of Birmingham's Institute for Local Government.

The background to this involves the same disillusionment and dealignment that have damaged the two main parties and helped the

Box 7.1 Membership of the peripheral parties

Source: John Marshall, *Membership of UK Political Parties*, House of Commons Standard Note, 17 August 2009

Party membership: BNP, Green and UKIP (in 000s)

	BNP	Green	UKIP
2002	3.1	5.9	10.0
2003	5.5	5.3	16.0
2004	7.9	6.3	26.0
2005	6.5	7.1	19.0
2006	6.3	7.0	16.0
2007	9.8	7.4	15.9
2008	N/A	8.0	14.6

Over the past twenty years there has been an upsurge in membership for some smaller political parties. Over the 2002–8 period, the Green Party has experienced steady growth – seeing membership increase by approximately 60 per cent. Following dramatic rises in its membership in 2003 and 2004, UKIP has since experienced a year-on-year decline. The BNP, however, has shown by far the most rapid membership expansion up to 2007, registering a near five-fold increase since 2001. The Growth in BNP membership has not been uniform; in particular, it appears to decline or slow after national-level elections. The Green Party's membership has shown a fairly persistent expansion, experiencing the largest gains during 2004 and 2005 – the years of European and Westminster elections. Unsurprisingly, UKIP registered its highest membership figures in 2004 – a year of elections to the European Parliament.

Question: What do this study of minor party membership and other evidence indicate about the significance of the appeal of the parties concerned?

third and fourth parties to grow, as we saw in Parts I and II. There is a number of other factors, however, which help to determine the success or failure of small parties in capitalising upon that disillusionment, as described below.

Leadership

Most successful peripheral parties have relied at some point upon their association with a familiar, charismatic personality – Arthur Scargill, Tommy Sheridan, David Owen or James Goldsmith, for example – as the focal point of their campaigns. Leadership is a double-edged sword, however: it has a limited shelf life (as the BNP has discovered with Nick Griffin) and small parties find it difficult to compensate for its loss, or to neutralise its unfavourable aspects, as the examples of George Galloway and Robert Kilroy-Silk illustrate. Nevertheless, even the Greens, who suffered by their association with David Icke, have now conceded that clear leadership is essential to any success beyond a certain level.

Media sympathy

Strong leadership wins publicity but the media must be willing to give coverage to it and to the issues in which a peripheral party is interested if it is to prosper. Press interest in the issues of asylum-seekers and the demand for a referendum over the European Constitution undoubtedly gave credibility to far-right peripheral arties after 2000; the Greens rely upon the media to maintain public attention on the environment, and to treat them seriously as defenders of it. Like charismatic leadership, however, this is an asset that can disappear without notice and out of the control of the peripheral party benefiting from it.

Organisation and resources

The Referendum Party was able to make an impact partly because of the funds provided by its leader, and representation has brought more funds to parties like UKIP. But other kinds of resource are important, too: a committed membership and strong branch organisations can see peripheral parties through very hard times, and maintain small parties that do not have great hopes of success.

Electoral systems

Peripheral parties have benefited from the introduction of more proportional systems of election for European and devolved elections. This has allowed the BNP and the Greens to win seats on the Greater London Assembly, the SSP to have six seats in the Scottish

Parliament, and UKIP, the Greens and the BNP to win seats in the European Parliament where they would have failed – and, indeed, with 15 per cent of the vote, the Greens did fail in 1989 – under the first-past-the-post system. This has provided a profile for peripheral parties on a bigger platform than council elections, the only ones they have any prospect of winning under first-past-the-post.

Relationships with competitors
Some peripheral parties have survived through arrangements with larger competitors. The Communist Party acknowledged that its role was to work alongside Labour; the Referendum Party left Eurosceptic Tory MPs alone in 1997; the Greens have worked in alliance with Plaid Cymru in Wales. This strategy, however, can make peripheral parties vulnerable to the whims of their patrons, undermines the 'purity' of their appeal, and runs the risk of seeming defeatist. It is, therefore, not suitable for highly ambitious or confrontational peripheral parties.

Clear agenda
The success of peripheral parties relies upon their association with niche issues that command public attention and sympathy. This may be localised – the defence of a hospital in Worcestershire or post offices in Cornwall – or it may be national, such as the demand for a referendum on Europe, opposition to war in Iraq, or greater government action to protect the environment. If it is too limited and specific, however, this factor may fade from public view or even become obsolete. Mebyon Kernow have maintained a very small but continuous appeal based on Cornish identity; it remains to be seen whether the KHHC can do the same with hospital services in Kidderminster.

The tortoise and the hare

Reviewing the factors highlighted above, it is possible to see a broad typology of peripheral parties based on Aesop's fable of the tortoise and the hare. In each part of the political spectrum there are parties like the tortoise – unobtrusive, slow but persistent in their progress – and others like the hare – experiencing sudden and highly visible surges of energy, only to run out of steam or become distracted. Those that rely upon media coverage and charismatic leadership, such as Respect, the Referendum Party or the continuing SDP, tend to be hares. The tortoises, like the Greens, UKIP and Mebyon Kernow, base their longer-term, less-spectacular impacts upon clear core appeals, good organisation, and on good relations with other parties. Like all analogies, this does not work categorically or for all parties (tortoises sometimes briefly have charismatic leaders and, in the end, even tortoises can die off) but it illustrates the difference between peripheral parties with short-term, dramatic impacts and those that have long-term, low-level policy influences.

Box 7.2 The status of peripheral parties

'Tortoise'	'Hare'
Green Party	Respect
Continuing Liberals	Continuing SDP
Mebyon Kernow	KHHC
UK Independence Party	Referendum Party

The impact of peripheral parties' growth can be identified as both indirect and direct. Indirectly, the peripheral parties have taken votes and some seats from their larger rivals and, therefore, have forced them to adapt to their agendas. The number of votes won by the Referendum Party in 1997 was less important than its impact in inhibiting John Major's attempts to resolve Conservative European policy; the shift of the major parties away from multiculturalism and towards tighter control of immigration and asylum follows the rise of parties of the Far Right since 2001; and Cameron's attempts to strengthen Conservative environmental policy were given greater urgency by the Greens' success among the metropolitan middle class.

More than all this, however, peripheral parties have begun in rare cases to edge towards taking real power, becoming the official Opposition on councils, or participating in local government administration in coalition with other parties. As well as influencing policy in other parties – the activity that led to peripheral parties being dismissed as pressure groups in the past – they are, in places, making policy themselves. To appreciate the potential significance of this, it is only necessary to refer to Part II in which we saw that, in the 1950s, the forerunners of the Liberal Democrats had, at one stage, five seats in the Commons, four of which had been won without a Conservative opponent; in the 1960s the SNP and Plaid Cymru were fringe parties putting up only a handful of parliamentary candidates, and now they are parties of government in their own countries. Most of the peripheral parties of today look every bit as serious as the Liberals and the nationalists did two generations ago. The representation they have won is, of course, tiny and can be fleeting but the 'others' cannot any longer be dismissed simply as Monster Raving Loonies.

✔ What you should have learnt from reading this chapter

- The number, profile and support of peripheral and independent candidates remain low but have grown at recent elections.

- The reasons for this can be found in constitutional change, conduct of the main parties, strategy of the peripheral candidates, and decline in public deference for other parties.

- Debate exists about whether any of these parties or movements represent significant forces in politics at other than local and temporary levels.

🔎 Glossary of key terms

Breakaway party A party formed from a disillusioned part of the membership of a larger party.
Independent A political figure or movement not obliged to conform to any prior agreement to policies other than their own, or to a whip in office.
Joke candidate A term of abuse directed at an independent or peripheral candidate with no public recognition or prospect of success.

❓ Likely examination questions

Why have more new candidates and parties appeared recently claiming the heritage and votes of the established parties?

Do independents in British politics have any future?

Helpful websites

The websites of the KHHC and the Liberal Party are: www.healthconcern.
org.uk/ and www.liberal.org.uk/. www.independentnetwork.org.uk/ is the
website of a network of independent candidates at the 2010 election.

 Suggestions for further reading

Moss, S., 'Election 2010: Can independent candidates change the political
landscape?', *The Guardian*, 2 April 2010.

Sainsbury, L., 'Are Independent Candidates the Source of Real Change?',
www.totalpolitics.com/, 9 April 2010.

Conclusion: What Kind of Party System?

Contents

Overview

A sustained academic debate has raged over the last generation as to what 'system' of parties Britain has and should have. This chapter explains the terminology of this debate and the arguments on each side, and highlights the different evidence focused on by different commentators. Finally, it assesses the value of parties collectively and in isolation to politics in Britain.

Key issues covered in this chapter

- What is meant by referring to the 'party system' in Britain?
- What types of party system are there?
- How are ideas of party systems useful to political analysis?
- How can we judge the nature of Britain's party system?
- How well are British parties serving their public, between them?

What party systems are and why they matter

The preceding chapters have examined the internal organisation and distinctive policies and support bases of the different parties in Britain. One of the recurrent themes of the discussion, however, has been the interdependence and interaction of parties – sometimes conscious and even deliberate, sometimes unwilling and even imperceptible. Just as the popularity of Thatcherism forced the Labour Party to begin the process of Labour's modernisation under Neil Kinnock, for example, so the success of Blair in broadening Labour's appeal first painted the Tories into a corner to retain 'clear blue water', and then dragged them on to the centre ground under David Cameron. The growing significance of the Liberal Democrats, nationalists and Greens, among others, has brought constitutional reform and environmental issues on to the agenda of government, even though those parties have participated in government only occasionally or at the periphery. So the relationships between parties are at least as important as their independent actions. That is what is meant by the party system.

When political analysts speak of a 'party system', it is easy to gain the wrong impression about what is being discussed. The term 'party system' does not refer to any consciously created constitutional structure but, rather, to the relationships between a country's political parties – their number, relative size and ideological proximity. In this sense, politicians and commentators do not have any significant control over the party system they are analysing. The party system in a democracy is ultimately a reflection of the preferences of voters and the effectiveness with which the parties themselves and the constitution give expression to those preferences. It is less like a tactical system used by a football team and more like a weather system.

The nature of the political weather is important, however, because an understanding of it enables us to predict and to respond to our circumstances even if we cannot control them. To maintain an effective democracy, we must tailor our constitutional arrangements to the type of party system we have. These arrangements include: the structure of Parliament and local government; the electoral system; and the legal controls around parties' campaigns and fundraising. Many of the criticisms directed at the British constitution over the last generation, and the reforms to it attempted in the last decade, have arisen from its being built upon the assumption that Britain has two main parties. The **adversarial** structure of the Commons, the tendency of the electoral system to exaggerate those parties' representation, and the largely self-funded nature of the parties have been progressively less appropriate to a system in which an increasingly changeable multiplicity of parties has support and influence.

If we can understand the nature of the relationships between parties, we can hold the parties accountable, we can create a constitution which facilitates the expression of their status, and we can introduce constraints on them which limit the potential dangers presented by whatever party system is in operation. Like the weather, the party system cannot in the end be controlled but it is vital that we prepare for the promise and the perils it offers.

Types of system

Not being artificially made, party systems do not fit simply into one category or another. At any given time, there will be evidence of more than one type of system in operation in Britain. Certain labels, however, function as an essential shorthand for the nature of the relationships between the parties, and each has had its advocates as a model to describe the British party system in recent decades. Three key types can be identified.

Two-party systems

In 1976, Giovanni Sartori defined a two-party system as one in which only two parties are capable of forming governments.[1] The classic case of such a system today is the United States where the role of the Republican and Democrat Parties is heavily institutionalised. For three decades following World War II, Britain had a strong two-party system. In the 1950s, the Labour and Conservative Parties held 98 per cent of the seats in the Commons, won 96 per cent of the vote at some general elections, and even provided 90 per cent of the candidates. They won relatively equal shares of the vote, neither party dropping below 40 per cent of the vote at any general election between 1945 and 1970. Minor parties, such as the Liberals, were reduced to a handful of Commons seats and disappeared from most local councils. Robert McKenzie's 1955 study even relegated the Liberals to a two-page appendix because they were 'of only very limited interest'.[2] Most obviously, and fulfilling Sartori's key requirement for a two-party system, only Labour and the Conservatives held power in government after 1945, a pattern which remained unbroken at national level until 2010. This was always the justification offered by the broadcasting authorities when excluding Liberal Democrat leaders from televised debates between 'the two prime ministerial candidates' at general elections before 2010.

Contemporary academic observers of this system were impressed not merely by its indisputable existence but also by its virtue. Ivor Bulmer-Thomas and Sir Ivor Jennings were part of a tradition that saw the two-party system as giving effective representation to all key interests in society, mobilising voters effectively and sharing power alternately.[3] They were adversarial enough to provide choice but shared enough ground to ensure stability of policy. Their ideological breadth meant that, between them, the two main parties reflected all significant points of view and could subsume and constitutionalise any new demands presented to the political system, such as controls on immigration, an end to unpopular wars, the rights of women, or protection of the environment. In the 1960s, Bulmer-Thomas dismissed Liberal success at by-elections as 'a protest vote against the other parties rather than evidence of a genuine revival'[4] and, at the end of that decade, Samuel Beer foresaw that 'the old party dualism would seem likely to have a long, vigorous and useful future'.[5] S. E. Finer also saw the United Kingdom as 'still a two-party system' but, by 1980, he was becoming doubtful as to its effectiveness and was urging electoral reform to ease transition to a new set of relationships between parties.[6]

The evidence on which the presumption of a two-party system rested was deteriorating by the 1970s, however. In 1974, the main parties won little more than 70 per cent of the vote between them and, after the Conservatives' failure to agree coalition terms with the Liberals, Labour ran a minority government which, within three years, was again turning to the Liberals and nationalists for support. In the 1980s, the ideological breadth of the main parties came into question as the **consensus** between them broke down, and their share of the vote fell again as the SDP–Liberal Alliance stepped into the void to gain a quarter of the vote. The Conservatives and Labour had lost sizeable portions of their core votes, too; at no general election since 1970 has either party secured 40 per cent of the vote, and each has proved capable of falling below a third of the popular vote on more than one occasion.

The background to this development is the pattern known as party **dealignment**. Voters' willingness to support the same party at all elections, regardless of performance, candidate, leader or policies, has declined since the 1950s so that an increasing share of the vote is cast for different parties at different elections, for minor parties, or for no party at all. The attitude of voters to parties has become less like the unchanging loyalty of the supporter of a football club and more like the choice of a consumer buying breakfast cereal in a supermarket. This trend was first identified in the 1970s by the work of Ivor Crewe and others, and has been attributed to: the rise of television and later the Internet as key campaign platforms because of the relatively even access to the electorate that they give to parties of all sizes; to the decline in our strict sense of class identity and our readiness to vote in conformity with it; to the nation's economic decline and the decline in deference as part of British political culture; and to the rise in the number and resources of minor parties and other candidates. Changes in party policy, which have been both cause and effect of this dealignment, are explored below.

Those analysts who continued to talk of a two-party system after 1970 did so in uncertain or conditional terms, or acknowledged that it was increasingly reliant upon the first-past-the post electoral system to sustain it. Alan Ball claimed in the 1980s that 'the British party system could still be characterised as a two-party system in that the majority of seats in the House of Commons were won by the two main parties, one of them having won the majority of seats at the last election and willing to govern alone'.[7] Even at the height of the two-party system the electoral weakness of other parties may be explained partly by their organisational limitations: when only one voter in six had the chance to vote Liberal or Nationalist, it was difficult to make reliable statements about the level of their support. Nonetheless, in governmental, representational and organisational terms, the Labour and Conservative Parties were clearly the only major players in British politics until the 1970s. Since then, however, matters have been far less clear.

One-party or dominant-party systems

A one-party system in its purest form is one in which only one party is permitted to be active. Such systems include those of Nazi Germany, the Soviet Union, or any of a number of African and Middle Eastern dictatorships in the post-war era. Even in these states, smaller parties are sometimes permitted to exist within a limited scope of ideological and electoral activity.

In liberal democracies, however, the term is sometimes used to describe what are more accurately called predominant- or dominant-party systems. These are ones in which only one party regularly exercises power or has any prospect of doing so. It dominates representation in Parliament and its core ideological values are shared by most voters. Indeed, if such a situation persists, in dominant-party systems, it is common for political argument to be conducted to a large extent within the main party rather than between it and its rivals. Opposition parties may become electorally unrealistic or unambitious because they anticipate defeat. Other dangers of such a system are that constitutionally neutral institutions, such as the courts, senior civil service, and public broadcasting, may become partisan over a period of time if only exposed to governments of one party.

This description is usually accepted as being true of post-war Japan where the Liberal Democrat Party held sway, divided into competing factions and, in Sweden, the Social Democrats governed uninterrupted from 1932 to 1976. A similar situation developed in India after independence, with the Congress Party being the leading party.

The argument that the United Kingdom was experiencing a dominant-party system gained momentum in the late 1980s, after a third substantial Conservative victory in 1987 left the Labour Party struggling for direction in its policy review, and the Social and Liberal Democrats descended into internecine warfare over the merger of their parties. Arguments over Europe, the poll tax and welfare were hammered out largely within Tory ranks, sparking the leadership battle of 1990. This scenario was being pointed out in Geoffrey Alderman's *Britain: a One Party State?* and Gareth Smyth's *Can the Tories Lose?* before the 1992 General Election.[8] When it came, Professor Anthony King argued after the Conservatives' fourth consecutive victory in 1992 that 'Britain no longer has two major political parties. It has one major party, the Conservatives, one minor party, Labour, and one peripheral party, the Liberal Democrats.'[9]

King argued in a fuller study later that year[10] that Britain now satisfied Sartori's criteria for a dominant-party system and, in 1993, Stephen Ingle agreed and went on to say that 'it can be argued that in recent years the party system has failed to offer choice on crucial policy issues; has ceased to provide for alternative parties in government regularly; has been unable to hold to account governments that have pursued almost universally unpopular policies' and that 'the modern British Party system is in serious need of reform'.[11] A major study of the party at the time suggested that there had been not only a Conservative decade but a 'Conservative century' since 1886 in which the party had formed sixteen out of twenty-three governments and had been out of government for only thirty out of 110 years.[12] This anxiety was reflected in the most dramatic of Labour's party election broadcasts in the 1997 campaign, which – to the sarcastic sound of 'Land of Hope and Glory' – made a series of speculative claims about the extreme policies a Conservative government might pursue, and ended with the warning that 'If the Tories win again, nobody will be safe and nothing will stop them', implying that the very existence of the second party was in jeopardy if Tory dominance continued.

Evidently the period of Conservative sway came to an end, though advocates of the dominant-party view of Britain might argue that their ideological dominance persisted in elements of Blair's 'Third Way' and in his 'Big Tent' approach to party politics. The Labour government itself seemed at times unmovable, winning an unprecedented hat-trick of general elections despite deep unpopularity over Iraq, taxation and public services. The Opposition was, as it was against Thatcher and Major, divided, weak and lost for strategy. Some analysts, such as Norris and Lovenduski, doubted whether the party could recover the ability to win.[13] Again, events proved that they could, and it seems to be a pattern that, if Britain can be said to be in a dominant-party system, the dominance of a party appears to be at its greatest just before its division and collapse occurs. Though party dealignment has ironically allowed one or other of the main parties to enjoy greater control than in the past, the pluralism of the British Party system nonetheless reasserts itself in time.

Clearly there have been longer periods of continuous government by one party since 1979 than before; even those who call this a dominant-party system, however, acknowledge that it does not reflect the work of parties at all levels. The operation of the electoral system and the distribution of the opposition parties' votes allowed the Thatcher and Major governments to dominate with smaller shares of the vote than had been secured by Heath and Douglas Home when they lost. Blair won in 2005 with the smallest share of the vote ever gained by a government in modern times. Thus, the dominance of these parties was chiefly parliamentary and, thereafter, ideological. At the electoral level, and at other levels of representation, the British system has been more varied.

Three-party or multi-party systems

Since the 1970s, it has been increasingly widely accepted that Britain's two-party system is first of doubtful effectiveness and then of arguable existence. Henry Drucker warned the main parties in 1979 that 'electoral support for them, the dependable alternation of the two of them in office, and the usefulness of office to them, are no longer assured',[14] and four years later Vernon Bogdanor discussed the constitutional consequences of 'the development of a challenge to the two-party system'.[15] It is Professor Patrick Dunleavy, however, who has provided the most recent and thoroughgoing argument that 'at different types of elections we now have over-lapping party systems with up to five or six serious contenders for elected office'. Dunleavy shows that, following the use of various systems of proportional representation in the United Kingdom, the 'effective number of parties' rose from 2.2 at the 1992 General Election to between 3 and 5.8 at elections since 1999 – and over 3 at the 2005 General Election.[16] Sarah Childs refers to five 'main parties' and concludes that 'the British party system can no longer be classified as a two-party system'.[17]

More basic data confirm the same pattern over a longer period. The support for parties other than the main two has been growing over the last four decades, accounting for 10 per cent of the vote in 1966, 25 per cent in 1974, 30 per cent in 1983 and, in 2010, reached over a third of the votes cast. In the European elections of 2004 and 2009, the Conservative and Labour parties were unable to win half the vote between them. By 2007, over a third of local councils – including all but two councils in Scotland – were controlled by 'minor' parties or by minority administrations of the two main parties. In Scotland and Wales since 1999, the two main parties have either given way to the nationalists, or shared power with them or the Liberal Democrats.

Associated with this growth in minor-party strength has been a change in the political agenda to accommodate new issues, such as constitutional reform, the environment, social equality in race and gender, and a multiplicity of single-issue campaigns on European integration, the livelihood of the rural population, law and order, and the rights of motorists. The swollen ranks of certain pressure groups, and the outspoken campaigns in the press, were only the more obvious illustrations of this. The major parties found themselves buffeted from the demands of one issue-based lobby to another, and struggled to modernise and to adapt their identities to cope.

As Chapters 1 and 2 confirmed, the fortunes of the 'other' parties have prospered accordingly. The Liberal Democrats, Greens, nationalists, UKIP, the BNP, breakaway socialist parties, and independents have all gained representation at some level of the political system. In contrast with general elections of the 1950s, the Conservatives and Labour provided only 35 per cent of the candidates at the 2005 contest. The majority was from other parties whose candidates often took second place, leaving a 'major' party trailing. In eighty-six seats, other parties now hold first place, forming a significant block in the Commons, and forcing change in parliamentary procedure: the Liberal Democrats, for example – even before they entered government – had two seats on most departmental select committees, and hold the chair of three whereas, in 1979, they had only two seats on all of the committees put together; the Liberal Democrat leader was guaranteed the opportunity to ask the prime minister at least three questions at prime ministers question times where no such right was accorded to 'minor' parties in the past.

Even at the level of executive office – the last bastion of the two-party system – diversity has begun to appear. The governments of Edward Heath, James Callaghan and John Major all sought the support of 'minor' parties to pursue their programmes, and were forced to sacrifice some control over policy to achieve this. Tony Blair tried unsuccessfully to bring Liberal Democrats into his government in 1997 but was allowed by his colleagues to recruit them on to a cabinet committee. His successor directly invited Paddy Ashdown to join the cabinet and, though the offer was turned down, Gordon Brown appointed Liberal Democrats, including Lords Lester and Carlile and Baronesses Williams and Neuberger, as senior government advisers. He went on to create a 'government of all the talents' including non-Labour Party figures such as former CBI leader, Digby Jones, and Admiral Sir Alan West, surgeon Professor Sir Ara Darzi and economist Shriti Vadera. Multiparty and non-party politics were a reality, if only a limited one, in all parts of the British system before 2010; in some parts they were already the normal way of life.

The Liberal Democrat–Conservative coalition government of 2010 was in some respects, therefore, neither unprecedented nor even entirely surprising: events at the electoral level, in local government and increasingly at Westminster had been preparing politicians for the prospect of working together in cabinet. The coalition was, in effect, the culmination of a trend that was observed by psephologists and party analysts from 1970 onwards but which circumstances, personalities and British constitutional arrangements had delayed. The coalition was the realisation of the multiparty system at the highest level of British politics. The main study of the 2010 election asserted that:

> The hung parliament did not occur by chance. Whilst the individual aspects of the 2010 election are important, it also needs to be seen in the broader context of political change in Britain, especially the fragmenting of the party system, decade-on-decade. A hung parliament was increasingly likely as a result of changes to electoral geography and the increasing inability of the two main parties to maintain voters' affection and loyalty. The election results and the formation of the coalition bring Westminster into line with what is happening in other parts of the UK. As of 2010, ten parties exercise national-level power and none of the four arrangements has one-party majority government, for so long seen as an essential feature of the British model of party government.[18]

Measuring party systems

How can we make sense of this competing evidence? One evident conclusion is that our perception of the British party system depends heavily upon the kind of evidence we examine, and this explains some of the differences of opinion among analysts of the parties. At least five determinants are used at different times to assess the relationships between parties:

Government

Traditional writers who argue that Britain still has a two-party system base this on the assertion that holding office in national governments is the key test of party strength. Only Labour and the Conservatives have done so, and only they look likely to be able to lead governments in the near future. In this sense, therefore, the British system remains a two-party one. It is noticeable, however, that this view has been commonest and strongest among those, like Harrison and Jennings, who set their observations in a long-term historical context, and it might be said in criticism that they assumed falsely that what has gone before will be – perhaps even should be – continued. Even before the coalition of 2010, the two main parties sometimes found it hard to govern alone, or they have perceived image benefits from broadening government personnel beyond the bounds of their own party, and the possibility of coalition government in future is one which the main parties' leaders would be unwise to discount. Ed Miliband has studiously avoided criticising the Liberal Democrats wholesale, preferring to isolate Nick Clegg, and encouraging his MPs to refer to the government as 'Tory led'. The assumption that Britain has a two-party system of government was therefore always an analysis limited in scope and time.

Parliament

Examination of representation in the House of Commons (and also the Lords) also reinforces the idea that Britain is principally a two-party system, though a less secure one than has been implied by the composition of governments until recently. While from 1950 to 1970 there were never more than a dozen MPs from outside the two main parties, there have been over seventy-five in each of the last four parliaments. Nonetheless, this leaves the two main parties with overwhelming predominance in the chamber, and is consolidated by the adversarial structure of parliamentary procedure – the whipping system, the arrangement of government and opposition, the timetable and so on. A year after the formation of the coalition, Nick Clegg complained that the Civil Service had not yet adapted to the condition of having two different parties in government. Recent innovations, including the departmental select committees, Westminster Hall debates and reform of the Lords, have weakened this a little but the sovereign body of the political system remains mainly two party in form. Critics of this approach, however, point out that its evidence is dependent upon the electoral system as much as on public opinion and the political climate. There may be a two-party system at Westminster but its strength in the rest of the country has to be tested by other methods.

Representation at other levels

The pattern of success in elections varies if we look at elected institutions other than the House of Commons. While the two main parties still dominate in the Commons, neither has been able to gain a majority of British seats in the European Assembly, or of the Welsh Assembly or Scottish Parliament, since 1997. Nor is this simply a result of the use of proportional systems for these elections because, in 2007, over a third of councillors elected under first-past-the-post were from the minor parties. This means that the experience of co-operation between parties – a key feature of multiparty politics – is commonplace at all levels of elected representation other than Westminster. It also highlights the differences between regions of the United Kingdom and levels of election: UKIP has the third largest number of MEPs but very few councillors; the BNP has over fifty councillors but has struggled to win at a higher level of representation. The nationalists perform noticeably better in elections to devolved institutions than at general elections, and the Liberal Democrats are stronger in local government and in Westminster by-elections than at general elections.

Votes

It might be argued by two-party analysts that the common feature of elections at other levels than the nation state is that they are second order – that, because they do not determine who holds the levels of power at national level, they are treated less seriously and more experimentally than general elections are. Even within the Westminster level of election, however, wholly separate party systems operate: the urban north is largely a Liberal Democrat–Labour battleground; the south-west a contest between the Conservatives and Liberal Democrats; in London and the Midlands, the two 'main' parties are the chief contenders in most seats; and Scotland and Wales have entirely different systems, involving four key players, within which there are yet more detailed geographical patchworks. The minor party in Devon and Cornwall is Labour which gained less than a fifth of the vote and fewer than ten MPs in 2010 but, at the same election, that fate befell the Liberal Democrats in the Midlands and the Conservatives in Scotland.

Indeed it is in the electoral arena that the multiparty analysis finds its strongest evidence. Here, the undoubted dominance of the Labour and Conservative parties in the 1950s and 1960s has been replaced by fragmentation among a wide range of parties, even at general elections, where the need for a clear executive winner and the tactical considerations of voting under first-past-the-post are at their strongest. If the party system is to be measured meaningfully in a democracy, the multiparty analysts argue, it must be judged at the electoral level where the distribution of public opinion is at least ostensibly reflected. Whatever happens in Parliament or in government after that must be a reflection of that or else a distortion of it and, therefore, commensurately irrelevant. It would be difficult, taking voting behaviour since 1970 as a test, to see the British system as either a dominant-party or a two-party system. Some have preferred to see it as a 'two-party-plus' system, given that no single remaining party yet matches the scale of support for Labour and the Conservatives consistently.

Policy

In the post-war two-party system, Labour and the Conservatives acted as 'broad-church' parties embracing a wide range of opinions from the centre ground, where they converged on 'Butskellite' territory, to Powellite nationalism and free-market economics for the Conservatives, to associations with communism through some trade union leaders in the Labour Party. Though in office the parties undid relatively little of each other's work, their long-term objectives were clearly enough understood by the public and were stable and distinctive: Labour favoured greater equality of standards of living and proposed higher progressive taxes, higher public expenditure on welfare and greater state control of industry; the Conservatives were sceptical about social change, favoured the protection of private enterprise, and wanted more limited taxation and public spending than Labour.

The two parties covered most of the ideological territory of British politics and offered choice to the electorate. Here it is important to distinguish between day-to-day policy, in which the leaderships of the parties were quite similar, and party image and identity based on long-term principles and support, in which Labour and the Conservatives were quite distinct. Jean Blondel wrote in the later part of this period that 'images differ from issues, but they are connected to them':

> Images are influenced by issues in a general fashion; they are influenced by what is going on. They are also influenced by leadership and party dynamism, as by the image of 'newness' which prevailed for a while in the middle of the 1960s. But they are more persistent than issues and some of them, for instance the image of class, are so persistent that they seem to be permanent. They are much vaguer than issues; they indicate that the electors have a general view of society and of the way in which the parties fit in the framework of society.

'One of the difficulties of the Liberal party', added Blondel, 'seems to be that it does not evoke any images in the minds of the electors.'[19]

This apparently virtuous scenario began to change in the 1970s because of a chain of mutually supportive factors: economic decline and social change; decline in support for the main parties; and more dramatic policy change – both towards and away from each other – by those parties. Whichever of these came first, each drove the other forward to a point where the electorate was less certain about the ideological identity of the main parties.

The polarisation of Labour and the Conservatives over the miners' strike in 1974 was merely the curtain-raiser to the long-term shift of the Conservatives to a free-market agenda under Margaret Thatcher whose victory in 1979 drove Labour in the 1980s to the Left on the issues of defence, public ownership, European integration and taxation. This partly accounts for the growth in the third-party and nationalist vote during these years, and the development of a three-party ideological split in which incomes' policy, constitutional reform and a mixed economy were neglected or abandoned by the main parties and taken up by their new rivals.

The attempted return of the two main parties to the ground of 'consensus' – under Blair's 'Third Way' and Cameron's 'modernisation' – has been an incomplete and, in some ways, confused journey. Firstly the consensus is no longer what it was: it entails less nationalisation but more progressive policy on social and constitutional reform. Secondly, the path to it has been a troubled one for both parties, involving the enforced resignation of two prime ministers in the middle of their third terms, repeated cabinet splits, and challenges to the leaderships of Thatcher, Kinnock, Major and Iain Duncan Smith. In fact, parties have not so much returned to the centre as tried to become '**catch-all**', flexible and open-ended vehicles appealing through leadership personality and superficial 'brand' images rather than through long-term social and political identity. Unsurprisingly, the public's sense of what the parties stand for has been undermined. Conservative deputy chairman and benefactor Lord Ashcroft attributed Cameron's failure to win an outright majority in 2010 to the fact that 'going into the election, many voters had little clear idea of what we stood for or what we intended to do in government';[20] Tony Blair blamed his successor's defeat on movement away from the centre ground rather than on failure to reach it clearly: 'Labour won when it was New Labour. It lost because it stopped being New Labour. Just as the 2005 election was one we were never going to lose, 2010 was one we were never going to win – once the fateful strategic decision was taken to abandon the New Labour position.'[21]

One feature of this unstable policy landscape is the willingness of parties to acknowledge shared policies: the coalition programme – and the difficulties it presented the Liberal Democrats in differentiating themselves from the Conservatives by 2011 – is only the most advanced version of a syndrome that was witnessed in: the constitutional proposals agreed by Labour and the Liberal Democrats in 1997; the Liberal Democrats' support for Major's policy of European integration against his own Eurosceptic rebels; or the limited shared objectives of the Labour Right and the Liberals in the 1970s which foreshadowed the formation of the SDP–Liberal Alliance. In policy terms, the multiparty system involves more intraparty division, more interparty agreement, more fluctuation over time than before – and perhaps more confusion. 'Trying to capture the ideological terrain of British interparty competition in the UK', writes Sarah Childs, 'is a complicated matter.'

Detailed polling data show that the public perceived the movements of the parties away from and back towards each other which took place between 1974 and 1997, and Paul Webb notes that 'this pattern accords closely with orthodox accounts of party programmatic development in the period'.[22] At the 2010 General Election they identified Labour as being the party most likely to help the poor, single parents and non-white Britons, whereas the Conservatives were thought more likely to help the rich and traditional families. By a small margin, but significantly, more people thought the Conservatives would help 'ordinary working people'.[23] These figures reinforce conventional, if somewhat stereotyped, impressions of the choice on offer from the main parties. It offers no explanation, however, for the decline in turnout, membership of parties and trust in their ability to serve the country which we have seen throughout this book.

An assessment of the parties

Recent analyses of the party system, and the extent to which it means parties are fulfilling the functions outlined in the Introduction, have expressed a range of reactions running from bemusement to despair. Richard Kelly mused in 2001 that 'the old two-party system has not been replaced by anything comparably "systematic". Far from being reshaped, the British "party system" has simply disappeared.'[24] More positively, Sarah Childs, who identified five 'main' parties, conceived five years later that the party system was in transition: 'Having a multiplicity of political parties is nothing new', says Childs, pointing to the variety of party configurations during the interwar period. Most recent commentary has agreed that evidence from different areas and levels of the political system has presented different, overlapping pictures over the last three or four decades.[25] It is fair now to say that a multiparty system has been growing upwards from the electoral level since the 1970s; it flourished in local government and under devolution; and, in 2010, it reached the executive in the form of full coalition. Multiparty Britain has arrived in a characteristically British evolutionary way: it seems difficult to imagine that it will disappear spontaneously.

Public opinion remains unconvinced by the parties, and there is some evidence that coalition has done further damage to trust in the traditional conception of parties as vehicles of the mandate. But we have yet to find an alternative method of communicating our priorities. A study by the Young Foundation in 2006 found that only 26 per cent of respondents saw political parties as among the two or three organisations that 'have the most impact on meeting the long-term needs of people in this country' and that just 13 per cent – about the same proportion that names pressure groups – chose joining a political party as the most effective way in which to have an impact on decisions about how the country is run (contact with government ministers and officialdom was thought more useful in both cases). In principle, 45 per cent think parties are good for a democratic system and only 6 per cent think they are bad; but, reflecting on the parties Britain actually has, 22 per cent think they are 'open and transparent', and a quarter of respondents say we would be better off without them and would prefer that all politicians were independent, and a similar number say the parties are 'a hindrance to democracy'. Most positively, 49 per cent agree that parties in Britain enable people to have a choice, and only 29 per cent disagree.[26]

The enthusiasm which greeted the formation of the coalition in 2010 was quickly replaced by disillusionment at the promises that were traded away and the divisions in party co-operation that opened up in both elements of the government. The British public recognises that parties are – as Edmund Burke, Paul Webb and others insist – a necessary feature of a mass democracy yet, at the same time, the public is increasingly disillusioned with the particular ones they have. Specific issues of policy and leadership have given this expression but the underlying trend is a long-term one away from the uncritical and unthinking loyalties of the post-war era to a more nuanced sort of political identity in which voters have moved between parties, and a significant minority is now moving away from parties altogether.

Precisely because of their importance, only parties can solve this problem by more energetic, more modern and more effective campaigning and mobilisation. Mostly, they must abandon the claim that they can and will fulfil detailed policy promises made in campaigns: they must credit the public with the ability to understand that politicians – even ones who are elected – are not omnipotent but must conciliate with economic and political forces they do not control. Parties must offer priorities, not promises. Webb and others are right that only parties can fulfil properly the vital functions outlined in the Introduction but it is wrong to assume that the public has to endorse them in doing so. Parties are, indeed, the only show in town but voters do not have to go to a show at all.

✔ What you should have learnt from reading this chapter

- Party systems describe the relationship in terms of size and character between parties in a country.

- Party systems change over time.

- Party systems can be measured by various criteria and, at times, their identity can be open to dispute.

- The United Kingdom had a two-party system until the 1970s but its features have been harder to assess since then.

🔎 Glossary of key terms

Adversarial A relationship in which parties naturally contradict each other and their policies are usually mutually exclusive.
Catch-all party A party which widens its appeal as far as possible, if necessary by the dilution or blurring of policies
Consensus A relationship in which major parties agree on the fundamental questions of policy, and differ only on matters of degree or detail.
Dealignment The weakening of the loyalty between voters and their parties

 **Likely examination questions**

What sort of party system exists in Britain?

Account for changes in the party system in Britain.

What advantages is a two-party system said to have?

How and why do political scientists identify party systems?

'Multi-party politics is here in Britain for the foreseeable future.' Discuss.

 Helpful websites

The party system in Parliament is briefly outlined at www.parliament.
uk/about/mps-and-lords/members/partysystem/. A wide-ranging list of
election results over time is available at www.election.demon.co.uk/.
Recent election results at all levels are presented and analysed on the
BBC News website. Current standings of the parties can be found at
www.ukpollingreport.co.uk/. www.earlhamsociologypages.co.uk/vbint.htm
gives information about voting behaviour and analyses of trends within
Britain, and www.ipsos-mori.com/researchpublications/researcharchive/
poll gives analysis of patterns of UK voting behaviour and looks at voting
at the 2010 election.

Suggested further reading

Childs, S., 'Political Parties and Party Systems' in Dunleavy et al. (eds),
Developments in British Politics 8 (Palgrave Macmillan, 2006).

Cowley, P., 'Political Parties and the British Party System', in Heffernan, R.
et. al. *Developments in British Politics* 9 (Palgrave Macmillan, 2011)

Cowley, P. and Kavanagh, D., *The British General Election of 2010*
(Palgrave Macmillan, 2010).

Denver, D., 'Results: How Britain Voted' in *Britain Votes 2010* (Hansard
Society and Oxford University Press, 2010).

Ingle, S., *The British Party System: an Introduction* (Routledge, 2008).

Webb, P., *The Modern British Party System* (Sage, 2000).

References

Introduction

1. Edmund Burke, 'A Speech on Conciliation with the Colonies', 22 March 1775.
2. Of these, three were former Labour MPs re-elected under new labels, and a fourth, Green MP Caroline Lucas, represents a nationally recognised party.
3. Jennings, I., *Political Parties* (1960).
4. www.lifeintheunitedkingdomtest.co.uk/?page_id=10
5. Major, J., *The Daily Telegraph*, 24 October 2003.
6. *Power to the People: the of an independent inquiry into Britain's democracy* (London: Power Inquiry, 2006).
7. *Strengthening Democracy: Fair and Sustainable Funding of Political Parties* (HMSO, 2007).
8. Rose, R., *Do Parties Make a Difference?* (London: Macmillan and Chatham, NJ: Chatham House, 1980).
9. Phillips, M., 'The not-the-Conservative Party', *Daily Mail*, 2 January 2006.
10. Booker, C., 'Election 2010: the Tory Gamble that failed us all', *Daily Telegraph*, 11 May 2010.
11. *Daily Telegraph*, 5 February 2007.
12. Meadowcroft, M., 'Ground Rules for Coalition Governments', letters, *The Guardian*, 23 March 2011.
13. Bogdanor, V., 'The Rise and Fall of the Political Party', *New Statesman*, 23 October 2006.
14. *Power to the People:* The report of Power: an independent Inquiry into Britain's democracy (2006).
15. These MPs made their arguments against the Labour Party's whips in 'New MPs beware: if you think you can express an opinion, forget it', Tess Kingham, *The Independent on Sunday*, 10 June 2001; Paul Marsden, *The Mail on Sunday*, 21 October 2001; and 'I quit because this is not a Labour government', Clare Short, *Independent on Sunday*, 22 October 2006.

16. Wollaston, S., 'Creeping patronage, new politics and the payroll vote', guardian.co.uk, 10 February 2011.
17. *Members Only? Parliament in the Public Eye*: Report of the Hansard Society Commission on the Communication of Parliamentary Democracy (2005).
18. YouGov and *The Sun*, 8 March 2010.
19. Richards, P., *Is the Party Over? New Labour and the Politics of Participation* (Fabian Society, 2000).
20. Putnam, R., *Bowling Alone* (Simon and Schuster, 2001).
21. Norris, P. and Lovenduski, J., 'Why Parties Fail to Learn', *Party Politics* Vol. 10, No. 1, Sage, 2004.
22. Strafford, J., 'The Conservative Party has become an oligarchy, controlled by a small group of people', *The Observer*, 14 February 2010.
23. Sutherland, K., *The Party's Over: Blueprint for a Very English Revolution* (Imprint Academic, 2004) p. 21.
24. Webb, P., *Democracy and Political Parties* (Hansard Society, 2007) p. 8.

Chapter 1

1. Thorpe, A., *A History of the Labour Party* (Macmillan, 1997) p. 5.
2. www.labour.org.uk/history_of_the_labour_party 23/1/11.
3. Thorpe, *A History of the Labour Party*, pp. 125–66.
4. Jones, B., Gray, A., Kavanagh, D., Moral, M., Norton P. and Seldon, A., *Politics UK* (Prentice Hall, 1998) p. 27.
5. Sandbrook, D., *White Heat, a History of Britain in the Swinging Sixties* (Abacus, 2006) pp. 333–4 and 698–9.
6. Jones, Gray, Kavanagh, Moral, Norton and Seldon, *Politics UK*, pp. 28–9.
7. McNaughton, N., *Success in Politics*, 2nd ed. (Hodder Headline, 2001) p. 94.
8. Callus, G. and Dale, I., *Total Politics Guide to the 2010 General Election* (Biteback, 2009) p. 30.
9. Geddes, A. and Tonge, J., *Britain Votes 2010* (Oxford University Press, 2010) p. 240–1.
10. 'Tony Blair's "New" Labour Party in Modern Britain', *Politics Review*, 16.4, April 2007, p. 17.
11. McNaughton, *Success in Politics*, p. 83.

12. Heywood, A., *Political Ideologies, an Introduction,* 2nd ed. (Macmillan, 1998), pp. 110–18.

13. Hirsch, D. and Miller, J., *Labour's Welfare Reform* (Joseph Rowntree Foundation Publications, 2004), p. 1.

14. Beackon, S., 'Labour Party Politics and the Working Class', *British Journal of Political Science* (1976), 6, p. 231.

15. Geddes, A. and Tonge, J., *Britain Votes 2010* (Oxford University Press, 2010), p. 21.

16. Beackon, *Labour Party Politics,* Article author query beackon s p. 231.

17. Philp, C. (ed.), *Conservative Revival: Blueprint for a Better Britain* (Politico's Publishing, 2006), p. 33.

18. Philp, C. (ed.), *Conservative Revival,* p. 34.

19. www.ipsos-mori.com/researchpublications, 28/7/11.

20. www.earlhamsociologypages.co.uk, 28/7/11.

21. Geddes and Tonge, *Britain Votes 2010,* pp. 6–18.

22. www.electoralcommission.org.uk/party-finance, 27/5/11.

23. BBC, 'Labour facing Membership crisis', www.news.bbc.co.uk, 27/5/11.

24. Fisher, J. and Cowley, P., 'The Labour Party (History and Future)', *Politics Review,* 10.1 (September 2000), p. 27.

25. Fisher and Cowley, 'The Labour Party', p. 27.

26. Callus and Dale, *Guide to the Election* , pp. 54–5.

27. David Simpson, *Political Parties* (Hodder and Stoughton, 2000) p. 127.

28. Kavanagh, D. and Cowley, P., *The British General Election 2010* (Palgrave Macmillan, 2010), p. 309.

29. Geddes and Tonge, *Britain Votes 2010,* p. 23.

30. www.parliament.uk/documents/commons/lib/research/briefings, 28/12/10.

31. Grice, A., 'Miliband plans to sever "big money" ties with the unions', www.independent.co.uk/news/uk/politics/miliband-plans-to-sever-big-money-ties-with-unions-, 28/12/10.

32. Simpson, *Political Parties,* pp. 74–5.

33. 'The Labour Party', www.labour.org.uk/home, 29/5/11.

34. 'The Labour Party', www.labour.org.uk/home, 29/5/11.

Chapter 2

1. Murphy, D., Station, R., Walsh Atkins, P. and Whiskerd, N., *Britain 1815–1918* (Collins Educational, 1998), p. 218.
2. Ball, S., *The Conservative Party and British Politics, 1902–1951* (Longman, 1995), pp. 32–3.
3. Budge, I., Crew, I., McKay, D. and Newton, K., *The New British Politics* (Longman, 1998), pp. 70–2.
4. www.news.bbc.co.uk/onthisday/hi/dates/stories/october/10, 29/5/11.
5. Budge, Crew, McKay and Newton, *The New British Politics*, pp. 70–4.
6. www.guardian.co.uk/politics/1993/jul/25/politicalnews.uk, 29/5/11.
7. Philp, C., *Conservative Revival: Blueprint for a Better Britain* (Politico's Publishing, 2006), p. 39.
8. BBC, cdnedge.bbc.co.uk/news/vote2001, 27/5/11.
9. Denham, A. and O'Hara, K., *Democratising Conservative Leadership from Grey Suit to Grass Roots* (Manchester University Press, 2008), pp. 5–7.
10. Ashcroft, M., *Minority Verdict: the Conservative Party, the Voters and the 2010 Election* (Biteback, 2010).
11. McNaughton, N., *Success in Politics*, 2nd ed. (Hodder Headline Group, 2001), pp. 60–1.
12. Ibid., p. 62.
13. Ball, *The Conservative Party 1902–1951*, p. 30.
14. Geddes, A. and Tonge, J., *Britain Votes 2010* (Oxford University Press, 2010), pp. 17–19.
15. www.earlhamsociologypages.co.uk/vbint.htm, 29/7/11.
16. www.ipsos-mori.com/researchpublications/researcharchive/poll, 27/5/11.
17. Geddes and Tonge, *Britain Votes*, pp. 6–16.
18. www.theconservativefoundation.co.uk, 5/2/2011.
19. Hanson A. H. and Walles, M., *Governing Britain: A Guidebook to Political Institutions* (Collins, 1978), p. 64.
20. Garner, R. and Kelly, R., *British Political Parties Today* (Manchester University Press, 1998), p. 76.
21. Clark, A., *The Tories* (Phoenix, 1998), p. xxiii.
22. Kavanagh, D. and Cowley, P. *The British General Election 2010* (Palgrave Macmillan, 2010), p. 72.
23. Philp, *Conservative Revival*, pp. 62–3.
24. Simpson, *Political Parties*, p. 71.

25. Philp, *Conservative Revival*, pp. 62–3.
26. Philp, Conservative Revival, p. 39.
27. Geddes and Tonge, *Britain Votes*, p. 241.
28. Geddes and Tonge, *Britain Votes*, p. 241.
29. BBC IDS think tank, www.bbc.co.uk/news/education, 26/5/11.
30. Geddes and Tonge, *Britain Votes*, p. 243.
31. Griffiths, S. and Hickson, K., *British Party Politics and Ideology After New Labour* (Palgrave Macmillan, 2010), p. 126.
32. blogs.channel4.com/gary-gibbon-on-politics, 27/7/11.

Chapter 3

1. Russell, A., and Fieldhouse, E., *Neither Left nor Right? The Liberal Democrats and the Electorate* (Manchester University Press, 2001), pp. 257–8.
2. Russell and Fieldhouse, *Neither Left nor Right?* (Manchester University Press, 2001), p. 102.
3. Denver, D., 'How Britain Voted', in Geddes, A., and Tonge, J. (eds), *Britain Votes 2010* (Hansard Society, 2010), pp. 17–18.
4. MacAllister, I., Fieldhouse, E. and Russell, A. 'Yellow Fever? The Political Geography of Liberal Voting in Great Britain', *Political Geography*, Vol. 21, No. 4 (2002).
5. A detailed review of this topic can be found in Hickson, K. (ed.), *The Political Thought of the Liberals and Liberal Democrats since 1945* (Manchester University Press, 2009).
6. Marshall, P. and Laws, D. (eds), *The Orange Book: Reclaiming Liberalism* (Profile, 2004); Brack, D., Grayson, R., and Howarth, D. (eds), *Reinventing the State: Social Liberalism for the 21st Century* (Politico's Publishing, 2007).

Chapter 4

1. Balsom, D. et al., 'The Red and the Green', *Journal of Political Studies*, 1983.
2. McEvoy, J., *The Politics of Northern Ireland* (Edinburgh University Press, 2008).
3. Sandry, A., *Plaid Cymru: an Ideological Analysis* (Welsh Academic Press, 2011).
4. Pittock, M., *The Road to Independence: Scotland since the Sixties* (Reaktion Books, 2008).

5. Bogdanor, V., *Devolution in the United Kingdom* (Oxford University Press, 2001).

Chapter 5

1. Hinsliff, G., 'It feels like the BNP – only in Blazers', *The Observer*, 30 May 2004.
2. Stoke-on-Trent Governance Commission Report to John Healey, May 2008.
3. *The Independent*, 4 May 2002.

Chapter 6

1. 'Left candidates can offer hope', *The Guardian*, 8 April 2010.

Chapter 8

1. Sartori, G., *Parties and Party Systems* (Cambridge University Press, 1976).
2. McKenzie, R., *British Political Parties* (Heinemann, 1955).
3. See, for example, Bulmer-Thomas, I., *The Party System in Great Britain* (Phoenix House, 1953) and Jennings, I., *Party Politics* (Cambridge University Press, 1960).
4. Bulmer-Thomas, I., *The Growth of the British Party System*, Vol. II (John Baker, 1965).
5. Beer, S., *Modern British Politics* (Faber & Faber, 1966).
6. Finer, S. E., *The Changing British Party System 1945–79* (AEI Press, 1980).
7. Ball, A. R., *British Political Parties: the Emergence of a Modern Party System* (Macmillan, 1987).
8. Alderman, G., *Britain: A One-Party State* (Christopher Helm, 1989); Smyth, G. (ed.), *Can the Tories Lose?* (Lawrence & Wishart, 1991).
9. King, A., 'Tory "Super-Party" born out of last-minute switching', *Daily Telegraph*, 13 April 1992.
10. King, A., 'The Implications of One-Party Government' in King et al., *Britain at the Polls* (Chatham House, 1992).
11. Ingle, S., 'Political Parties in the Nineties', *Talking Politics*, Vol. 6, No. 1 (Politics Association, 1993).

12. Seldon, A. and Ball, S. (eds), *Conservative Century* (Oxford University Press, 1994).

13. Norris, P. and Lovenduski J., 'Why Parties Fail to Learn', *Party Politics*, Vol. 10, No. 1 (Sage, 2004).

14. Drucker, H., *Multi-Party Britain* (Macmillan, 1979).

15. Bogdanor, V., *Multi-Party Politics and the Constitution* (Cambridge University Press, 1983).

16. Dunleavy, P., 'Facing up to Multi-party Politics, How Partisan Dealignment and PR Voting Have Fundamentally Changed Britain's Party Systems', *Parliamentary Affairs*, Vol. 58, No. 3 (July 2005).

17. Childs, S., 'Political Parties and Party Systems' in Dunleavy et al. (eds), *Developments in British Politics*, 8 (Palgrave Macmillan, 2006).

18. Kavanagh, D. and Cowley, P., *The British General Election of 2010* (Macmillan, 2010).

19. Blondel, J., *Voters, Parties and Leaders* (Penguin, 1975), pp. 80–1.

20. Lord Ashcroft, *Minority Verdict: The Conservative Party, the voters and the 2010 election* (2010)

21. Blair, T., *A Journey* (Hutchinson, 2010), p. 67.

22. Webb, P., *The Modern British Party System* (Sage, 2000), p. 113.

23. YouGov poll, 2010.

24. Kelly, R., 'The Defunct Party System', *Talking Politics*, September 2001.

25. See, for example, P. Lynch and R. Garner, 'The Changing Party System', *Parliamentary Affairs*, Vol. 58, No. 3 (July 2005).

26. *Parties for the Public Good*, The Young Foundation, October 2006.

Index